What Was Man Created For ?

What Was Man Created For ?

The Philosophy of the Common Task

N.F. Fedorov

Selected works translated from
the Russian and abridged by
Elisabeth Koutaissoff and Marilyn Minto

Honeyglen Publishing
L'Age d'Homme

© 1990 Honeyglen Publishing / L'Age d'Homme

All rights reserved. No part of this publication may be reproduced, stored in a retrieval system, or transmitted, in any form or by any means, electronic, mechanical, photocopying, recording or otherwise, without the prior permission of the copyright owner.

First published 1990 by Honeyglen Publishing Limited/L'Age d'Homme

British Library Cataloguing in Publication Data
Fedorov, N.F. (Nikolai Fedorovich)
What was man created for ? : the philosophy of the common task : selected works.
1. Russian philosophy
I. Title II. Koutaissoff, Elisabeth III. Minto, Marilyn 197

ISBN 0-907855-09-1

Typeset by l'Age d'Homme (Lausanne)

Printed and bound by Bookcraft (Bath) Ltd.

'God has granted to me to make friends with two of the people here : one is Orlov, and the other and principal one is Nikolai Fedorovich Fedorov. He is a librarian at the Rumyantsev Library... He has devised a plan for a common task for humanity, the aim of which is the bodily resurrection of all humans. First, it is not as crazy as it sounds (don't worry, I do not and never have shared his views, but I have understood them enough to feel capable of defending them against any other beliefs of a similar material nature). Secondly, and most importantly, because of these beliefs he leads the purest Christian life... He is sixty, a pauper, gives away all he has, is always cheerful and meek.'

L.N. Tolstoy writing to V.I. Alexeev, 1881

'I accept your project unconditionally... I have much to say to you. But for the time being I will say only that since the emergence of Christianity your "project" is the first step forward of the human spirit along the path of Christ. As to myself, I can only recognise in you my teacher and spiritual father.'

Vladimir Solov'ev writing to N.F. Fedorov, 1881

'He was a Russian searcher for universal salvation. In him the feeling of responsibility of all for all reaches the ultimate and acutest expression... What was that "project" of Fedorov ? What were these striking ideas that impressed some of the most outstanding Russians ? At the basis of his philosophy was his grieving for the human predicament, and there was no man on earth who felt such sorrow at the death of people and such thirst to return them to life.'

Nicholas Berdyaev, *The Russian Idea* (N.Y., 1948)

CONTENTS

Introduction by Elisabeth Koutaissoff 11
The Philosophy of the Common Task
    Part I 33
    Part II 65
    Part III 77
    Part IV 89

Essays and other writings

Supramoralism 105
Ways of solving the paschal questions 137
Disarmament 144
Foreword to a letter from F.M. Dostoevsky 159
Faith, deed and prayer 169
Weather regulation... 'Give us this day our daily bread' 173
The Orthodox burial rite and its meaning 175
The daughter of humanity as reconciler 178
The agapodicy and the theodicy 180
Physical and moral sinlessness 182
How did art begin... ? 184
The art of imitation and the art of reality 187
Parents and resurrectors 191
On the unity of the meteorological and cosmic processes 195
What the most ancient Christian monument in China can teach us 196
On Turkestan 205

Paradise and hell ? Or purgatory ? 220
The conditionality of prophecies concerning the end of
   the world 222

Appendices 227
Select Bibliography 237
Index 245

INTRODUCTION

Nikolai Fedorovich Fedorov (1828-1903), one of Russia's most original thinkers, lived at a time of intense intellectual controversies, artistic creativity and scientific 'take-off' in Russia. Yet it was also a time of growing worldwide militarism when increasingly lethal weapons were being developed, of civic strife, of labour unrest in the rapidly industrialising countries of the West, and of revolutionary rumblings in Russia. Fedorov was deeply distressed by this state of discord and lack of brotherly feeling, which was bringing so much misery to the common people. How could brotherhood be achieved ? Would it be possible to divert human energies from wars and dissension towards measures for protecting mankind against natural disasters such as floods, droughts, earthquakes and hurricanes, and to transform nature from 'a temporary enemy into an eternal friend'?

Fedorov believed that if the causes of disunity, discord and war were elucidated and a common purpose found to deflect human energies away from dissensions towards a common goal of overwhelming importance to all human beings, it would fire their imaginations, enlist all their energies and bring about universal cooperation. This goal, of concern to all, was nothing less than to rationalise the blind forces of nature 'which bring famine, disease and death'. Since death is a natural phenomenon it, too, could and should be overcome by 'knowledge and action'. God had not created *mortals*. Death was the wages of sin, the penalty inflicted by nature for man's slothful ignorance and discord. In the absence of a common cause peace was impossible, because inaction is contrary to human nature.

Man is an active creature and cannot not act. If he does not know what to do, he will do what he should not do. We will cease doing what we should not do only when we know what to do. Then we will give our energies to a cause which we will regard as a duty. We will stop fighting when we acknowledge it as possible, and therefore obligatory, to redirect our energies now squandered on wars and mutual struggles towards the act of universal salvation.[1]

This duty, this Common Task, this universally accepted 'project', was to regulate the forces of nature, to defeat death and bring ancestors back to life, so that they too would participate in the general resurrection. Fedorov's views could be described as Promethean utopianism because of his faith in science and human reason. Moreover, his utopianism went far beyond most utopias, which envisage equitable and rationally organised societies, healthy, prosperous and happy, living within a natural environment which they are capable of exploiting wisely for their economic needs. Such utopias do not question what purpose these good societies should serve apart from the welfare of their own citizens ; whereas Fedorov, who was a deeply religious man, believed the world had been created by God to some purpose and that man, endowed with reason and consciousness, had a divine mission to accomplish.
What was that mission ? And, more generally, *'What was man created for ?'*, as the age-old Russian phrase would have it, and as quoted by Fedorov on pages 128 and 142.

1. *Filosofiya obshchago dela* (*The Philosophy of the Common Task*). All references are to the reprint of the first edition, vol. I, Verny, 1906, and vol. II, Moscow, 1913, reprinted by L'Age d'Homme, Lausanne, 1985. Hereafter referred to as *FOD*.

The spectacular advances of modern science such as the landing of men on the moon, spare-parts surgery, genetic engineering, and so on, make many ideas put forward by Fedorov in the nineteenth century sound less extravagant than they seemed to his contemporaries. Indeed, it is increasingly felt that humanity is taking over from nature the course of evolution and the fate of the planet Earth. To use the word coined by P. Teilhard de Chardin, our era is that of the *noosphere*. Hence the growing interest in Nikolai Fedorov, this much neglected Russian thinker, both in the USA and — despite his religious views — in the Soviet Union. For the first time since the Revolution, a 700-page volume of his selected works was published in 1982 on the initiative of the Soviet astronaut V.I. Sevast'yanov, under the auspices of the Institute of Philosophy of the Academy of Sciences of the USSR. However, when this came to the notice of M.A. Suslov, then member of the central Committee of the CPSU in charge of ideology, he declared this publication to be 'untimely' and 'misguided', and all unsold copies were withdrawn and probably destroyed.[2]

Several causes contributed to Fedorov's earlier neglect: the boldness and eccentricity of his 'project', his religious and monarchical convictions, so completely alien to the political radicalism and philosophical materialism prevalent among the Russian intelligentsia of the second half of the nineteenth century, and the fact that he published very little during his lifetime, and always anonymously and mostly in provincial journals. His heavy repetitive style did not help matters.

2. Stephen Lukashevich, *N.F. Fedorov (1828-1903), A Study in Russian Eupsychian and Utopian Thought*, Newark, 1977 ; George M. Young Jr, *Nikolai F. Fedorov : An Introduction*, Belmont, 1979 ; Liudmilla Koehler, *N.F. Fedorov : The Philosophy of Action*, Pittsburg, 1979 ; Ayleen Teskey, *Platonov and Fyodorov : The Influence of Christian Philosophy on a Soviet Writer*, Avebury (England), 1982 ; S.G. Semenova (ed.), *Nikolai Fedorovich Fedorov : Sochineniya* (*Works*), Moscow, 1982 ; *Literaturnaya gazeta*, 18 January 1989, p. 5.

For recent articles see the Bibliography and for a complete list of Fedorov's writings see George Young, op. cit., pp. 248-55.

His friend and later editor, N.P. Peterson,[3] explained Fedorov's reluctance to publish as resulting from his innate modesty, his realisation that the time was not yet ripe for his project to be understood and accepted, and from his inability to present it in a systematic and streamlined form, and in particular to provide sufficient scientific evidence to support his forecasts. It was in fact without the consent of Fedorov that in 1897 Peterson sent to the journal *Don* (published in the provincial town of Voronezh) a copy of a letter he had received from Dostoevsky in 1876, together with a foreword to it written by Fedorov. It was in that year that Peterson had first approached Dostoevsky, sending him an exposition of Fedorov's ideas and asking him to have them discussed in the *Diary of a Writer* published by Dostoevsky during the 1870s. Dostoevsky complied partially with this request by publishing in the March 1876 (volume 2) issue a long extract about associations and trade unions, which Fedorov regarded as

3. N.P. Peterson, *N.F. Fedorov i ego kniga* 'Filosofiya obshchago dela' *v protivopolozhnost' ucheniyu L.N. Tolstogo o neprotivlenii i drugim ideyam nashego vremeni* (*N.F. Fedorov and his Book* The Philosophy of the Common Task *in Opposition to the Teaching of L.N. Tolstoy on Non-Resistance and to other Ideas of our Time*), Verny, 1912, p. 89.

Nikolai Pavlovich Peterson (1844-1919) was, like Fedorov, the illegitimate son of a wealthy landowner. When a student at Moscow University he joined a revolutionary group and was expelled, though later he was allowed to complete his course. For a short time he taught at the school for peasant children organised by Tolstoy in Yasnaya Polyana, then at Bogorodsk (now Noginsk). There he met Fedorov and became his lifelong friend and first disciple. He had been impressed by Fedorov's statement that the slogan of the French Revolution — liberty, equality, fraternity — was self-contradictory because 'liberty for all to follow their personal inclinations and envious equality could engender only discord and not fraternity' (restated in *FOD* ; see page 85). In 1869 Peterson moved to the Ministry of Justice and for twenty years worked at the law courts in Kerensk, Perm' province, then in Voronezh, and eventually became a district judge in Askhabad and Verny. Fedorov often spent his holidays in these places with Peterson and very occasionally contributed to local publications. There is reason to believe that Tolstoy had Peterson in mind when he created the character of Simonson in his novel *Resurrection*.

unbrotherly since they catered for their own members to the exclusion of everybody else. Dostoevsky asked Peterson for more details about the author,[4] whose ideas fascinated him so much that he discussed them for two hours with the philosopher Vladimir Solov'ev. Solov'ev also became enthusiastic, but later raised serious objections which infuriated Fedorov.[5] It has been suggested that the scene at Ilyusha's graveside in *The Brothers Karamazov* echoes Fedorov's faith in bodily resurrection.[6]

Biographical data about Fedorov are scanty and uncertain. He was probably the illegitimate son of a Russian diplomat, Prince Paul Gagarin, and a girl of humble birth about whom nothing is known. His origin deprived him of his patronymic, let alone his father's surname. Instead he was given those of the man who stood godfather to him. At the age of four he lost his father and a few months later his grandfather, Prince Ivan Gagarin, a distinguished eighteenth-century freemason, book collector and patron of the arts, whose second wife was the famous dramatic actress — much admired by Pushkin and others — Catherine Semenova. Presumably, Fedorov, his mother and two little sisters now had to leave the Gagarins' fine country house, Okna (Kherson province).[7] Some provi-

---

4. See Appendix I.
5. See Appendix II. Fedorov was particularly incensed that at the 1891 October meeting of the Psychological Society Solov'ev should have given a watered down account of his ideas. The letter that he then wrote to Solov'ev, but apparently did not post, has been published by Semenova, op. cit., p. 651. For other critical remarks, see *FOD*, vol. I, pp. 479-90 and three unfinished drafts : *FOD*, vol. II, pp. 163-75, the shortest of which is included in the present volume on p. 180.
6. R. Lord, 'Dostoevskii and N.F. Fedorov', *Slavonic and East European Review*, June 1962, pp. 409-30 ; A.K. Gornostaev (pseudonym of A.K. Gorsky, another admirer of Fedorov who had not emigrated), *Rai na zemle : k ideologii tvorchestva Dostoevskogo : F.M. Dostoevsky i N.F. Fedorov (Paradise on Earth : Some Ideological Aspects of the Works of Dostoevsky : F.M. Dostoevsky and N.F. Fedorov)*, Harbin, 1928, pp. 37-67.
7. A. Ostromirov (another pseudonym of A.K. Gorsky), biographical preface to the 2nd edn of *FOD*, Harbin, 1928. See also *Russky biografichesky slovar'*, Moscow, vol. 4, 1914, pp. 67-8 and vol. 18, St Petersburg, 1904,

sion must have been made, however, for the boy's education, since he first studied at the Tambov secondary school, then at the Richelieu Lyceum in Odessa. He left without completing the course, allegedly after quarrelling with his examiners. For several years he taught history and geography in various provincial schools. Later he became a librarian at the Rumyantsev Museum Library (now the Lenin Library, Moscow), and he then worked as the librarian in charge of the reading room of the Moscow Archives of the Ministry of Foreign Affairs.

The painter Leonid Pasternak (father of Boris, the poet) was so fascinated by Fedorov's austere features and fiery eyes, which reminded him of St Francis of Assisi, that he surreptitiously drew a sketch of the old librarian, later using it for his painting *The Three Wise Men*, the two other wise men being Tolstoy and Vladimir Solov'ev, both of whom admired Fedorov though disagreeing with many of his ideas.

Fedorov's work in public libraries brought him into contact with some of his most distinguished contemporaries. He impressed Tolstoy by the intensity of his religious faith, his ascetic life and legendary erudition — he was reputed to have read all the books he catalogued. When he noticed that a reader was a serious research worker he would bring him books whose existence the specialist did not suspect.

Among the readers whom he helped most, and even coached in mathematics, was K.E. Tsiolkovsky, now regarded as the forefather of Soviet space rocketry. Tsiolkovsky was partially deaf, so his parents sent him, aged sixteen, to Moscow to complete his education by private study, since his

pp. 299-304 ; Semenov Tyan'-Shansky, *Rossiya*, vol. 14, St Petersburg, 1910, p. 521. In an unpublished letter from Peterson to Kozhevnikov, dated 26 December 1903, Peterson mentions meeting Fedorov's sisters and having mistakenly thought that the husband of one (Astaf'ev) was a brother of Fedorov, whereas he was his brother-in-law. The other sister was married to a man called Poltavtsev. Neither seems to have had close relations with Fedorov. Lenin Library Archives, f. 657.

poor hearing handicapped his school progress. Did the two men ever discuss space flights ? Did Fedorov see any drafts of Tsiolkovsky's science-fiction story *Outside Earth*, written in 1898 though not published until 1910, or of his seminal article 'The probing of space by jet devices', published in 1903, the year of Fedorov's death ?[8]

Fedorov's ideas became more widely known after the posthumous publication of two volumes of his works entitled (by their editors, V. A. Kozhevnikov[9] and N.P. Peterson) *The Philosophy of the Common Task* (*Filosofiya obshchago dela*), sometimes translated as *The Philosophy of the Common Cause*. The editors had sorted out Fedorov's numerous notes, drafts and unpublished articles and put them together in some sort of order — which was no easy job, since Fedorov wrote in response to a variety of contemporary events. There were critical essays on, or rather against, German philosophical systems, especially Kant's school of criticism, and against Nietzsche and Schopenhauer as well as the positivism of Auguste Comte and Herbert Spencer ; there were disquisitions on the changing style of handwriting in ancient manuscripts, on the role of museums in education, on the card-indexing of library catalogues and on the then novel idea of international library loans ; on the need for the Russian Autocrat to become the Father of all nations ; on negative and positive chastity, the former being merely abstinence from sexual intercourse while the latter was the redirection of sexual energy towards 'knowledge and action' ; on Constantinople as the link between Asia and Europe and hence the

---

8. M. Arlazorov, *Tsiolkovsky*, Moscow, 1962, p. 28. K. Altaisky, 'Moskovskaya yunost' Tsiolkovskogo' ('Tsiolkovsky's youth in Moscow'), *Moskva*, 1966, n° 9, p. 181. Tsiolkovsky's article appeared in *Nauchnoe obozrenie*, St Petersburg, 1903, n° 5.

9. Vladimir Aleksandrovich Kozhevnikov (1852-1917), philosopher and religious writer ; his most important works are *Filosofiya chuvstva i very* (*The Philosophy of Feeling and Faith*), Moscow, 1897, and a two-volume *Buddizm v sravnenii s khristianstvom* (*Buddhism in Comparison with Christianity*), Moscow, 1914.

17

natural Christian Orthodox capital of the world ; on the struggle of the settled agricultural peoples, symbolised by Iran, against the predatory nomads (Turan), a conflict which had had its effect on Russia who had suffered throughout her history from the incursions of various steppe peoples — Pechenegs, Khazars, Polovtsy — even before the Mongol invasion and the long Tartar domination, and later from the depredations of the Crimean Tartars, who were not subdued until the end of the eighteenth century. Since Chinese, Indian and Semitic myths about the origins of their respective nations seem to point to the Pamir (that mountainous region of Central Asia, often referred to as 'the roof of the world', which may have had a less forbidding climate in an earlier geological era), it has been thought that the cradle of the human race might have been located there ; so Fedorov advocated sending an Anglo-Russian scientific expedition — uniting two usually hostile nations in a joint venture — to discover the bones of these early men and provide a tangible proof of human kinship. Like many Russians of his time he bitterly resented and often referred to the role of the Western powers, especially Great Britain during the Russo-Turkish war of 1877-8, fought for the liberation of the Balkan Slavs from Turkey. The Russian victory had been difficult and costly in lives, but the aim was achieved when Turkey agreed to grant independence to Serbia, Romania and Montenegro by the treaty of San Stefano. It was then that the Western powers intervened, depriving Russia of the fruits of her hard-won victories and limiting the independence of her Balkan brothers at the Congress of Berlin in 1878.

Whatever topic he wrote about, Fedorov brought in his main idea of the Common Task — how to achieve universal brotherhood, rationalise nature instead of merely exploiting her bounties, overcome death, resurrect the ancestors and create a united humanity worthy of governing the universe. The obsessive emphasis on the duty of the sons to resurrect their forefathers can possibly be ascribed to his traumatic childhood experience of losing both his father and his grandfather at the age of four, and to a subconscious guilt complex for having failed to keep them alive through adequate love. However, there is also a theoretical reason for his emphasis on filial love ; for although humans share with other animals both sexual love and love for their offspring, only human adults remain tied by affection to their parents when they no longer need their protection in order to survive.

Whilst preparing the first volume of *The Philosophy of the Common Task*, Kozhevnikov also published, between 1904 and 1906, a series of articles on Fedorov in the journal *Russky arkhiv*, which appeared in book form in 1908. The first volume of Fedorov's works was published in 1906 in the remote town of Verny, then a frontier fortress, now known as Alma-Ata, capital of Kazakhstan, where Peterson was a district judge at the time. The edition was limited to 480 copies, which were not for sale but were available to friends and libraries. A second volume came out in Moscow in 1913 in an edition of 620 copies. The third volume was never published, Kozhevnikov having died of cancer in July 1917 and Peterson in March 1919, though parts of it saw the light later.[10]

Among the first to review the book was Nicholas Berdyaev, in 1915, in an article entitled 'The religion of resurrection' ('Religiya voskreseniya') in the journal *Russkaya mysl'*, and he often referred to the subject later. In his 1928 article,

---

10. Parts of the third, unpublished, volume appeared in the Paris émigré journals *Put'* (*The Way*), 1928, n° 10, 1929, n° 18, 1933, n° 40 and *Versty*, 1928, n° 3. Other items came to rest in the archives of the Lenin Library in Moscow. A few are included in the volume of Fedorov's works edited by Semenova, op. cit., pp. 607-57. She also published an article by Fedorov on Goethe's *Faust*, in *Kontekst*, 1975, pp. 312-32. In the 1920s N.A. Setnitsky, lecturer at the Russian Faculty of Law in Harbin, attempted a second edition of *FOD* with a biographical introduction by A. Ostromirov. Only three out of the planned twelve parts appeared in Harbin, between 1928 and 1930. In 1970 *FOD* was reprinted by Gregg International, Farnborough, England, with a foreword in English by N.M. Zernov, under the title *The Philosophy of the Common Cause*, and in 1985 by L'Age d'Homme, Lausanne (without any preface).

'Three jubilees : L. Tolstoy, H. Ibsen and N.F. Fedorov',[11] he wrote :

> The novelty of Fedorov's idea, one which frightens so many people, lies in the fact that it affirms an activity of man incommensurably greater than any that humanism and progressivism believe in. Resurrection is an act not only of God's grace but also of human activity. We now come to the most grandiose and bewildering idea of N. Fedorov. He had a completely original and unprecedented attitude towards apocalyptic prophecies, and his doctrine represents a totally new phenomenon in Russian consciousness and Russian apocalyptic expectation. Never before in the Christian world had there been expressed such an audacious, such an astounding concept, concerning the possibility of avoiding the Last Judgement and its irrevocable consequences, by dint of the active participation of man. If what Fedorov calls for is achieved, then there will be no end to the world. Mankind, with a transformed and definitively regulated nature, will move directly into the life eternal.

Another ex-Marxist, later to become an Orthodox priest, Father Serge Bulgakov, was fascinated by Fedorov's vision of a solar economic system. He wrote of him enthusiastically : 'A most original mind and a most original man speaks to you from these pages, so variegated in theme, but imbued throughout with a unity of thought. An extraordinary feeling takes hold of you at once — a reverence and awe before a greatness that is genuine and unassertive in our vain, clamorous age.'[12]

---

11. N.A. Berdyaev, 'Tri yubileya : L. Tolstoy, Gen. Ibsen, N.F. Fedorov', *Put'*, 1928, n° 11, pp. 76-94. English translation of the section on Fedorov, *Russian Review*, New York, 1950, n° 9, pp. 124-30.
12. S.N. Bulgakov, *Svet nevecherny* (*Unfading Light*), Moscow, 1917, pp. 358-9. Quotation from 'Zagadochny myslitel'' ('An enigmatic thinker'), *Dva grada* (*Two Cities*), Moscow, 1911, vol. 2, p. 260 ; first published in *Moskovskie vedomosti* (*Moscow Gazette*), 5 December 1908.

Nor was Fedorov's impact limited to religious writers. Traces of many of his ideas can be found in Russian poets such as Mayakovsky, Bryusov, Andrei Bely and Klyuev, and in the Soviet short-story writer Platonov. The prototype of the character Varsonof'ev in Solzhenitsyn's *August 1914* may have been Fedorov himself. The Soviet agricultural economist A.V. Chayanov, who paid with his life for opposing collectivisation, published in 1920 a novelette entitled *Journey of my Brother Alexei to the Land of Peasant Utopia*. The story is set in Russia in 1984. All towns have been abolished and the people live in prosperous rural communities reminiscent of William Morris's *News from Nowhere*. When the Germans try to invade Russia, her scientists bring about such terrible storms that German planes have to be grounded and tanks sink in the mud. The German advance is halted and peace restored. The proletarian writer Maxim Gorky, though he regarded Fedorov as a religious eccentric, was impressed by the activism of his philosophy and by his view that in capitalist societies women are the promoters of consumerism, of 'toys'.[13]

13. V.V. Mayakovsky knew about Fedorov from the painter Chekrygin, whom he had met at his art classes ; see V.B. Shklovsky, *O Mayakovskom*, Moscow, 1940, pp. 30 and 89-100. In his 1923 poem *Pro eto* (*About This*), lines 1681-1710, a scientist ponders on whom to resurrect.
V.Ya Bryusov had once met Fedorov personally. In his poem *Khvala cheloveku* (*Praise to Man*), 1908, he forecasts that man will direct the course of his planet among other stars ; Bryusov also contributed a note, 'O smerti, voskresenii i voskreshenii' ('On death, resurrection and resuscitation'), to the first issue of *Vselenskoe delo* (*The Ecumenical Task*), Odessa, 1914, p. 49. This publication was designed to propagate Fedorov's ideas, but only two issues came out, the 2nd in Riga in 1934.
Apparently in 1912 Andrei Bely (pseudonym of B.N. Bugaev) had thought of writing a book on Fedorov, but left for Basle and turned to anthroposophy. On returning to Russia in 1916 he wrote a novel, *Moskva*, featuring the character of a Professor Korobkin vaguely modelled on Fedorov : see S.S. Grechishnikov & A.V. Lavrov, 'Andrei Bely i N.F. Fedorov', *Toimetiged : acta et commentationes Universitatis Tartuensis*, Tartu, 1979, n° 459, pp. 147-64.
On Klyuev, see Liudmilla Koehler, op. cit., p. 95 ; on Platonov, A. Teskey, op. cit. ; on Solzhenitsyn, Aleksei Kiselev, 'Varsonof'ev i N.F. Fedorov', *Novy zhurnal*, New York, 1977, n° 110, pp. 296-9.

Most of these authors picked out only some of Fedorov's — always controversial — views, and not always the same ones. Possibly the most interesting are the similarities and contrasts between Fedorov's vision and the preaching of the later Tolstoy. Both were religious thinkers, both were hostile to the secular industrialised society and longed for a return to the simpler village life of the peasantry with its traditional healthy moral values : for both, the ethical message of art was more important than aesthetic virtuosity, and both were hostile to the commercialisation of literature. A God-given talent should not be sold for money. After 1877 Tolstoy ceased to accept royalties for his works, except, for very special reasons, for the novel *Resurrection* — these royalties were to finance the emigration of the Dukhobors who, as conscientious objectors, had been in trouble with the Tsarist regime since the introduction of compulsory military service for all young men in the 1860s.

Fedorov sought to counter the efforts of Emile Zola, then President of the French Society of Men of Letters, to get Russia to sign the International Copyright Agreement, which Fedorov deemed to be detrimental to the spread of knowledge, since knowledge should be available to everybody free of charge. Above all, both Tolstoy and Fedorov were distressed by the growing militarisation of nations.

For A.V. Chayanov, writing under the pseudonym Ivan Kremnev, see his *Puteshestvie moego brata Alekseya v stranu krest'yanskoi utopii*, Moscow, 1920, translated into English by R.E.F. Smith, 'The journey of my brother Alexei to the land of peasant utopia', in *Journal of Peasant Studies*, 1976, n° 1, pp. 63-117 ; and in the same issue devoted to 'The Russian peasant 1920 and 1984', also by R.E.F. Smith, a 'Note on the sources of George Orwell's *1984*', pp. 10-11.

On Maxim Gorky, see L.I. Sukhikh, 'M. Gor'ky i N.F. Fedorov', *Russkaya literatura*, 1980, n° 1, pp. 160-8 ; 'Gor'ky i sovetskie pisateli ; neizdannaya perepiska' ('Gorky and Soviet writers : unpublished correspondence'), *Literaturnoe nasledstvo* (*Literary Heritage*), vol. 70, Moscow, 1963, pp. 134-6, 335, 584, 587 and 589 ; Michael Hagemeister, 'Neue Materialen zur Wirkungsgeschichte N.F. Fedorovs, M. Gor'kii und die Anhänger Fedorovs in Moskau und Harbin', *Studia Slavica*, Beiträge zum VIII Internationalen Slawistenkongress in Zagreb 1978, Giessen, 1981, pp. 219-43.

Yet they differed on many points. Tolstoy eventually rejected faith in life after death, whereas for Fedorov the cornerstone of Christianity was immortality and physical resurrection. They disagreed also on ways to achieve peace among nations. Tolstoy preached non-resistance to evil by force in accordance with Gospel teaching — 'Whosoever shall strike thee on thy right cheek, turn to him the other also.' This entailed non-participation in any form of institutionalised violence, such as military or jury service. It was essentially a form of passive resistance and non-cooperation with the powers that be which so impressed Gandhi, then a very young man. Fedorov argued that disarmament was not possible so long as the causes of mutual distrust and hostility persisted. He proposed that armies and their expensive and sophisticated equipment be put to a better use, such as the modification of the weather, designed to benefit agriculture and increase crop yields. This would put an end to one of mankind's scourges — famines resulting from droughts or floods. To control cloud formation and redirect winds over vast expanses would require the cooperation of the armies of neighbouring states, thus diverting them from mutual extermination towards the common beneficial task of 'irrigating and ventilating' the Earth.

Homo sapiens was a weak animal at the mercy of the forces of nature, subjected to a senseless and endlessly recurring cycle of birth, procreation, death and disintegration. Yet God had endowed him with Reason and it was, therefore, his duty to introduce some rational order into this irrational universe. He could and should further transform nature from 'a temporary enemy into an eternal friend'. Unfortunately — and this was one of the major causes of human disunity — knowledge had become divorced from action. The 'learned' were concerned with abstract speculations (Fedorov had Kant and other philosophers in mind), while the 'unlearned' toiled in the fields without active help from them. (It should be remembered that in nineteenth-century Russia there was a great gap between the highly educated upper classes and the largely illiterate peasantry.) Like Karl Marx, Fedorov thought that savants should not merely study nature, but change it, and Fedorov was equally dissatisfied with their inaction. However, he envisaged changes quite different from those propounded by Marx.

The 'learned', according to Fedorov, studied nature *as it is* without giving any thought to *what it should be* in order for the world to become perfect. They studied *causes* without considering the *ends*. No higher purpose guided their often random scientific research. So whenever the learned acted and applied their knowledge, it was to promote industry which manufactured unnecessary consumer goods (the possession of which merely increased the gap between the 'haves' and the 'have nots') ; or, worse still, they applied their knowledge to devise abominable weapons which increased distrust and hatred beween nations. Universities were nothing more than 'the backyards of factories and army barracks, that is, serving industrialism and militarism'.[14] To protect their wealth, the rich promulgated laws, set up courts of justice, established police forces and other unbrotherly institutions. As to the poor, they rationalised their envy, greed and frustration by turning to socialist theories and violent revolution. Fedorov was equally critical of both capitalism and socialism because both institutionalised the struggle for mere material possessions. Wealth and poverty were surely less important than life and death, and humanity's childish lust for 'toys' was the sign of its mental and spiritual immaturity.

To reintegrate knowledge and action a complete reform of the educational system was necessary. Knowledge should cease to be the privilege of 'some people carrying out observations and experiments sometimes and in some places'. It should be the concern of 'all, always and everywhere'. Even teachers and pupils in rural schools could observe and record local climatic conditions, study local flora and fauna, do their own research and add their modest contributions to the pool

14. *FOD*, vol. I, p. 198.

of general knowledge, instead of swotting up information from textbooks compiled by town-dwellers. Thus, 'everyone should be a student and everything an object of study'.

The study of the Earth's magnetism might lead to an understanding of the force which propels the planet through space and, perhaps, to the utilisation of that force for space travel and emigration to other planets from an eventually overpopulated earth. It was time we stopped being 'idle passengers' on our planet and became 'the crew of our celestial craft'. Indeed, the potential of humankind is boundless, provided men stop wasting their energies on discord and dissension which are both the consequence and the manifestation of immaturity, and unite in a common cause that will lead mankind to adulthood and participation in the creation of a New Heaven and a New Earth.

The present cosmos, which it would be more correct to call chaos, will cease to be a desert strewn with worlds, like sparse oases, most of which are probably inanimate, apart from one small planet destined perhaps to populate the other worlds.[15] For the resources of any planet, however great, are eventually limited, and consequently an isolated world cannot maintain immortal beings. And why should they not be immortal? Death is inevitable today because of man's ignorance and consequent helplessness. Death is a form of epidemic disease. Sometimes it is even difficult to diagnose at what moment a human being is actually dead. The only certainty comes with the decomposition of the body. A better knowledge of physiology and psychology should make it possible to prevent the decomposition of corpses and achieve bodily immortality — and immortality could not be the privilege of one generation only. So the ultimate goal of the Common Task was to achieve, scientifically and in accordance with God's design, the resurrection of the dead.

As a preliminary to the resuscitation of earlier generations, the memory of the departed should be kept alive by lovingly

15. *FOD*, vol. I, p. 613.

preserving their graves and artefacts as well as their thoughts embodied in their writings. So alongside rural schools there should be churches where prayers would be said for the souls of the departed, as well as graveyards forming a link between the dead and the living. The adjoining library and museum would preserve both their thoughts and the work of their hands. The early histories of primitive people consist of genealogies (similar to those of the Bible). Russian peasants still religiously tended the tombs of their forefathers, where they brought Easter eggs and sang 'Christ is risen', and they still attended the early morning liturgy when the names of the dead are remembered during the *proskomidia*. If they were leaving their village for good, they would take with them at least a handful of dust from the cemetery, to be thrown later into their own graves. Thus the symbolic chain of filiation was never broken. In Fedorov's scheme, apart from the history museum every school would have, adjoining it, a museum of natural history with an observatory, however modestly equipped. These museums would not be store-rooms of antiquated curios and lifeless exhibits, but centres of research run by teachers, pupils and local inhabitants. Eventually they would lure back 'the learned' out of their urban ivory towers to the countryside, to a simpler, harder and more communal way of life which, hopefully, would revive in them a sense of kinship with other people.

The resurrection of the dead was the supreme act of love of the living for the deceased fathers and ancestors : a love approaching the divine love which binds together God the Father, God the Son and the Holy Spirit into a Trinity which is One in Three. Just as the three Persons within the Holy Trinity are unmerged, so would humanity be united without individuals being depersonalised. In its growing wisdom and power of love mankind would at last reach adulthood. People would cease to be governed by childish desires of domination over kith and kin, sexual impulses and other 'natural' instincts. From being *zoo-anthropic*, morality would become *theo-anthropic*. Men would become God's conscious and willing tools, His co-workers in the creation of a universe that God, from the beginning of time, could only have destined to attain incorruptible beauty and ineffable perfection.

This grandiose project was no mere day-dreaming. Fedorov advanced various practical schemes, such as methods of artificial rain-making and the use of atmospheric electricity as a source of energy. In his stress on the transforming power of human reason and collective toil, Fedorov differs from other authors, like Winwood Reade[16] and Charles Stoffel,[17] who also foretold a united and immortal humanity floating through outer space, but without any attempt to indicate the long and difficult steps by which this could be achieved. Even Teilhard de Chardin, who comes so close to Fedorov's vision of universal scientific research and the unification of mankind, emphasises the cosmic forces of evolution rather than human endeavour in the achievement of human love *(amorisation)* and the eventual divinisation of humanity at 'point omega', where God becomes 'all in all'.

The first glimmer of hope that rain might be produced by human agency came in 1891, coinciding with a terrible famine, caused by drought, in Russia. That same year Edward Powers, an American engineer, published a revised and enlarged edition of his book entitled *War and the Weather*,[18] describing experiments to induce rainfall by shooting at the sky with guns. He contended that the pressure engendered by the explosions would condense the aqueous vapours dispersed in the atmosphere. His small-scale experiments proved inconclusive, and the US Congress refused a further grant of $20,000

16. Winwood Reade, *The Martyrdom of Man*, Trubner, London, 1872, pp. 514-15.
17. Charles Stoffel, *Résurrection*, Paris, 1840 ; especially p. 97. Contrary to his principle of never quoting his sources, Fedorov gives an actual reference to this strange book.
18. Edward Powers, *War and the Weather*, Chicago, 1871, 2nd rev. edn 1890 ; see also Horace E. Byers, 'The history of weather modification' in W.N. Hess (ed.), *Weather and Climate Modification*, New York, 1974, chap. 1.

needed to fire up to forty thousand rounds of ammunition. Fedorov argued that further investigations on a much larger scale should be carried out during army manœuvres. However, although Powers' experiments had been discussed by the Russian Technological Society, no action was taken. Back in 1814 the scientific elite had similarly failed to test another, possibly seminal, idea put forward by V.N. Karazin, founder of the University of Kharkov and an amateur meteorologist.[19] Karazin had proposed raising lightning conductors on balloons to bring down lightning from thunder clouds and to use it as a source of energy, and possibly as a method of altering air currents and eventually redirecting the moisture of the atmosphere to wherever it was most needed. Atmospheric electricity and rain formation had been studied also by Sir Oliver Lodge, professor of physics and first vice-chancellor of Birmingham University. The rejection without trial of projects of such momentous importance to mankind was proof of scholars' callousness and indifference to the needs of the toiling masses. Thus, while men laboured in dark and dangerous mines and though coal itself was the product of solar energy, no serious endeavour was being made to harness solar energy itself.

The century that has elapsed since Fedorov's days makes many of his ideas obsolete. The political map of the world has changed out of all recognition — India is no longer a British colony ; China is no longer on the verge of partition into

19. V.N. Karazin (1773-1842) put his idea in a letter dated 9 April 1814 to A.A. Arakcheev, the notorious favourite of Emperor Alexander I. Arakcheev dismissed it with contempt. The letter was later published in *Sbornik istoricheskikh materialov, izvlechennykh iz pervago otdeleniya sobstvennoi Ego Imperatorskago Velichestva kantselyarii* (*Collection of Historical Materials from Department I of His Imperial Majesty's Private Chancery*), St Petersburg, 1891, p. 461. Fedorov devoted three articles to Karazin and his invention. According to Fedorov, similar proposals were put forward by Arago, Bernard and Lodge. The only precise reference is to Arago in *Annuaire pour l'an 1838, présenté au Roi par le bureau de longitudes*, p. 570. Bernard may refer to Claude Bernard, the famous physiologist, and Lodge to Sir Oliver Lodge, *Lightning Conductors and Lightning Guards*, 1892, chap. 1.

spheres of Western influence ; Constantinople, now Istanbul, has lost in the eyes of a Russia officially atheist and culturally uprooted the aura of 'Tsargrad', the cradle of Orthodox Christianity, its faith and traditions. Fedorov's scientific ideas are also out of date and may even sound naïve. But he raised the fundamental and increasingly urgent questions regarding the responsibility of scientists and the aims of scientific research. Even more than in his day, the lack of any higher purpose results in science being geared to military objectives or to the commercial production of consumer goods (with inbuilt obsolescence), the 'toys' of mass culture, while people in the Third World remain at the mercy of droughts, floods and desertification.

For the modern reader Fedorov's work is valuable because of its unusual treatment of problems that are still with us : how to achieve disarmament and to manage (not merely to exploit and pollute) nature ; how to determine the purpose of scientific research in general and the conquest of outer space in particular ; how to achieve, if not brotherhood, at least friendly cooperation by working together on projects important to all — such as the elimination of smallpox sponsored by the World Health Organisation and other projects financed by the United Nations Environment Programme. He anticipated the question so neatly expressed by the Soviet geographer Igor Zabelin in an article entitled 'Humanity — what is it for ?'.[20] Indeed, has 'the planet of reason'[21] any mission to carry out ? Are the prophecies concerning the Last Judgement conditional on mankind reaching adulthood, as Fedorov hoped, or will men fall victim to their childish lust for domination over each other and to a man-made nuclear annihilation ?

As George M. Young says in his excellent book *Nikolai F. Fedorov : An Introduction*,[22] modern technology has given

20. I.M. Zabelin, 'Chelovechestvo — dlya chego ono ?' (*Humanity — what is it for ?*), *Moskva*, 1966, n° 8, pp. 173-86 ; especially with reference to Fedorov, ibid., 1968, n° 5, pp. 147-61.
21. I.D. Laptev, *Planeta razuma*, Moscow, 1973.
22. George Young, op. cit., p. 198.

us the power to alter life itself, but 'just what we should do with this Godlike power is a question that someone is going to have to answer. Fedorov's answer may not be the best one that will ever be proposed, but so far it seems the most thorough and deepest attempt at one.'

Elisabeth Koutaissoff

THE PHILOSOPHY
OF THE COMMON TASK

Part I

The problem of brotherhood or kinship, of the causes of the unbrotherly, unkindred, that is, the unpeaceful state of the world, and of the means for the restoration of kinship

A memorandum from the 'unlearned' to the 'learned', clergy and laity, believers and non-believers

> Why is it that the words 'peace' and 'world' are not synonymous ? Why does peace, according to some, exist only in the world beyond and, according to others, neither in this world nor beyond it ?
> Why is nature not a mother, but a stepmother who refuses to feed us ?
> Participation of all in material comfort or participation of all in the work — essentially voluntary — of understanding the blind force which brings hunger, disease and death, and transforming it into a life-giving force ?

§ 1

In 1891, the disastrous year when crop failure in many of the provinces constituting the granary of Russia caused a famine which threatened to become endemic, and when rumours of war were rife, we suddenly heard of experiments in rain-making by means of explosives[1] — that is, by the very

---

1. Reference to Powers's experiments in rain-making ; see note 18 to the Introduction.

substances which hitherto were used solely for wars foreign and domestic (such as revolutions, dynamite attacks and so on). The coincidence of this famine caused by drought and the discovery of how to combat it by means used hitherto only for mutual annihilation could not fail to produce a shattering effect on those on the verge of starvation as well as on those who had relatives of military age. And not on them alone.

Indeed, people have done all possible evil to nature (depletion, destruction, predatory exploitation) and to each other (inventing most abominable arms and implements of mutual extermination). Even roads and other means of communication — the pride of modern man — serve merely strategic and commercial purposes, war and gain. Profit-makers look upon nature as 'a storehouse from which to extract the wherewithal for a comfortable and enjoyable life, destroying and squandering nature's wealth accumulated over centuries'.*

This could lead to despair, because there was everywhere only evil to be seen, without a glimmer of hope. Now, suddenly, like a joyous ray of light for 'those dwelling in darkness and under the shadow of death', come the good tidings that those very means of mutual annihilation may become means of salvation from hunger. Here is hope that an end may be put to both famine and war — moreover an end to war without disarmament, for the latter is not possible.

Even unbelievers, even professed atheists, can hardly fail to see in this possibility of transforming a great evil into a great blessing a sign of Divine Providence. Here is a completely new proof of the existence of God and His Providence, a proof derived no longer from contemplating the purposefulness of the natural order, but from acting and from influencing it in real life. Is it not indeed a manifestation of God's great mercy to man, who seems to have reached the limits of perversity,

---

* From a sermon by Bishop Ambrosius of Kharkov, preached at the University of Kharkov and published under the title 'The Christian way in natural science', *Tserkovnye vedomosti*, 1892, n° 5.

sinning against both nature and his fellow beings and even rejecting the very existence of God ?

Yet from the pulpit comes a voice saying, 'Beware of this audacity which seeks to bring down rain from heaven by means of gunfire.' * But if gunfire cannot be condemned out of hand even when it brings death (for example, in the defence of the homeland), why should it be condemned when it brings life and saves people from starvation ? Is it not rather the carrying out of God's will ? Having created man, did He not enjoin him to possess the Earth and all that is upon it ? So why is it wicked insolence and even sacrilege to redirect a cloud from a place where its rain could be harmful, to one where it would be beneficial ? To channel water from a stream or river for irrigation is not regarded as obstructing God's will, so why should redirecting moisture for human needs, not from a stream but from atmospheric currents, be contrary to God's will ? The more so when this is done not for the sake of luxury or fun but to provide our daily bread.

If the censure expressed in the sermon 'The Christian way in natural science' referred solely to plans envisaged by the Americans to patent their discovery and thus make a holy act of succour into a financial speculation, then one could bow to the wisdom of the condemnation. However, our hopes are based not on the possibility of bringing about rain by firing a few cannon shots, but on that of controlling moist and dry air currents over vast territories by concerted action which would require the joint efforts of the armies of all nations. Consequently, it could not become a private financial speculation.

Even if our hopes of rain-making by means of explosions were to be thwarted, the value of the hypothesis would remain, since it points to an operation involving the whole human race. Other means used in warfare might be found to regulate meteorological phenomena : consider, for instance, the suggestion of V.N. Karazin (who pioneered the setting up

---

* Concluding remarks of Bishop Ambrosius of Kharkov.

of the Ministry of Education and the foundation of the University of Kharkov) for raising lightning conductors on balloons into the upper strata of the atmosphere. Balloons are not yet used as military equipment, but might be in future ; at the present time everything is put to the service of war. There is not a single invention which the military are not bent on applying to warfare, not a single discovery which they fail to turn to military purposes. So if it were made the duty of the armies to adapt everything now used in warfare for controlling natural forces, this duty would automatically become the common task of humanity as a whole.

§ 2

Crop failures and, in particular, the 1891 famine impel the 'unlearned' to remind the 'learned' of their origin and of the vocation that this entails, namely :

1. To study the force which produces crop failures and lethal diseases : that is, to study nature as a death-bearing force and to regard this study as a sacred duty and, moreover, as the most simple, natural and self-evident duty.

2. To unite both the learned and the unlearned for the purpose of studying and controlling this blind force. Indeed, can there be any other purpose or task for a being endowed with consciousness ? To expect that a blind force destined to be controlled by a conscious being, who fails to do so, will produce only good results such as rich harvests, is extreme childishness — and of this the Paris Exhibition of 1889 and the French Exhibition in Moscow in 1891, the very year of the famine, were manifestations. No wonder that the wrath of the Lord is upon us for the protracted infantilism of our behaviour. How can it be otherwise, since we fail to heed His command 'to come unto true wisdom', which consists in achieving a unity similar to that of God the Father and God the Son, a unity which can be achieved only through working for one common cause, that of our fathers ?

The learned, who have fragmented science into a multiplicity of branches, imagine that the calamities that strike and oppress us are within the competence of specialised disciplines to control, whereas in fact they constitute a single problem common to all of us, namely the lack of kinship relations between a blind force and rational beings. This blind force makes no demand on us other than to endow it with what it lacks : rational direction, or regulation. Yet no regulation is possible owing to our disunity, and our disunity persists because there is no common task to unite men. Regulation, the control of the blind force of nature, can and must become the great task common to us all.

§ 3

The regulation of meteorological processes is necessary not only to improve harvests and agriculture in general, but also to replace the inhuman underground toil of miners who extract the coal and iron on which modern industry is based. Regulation is necessary in order to replace this extraction with energy from atmospheric currents and solar radiation, which created the coal deposits in the first place. The position of miners is so miserable that it would be unpardonable to disregard it, and it is these conditions that the socialists — these foes of society — expose to stir up sedition. The regulation of the meteorological process could solve both the agricultural and the industrial problems.

§ 4

Since the consequences of the lack of kinship relations bear most heavily on the unlearned, they naturally turn to the learned to question them, because the educated are a class which exhibits alienation from its kin in an extreme form, and also because that class has the duty, ability and responsibility to restore kinship. But although it has within its grasp the understanding and, consequently, the solution of the problem, the learned class fails to solve it. Moreover, out of servility to feminine caprice the learned have promoted and are supporting the manufacturing industry, which is at the root of alienation ; and, furthermore, they invent weapons of destruction to defend this manufacturing industry.

The unlearned are in duty bound to question the learned on the causes of alienation, both because of their present attitude to the unlearned and because of the very origin of the learned class. Historically, we would be wrong to explain the emergence of the learned class as occasioned by the setting up of a commission with a definite assignment, just as it was wrong to explain the origins of the state by the social contract, as posited by eighteenth-century philosophers. Of course, there is no juridical evidence for the idea of such a commission. However, if one takes an ethical view of history, the separation of the urban from the rural classes, and the further separation of the learned from the mass of the urban class, could have had no other purpose than that of a temporary assignment — otherwise such a separation would be permanent and would constitute the complete negation of unity. Historically, we may be wrong to explain the origin of the learned class as the setting up of a commission for a definite purpose. One cannot contend that this happened in actual fact. Nevertheless, morally we are right, for that is how it should have happened.

A truly moral being does not need compulsion and repeated orders to perceive what his duty is — he assigns to himself his task and prescribes what must be done for those from whom he has become separated, because separation (whether voluntary or not) cannot be irreversible. Indeed, it would be criminal to repudiate those from whom one descends and to forget about their welfare. For the learned to behave thus would be to reject their own welfare, to remain prodigal sons for ever and be permanent hirelings and servants of urban caprice. This would lead them to disregard completely the needs of rural communities, that is, real needs, because the needs of such communities, unspoilt by city influences, are limited to those essentials that ensure survival in the face of hunger and illness, which not only destroy life but also displace kinship relations and replace love by enmity and hostility. Therefore the rural problem is (1) loss of kinship between men who, through ignorance, forget their relatedness, and (2) the hostility of nature to humans, which is felt most acutely if not exclusively in villages, where people confront the blind force directly ; whereas townsfolk, being remote from nature, may think that man lives at one with nature.

§ 5

The hateful division of the world and all the calamities that result from this compel us, the unlearned — that is, those who place action (action in common, not strife) above thought — to submit to the learned this memorandum concerned with lack of kinship feelings and the means of restoring them. In particular, we address it to theologians, those men of thought and ideology who rank thought above action. Of all divisions, the dissociation of thought and action (which has become the appurtenance of certain classes) constitutes a great calamity, incomparably greater than the division into rich and poor. Socialists and our contemporaries in general attribute the greatest importance to this division into rich and poor, assuming that with its elimination all of us would become educated. However, what we have in mind is not schooling, which will become more evenly available with the elimination of poverty. What we have in mind is universal participation in knowledge and research. The elimination of poverty is not sufficient to ensure such a universal participation. Yet it alone can bridge the chasm between the learned and the unlearned.

So long as participation in knowledge does not embrace everyone, pure science will remain indifferent to struggle and depredation, while applied science will contribute to destruction either directly by the invention of weapons, or indirectly by endowing things like consumer goods with a seductive appearance, thus fostering friction among people. Scientists, who take no direct personal part in the struggle or in actual war and who are outside the reach of natural disasters because they are sheltered against them by the peasantry — who bear the full brunt of nature — will remain indifferent even to the depletion of natural resources and to changes in climate. Indeed, changes in climate may be pleasant to town dwellers, even when they result in crop failures.

Only when all men come to participate in knowledge will pure science, which perceives nature as a whole in which the sentient is sacrificed to the insensate, cease to be indifferent to this distorted attitude of the conscious being to the unconscious force. Then applied science will be aimed at transforming instruments of destruction into means of regulating the blind death-bearing force.

E. Haeckel[2] accepts 'scientific materialism' and denies 'moral materialism'. He sees supreme bliss in the knowledge and discovery of the laws of nature. But even assuming that such knowledge were accessible to all, where would be the joy ? In contemplating everywhere the ruthless struggle of all against all ? Who could enjoy such hell ?

Solving the first problem, that of the segregation of the learned from the unlearned — that is, men of thought from men of action — will also solve the division between rich and poor. The root cause of this division lies in common calamities like sickness and death, and can be overcome only given a higher purpose — the participation of all in knowledge and in art, both directed towards solving the problem of loss of kinship and its restoration, that is, the search for the Kingdom of God.

§ 6

The question of 'brotherhood and the unbrotherly state of the world' implies the conditions under which brotherhood can and must be restored. These conditions constitute a practical problem, as in the case of the Eastern Question, or of colonialism or migration. The problem is how to find a way out of the unbrotherly state. Thus posed, the problem

---

2. Ernst Haeckel (1834-1919), German philosopher and scientist who sought to reconcile science and religion in the theory of monism.

becomes the concern of all the sons of man, particularly of those baptised in the name of the God of their fathers. Although it is directed at scholars because the problem of knowledge and science, that is, the theoretical problem, is contained within the practical one as its necessary prerequisite and integral part, this problem is not one of scholarship or research.

§ 7

By using the word 'question' in this memorandum to the learned from the unlearned, we admit our weakness in comparison to those to whom we address it. Those who ask are obviously those who do not know and who recognise their weakness. This is not an expression of modesty commonly found in introductions. It is the inevitable humility before the terrifying force which causes unbrotherliness, yet urges union and the need to speak for the least articulate. It is a humility in the face of a force which silences mere interest groups. And if Russia and Russian science address this question to other nations standing at a higher intellectual and moral level, there is nothing offensive in it for these high-ranking nations or for their pride.

§ 8

The unbrotherly state is conditioned, of course, by serious causes. The circumstances we live in render the question of unbrotherliness one of general concern. In speaking of the causes of unbrotherliness, we indicate that it is not rooted in caprice, that it cannot be papered over by words nor by the mere desire to wish away these causes. The combined effort of knowledge and action is needed, because such a persistent disease, with roots within and outside man, cannot be cured in the twinkling of an eye, as those who are moved solely by emotions would have it. Their disquisitions on unbrotherliness could be described as treatises on the absence of causality for the unbrotherly state. They would forbid us to think because thought and reasoning mean, in fact, the discovery of causes and conditions. To admit an absence of causality for the unbrotherly state leads not to peace and brotherhood but merely to playing at peace, to a comedy of reconciliation which creates a pseudo-peace, a false peace which is worse than open hostility because the latter poses a question whereas the former prolongs enmity by concealing it. Such is the doctrine of Tolstoy. Having quarrelled one day, he goes to make peace the next. He takes no measures to forestall clashes but apparently seeks them out, perhaps in order thereafter to conclude a fragile peace.

However, causality in the sense of determinism can be assumed only in respect of people taken individually, in disunion. The learned class accepts fatal, eternal determinism because they deny the possibility of common action. The impossibility of doing away with our state of unbrotherliness is a fundamental dogma of scholars, because to admit the contrary would imply that they must turn themselves into a commission with a purpose to fulfil.

§ 9

By unbrotherly relations we mean all juridical and economic relations, class distinctions and international strife. Among the causes of unbrotherliness we include 'citizenship' and 'civilisation', which have displaced brotherhood, and also 'statehood', which has replaced loyalty to the land of the fathers. Loyalty to the land of the fathers is not 'patriotism', which replaces love for the fathers with pride in their achievement, thus substituting pride (a vice) for love (a virtue) and self-love and vanity for love of the fathers.

People who take pride in the same object can form a knightly order but not a brotherhood of loving sons. However, as soon as pride in the exploits of the fathers is replaced by grief over their death, we will begin to perceive the Earth as a graveyard and nature as a death-bearing force. Then politics will yield to physics, which cannot be separated from astronomy. Then the Earth will be seen as a heavenly body and the stars as so many earths. The convergence of all sciences in astronomy is a most simple, natural and unscholarly phenomenon, demanded by feeling as well as by any mind not addicted to abstraction. In this convergence mythical patrification will become actual resuscitation, and the regulation of all the worlds by all the resurrected generations.

The problem of the force which brings the two sexes to unite and give birth to a third being is also a problem of death. The exclusive attachment to a woman leads the man to forget his fathers, introduces political and civil strife into the world and, at the same time, makes man forget that the Earth is a heavenly body and that heavenly bodies are stars.

So long as historical life was confined to the shores of oceans, to the seaboard, and encompassed only a small part of the earth enjoying approximately similar conditions, life was political, commercial and civil ; it was a civilisation — in other words, a struggle. Now the interiors of continents are drawn into a history which will embrace the entire Earth ; so political and cultural problems become physical or astrophysical, that is, heavenly-terrestrial.

§ 10

...There is only one doctrine which demands not separation but reunification, which sets no artificial aims but one common task for all — the doctrine of kinship... Only this doctrine can provide a solution to the problem of the individual and the masses. Union does not absorb but exalts each individual, while the differences between individuals strengthen unity, which consists in (1) the realisation by every person that he is a son, grandson, great-grandson or descendant, that is, a son of all the deceased fathers and not a vagrant in the crowd, devoid of kith and kin ; and (2) the recognition by each and everyone, together and not in disunity as in a mob, of one's duty to the deceased fathers, a duty which is limited solely by sensuality, or rather by its misuse, for it breaks up rural communities and transforms them into an amorphous mass.

The human mob with its mutual pushing and struggling will

become a harmonious force when the rural masses, the people, become the union of sons for the resurrection of the fathers, thus achieving kinship or *psychocracy*. The metamorphosis of a mob into a union of sons who find their unity in a common task does not entail loss of identity. By sharing in this task every man becomes a great man — because he participates in the greatness of the task — incomparably greater than those who have been called great men. Only the son of man is a great man, for he has measured up to the adulthood of Jesus Christ who called himself the Son of Man.

A humanist who calls himself a human and is proud of this denomination has evidently not yet achieved adulthood in Christ and has not become *a son* of man. Those who reject the veneration of ancestors are depriving themselves of the right to be called sons of man. Instead of participating in the Common Task they become the organs, the tools, of various industries — mere cogs, however much they may think that they live for themselves. In such a state no one can assert, says Noiré,[3] that the eternal existence of individuals X or Y has any exceptional importance or even any sense, so that it might have been better for them not to exist at all. This of course refers only to X and Y. It cannot refer to *the sons of man, the participators in resurrection*, whose existence is not only vitally important but absolutely indispensable if the purpose of life is to transform the blind force of nature into one governed by the reason of all the generations brought back to life. Then, of course, *each and everyone* is indispensable.

§ 11

The question posed by the present memorandum is twofold.

1. When the question of the causes of lack of kinship is likened to the Eastern Question or that of migration, for

---

3. Ludwig Noiré (1829-89), German philosopher and prolific writer on the history of philosophy, the theories of monism and the philosophy of language. It is difficult to tell to which of his many books Fedorov alludes in this passage.

instance, it is assumed that science must be a knowledge not only of causes, but of aims as well. And it must not be solely a knowledge of initial causes, but also of ultimate ones (that is, it must not be knowledge for the sake of knowledge, knowledge without action). It must not be a knowledge of *what is* without one of *what should be*. In other words, science must be a knowledge not of causes *in general* but specifically of that underlying *disunity* which makes us the tools of the blind force of nature and results in the displacement of the older generation by the younger, as well as in mutual constraints conducive to a similar displacement.

2. When the unlearned admit their ignorance and inquire about the causes of unbrotherliness, other questions arise too : namely, should the learned remain a separate caste or school, entitled to brush aside the questions of the ignorant on the grounds that science is the study of causes *in general* (pure speculation), or should they turn themselves into a commission for the elucidation and practical solution of the problem of disunity ? Should they regard their segregation from the mass of mankind as a temporary purposeful arrangement or as an ultimate end ? Should they consider themselves as 'co-spectators' of the path that lies before all, or are they the better and higher class, the flower and fruit of the human race ? Is the problem about scholarship and the intelligentsia, or is it about internal disharmony — in other words, about intelligence deprived of feeling and willpower ? And is the complete loss of a sense of kinship an essential characteristic of the learned inevitably resulting from the separation of intelligence from feeling and will ?

Internal discord reflects external disunion, that is, the separation of the learned and intellectual classes from the people. Intelligence without feeling becomes the knowledge of evil without any desire to root it out, and a knowledge of good without any wish to promote it. It is an admission of lack of kinship and not a plan to re-establish kinship bonds. The consequence of indifference is oblivion for the fathers and discord among the sons. The causes of lack of kinship extend to nature as a whole, for it is a blind force uncontrolled by reason.

However, as soon as intelligence combines with feeling, memories of the deceased fathers return (museum), as well as the union of sons with those still living (assembly) for the education of their progeny (school). The wholeness of feeling brings about the union of all the living (sons), while the force of their will and joint action leads to the resurrection of all the deceased (fathers). What then is needed for the museum and the assembly to achieve such wholeness ?

So long as the object of science is to solve the problem of causes in general, it remains concerned solely with the question, 'Why does the existing exist ?' This is an unnatural, a wholly artificial, question, whereas it would be quite natural to ask, 'Why do the living die ?' Because of the absence of brotherhood, this question is not posed, or even perceived, as requiring investigation. Yet this is the sole object of research which could provide a meaning to the existence of philosophers and scholars, who would cease being a caste in order to become a provisional commission with a specific purpose.

§ 12

By exchanging their status of upper class for that of a commission with a purpose, scholars would lose only imaginary advantages and gain real ones. The world would no longer be perceived as a mental image, a representation, the inevitable view of the scholars in their ivory towers, deprived of activity and condemned to mere contemplation or to desires with no means of implementing them. The new representation of the world would then become the blueprint for a better world, and the task of the commission would be the drafting and implementation of such a plan. Then pessimism would vanish, as would the kind of optimism that seeks misleadingly to represent the world as better than it is. It would be no longer necessary to conceal evil or to convince oneself that death does not exist. Yet while admitting the existence of evil in all its might, we would not lose hope that, through the union of all the forces of reason, we would find it possible to redirect the irrational force which produces evil and death and all the resulting disasters. By assuming immanent resurrection, we circumscribe man's curiosity directed towards the transcendental as well as towards thought without action. While objecting to spiritualism and similar aspirations to otherworldliness, we do not restrict man, because the field of the immanent within his reach is so wide that moral brotherly feelings and universal love can find in it complete satisfaction.

The segregation of scholars into a separate caste gives rise to three evils :

1. The fundamental one is the reduction of the world to a mere representation, a mental image ; in ordinary life egotism, solipsism and all ensuing crimes find a philosophical justification in the formula, 'The world is my representation of it' — the latest word in Kantianism. The reduction of the world to its representation is the outcome of inactivity and individualism ; it is the child of idleness — mother of all vices — and of solipsism (selfishness) — father of all crimes.

2 and 3. The consequences of this primary evil — the reduction of the world to its representation — are two other evils : drug addiction and hypnotism. If the world is merely one's representation of it, then the transformation of unpleasant into pleasant representations by means of morphine, ether and so on would solve the world's problems by replacing suffering by pleasurable sensations. (Hypnotism provides an even simpler solution. It claims to cure all sickness and vices by strength of will.) However, to resort to narcotics is to stupefy oneself and forgo reason and feeling. People resort to drugs because they fail to find in life a worthy use for their reason. They will stop doing so when their task becomes the transformation of a blind force into a rational one, thus making all life rational. The peculiar addiction of the learned, that is, the deliberate self-deprivation of reason by those who live by thought, is apparently their punishment for setting themselves apart from the rest of humanity, for their

indifference to calamities and for their unworthy use of rational thought.

On the other hand, we witness the drift of science towards magic, witchcraft, exorcism or suggestion in hypnosis. One well known professor advocating 'suggestion', that is, 'exorcism', rather than 'exhortation', seems not to notice that he relegates the mind to inaction. Indeed, a great intellectual effort is needed to make exhortation convincing, but none is required for suggestion. To replace rational argument by suggestion is an abdication of intelligence and rational willpower by both hypnotist and hypnotised. What will be the fate of a faculty reduced to inaction ? Will it be in danger of atrophy ? Why give preference to the irrational over the rational ? If admonitions prove ineffectual, other rational ways may be found : for instance, research into individual inclinations and abilities, or discoveries concerning the relations between inner and outer human properties, which may open up new insights into how and in collaboration with whom every human can give of his best in solving the problem of restoring universal kinship.

To replace exhortation by exorcism is to abdicate reason. Moreover, hypnosis is also an abdication of consciousness, that is, a submission to the blind, unconscious forces and a rejection of conscious work. Should we follow the advice of the Evil Spirit to turn stones into bread by uttering a single word ? Or shall we earn our bread by work and make sure of it by regulating nature ?

§ 13

Positivism — the latest in European thought — is not a way out of scholasticism because it too is based on the distinction between theoretical and practical reason. The helplessness of theoretical reason is explicable by inaction and by the absence of a common task to provide any proof. Positivism is merely a modification of metaphysical scholasticism, which arose, similarly, from a modification of theological scholasticism. Therefore, positivism is also scholasticism, and positivists form a school and not an investigative commission in the sense we imply.

However, if positivism were to oppose popular and religious attitudes, which consist not merely of knowledge and contemplation but of action, sacrifice, cult, and so on, which are mythical and miraculous (ineffective and illusory) remedies against evil, then positivism could contribute to transforming these mythical, miraculous, make-believe, symbolic acts into an effective, real remedy against evil. It would meet a need hitherto satisfied, or rather, stultified (through ignorance), by sham remedies against evil. If positivism, either Western (European) or Eastern (Chinese), actually opposed the mythical and fictitious, there would be nothing arbitrary about it. However, it sees its merit in limiting and negating. It turns out to be not a method of substituting the real for the imaginary, but merely the denial of the latter. It even denies the possibility of replacing the allegorical by the real, and hence of satisfying man's most legitimate craving — his urge to ensure his existence.

Critical philosophy — Kantianism and neo-Kantianism — is also a school and not a solution. The *Critique of Pure Reason* can be said to deal with science or philosophy only within the narrow limits of an artificial, particularised experience (confined to laboratory or academic study). Similarly, the *Critique of Practical Reason* can be said to deal with life only within the narrow limits of personal affairs and within the kind of disunity that is not regarded as vice ; it is a moral code for minors whose crimes would be called 'mischief' in popular Russian. The *Critique of Practical Reason* knows no united humanity, nor does it prescribe any rules for common action by mankind as a whole. Like the *Critique of Pure Reason*, it knows only experiments carried out *sometimes, somewhere and by some people*. It ignores those experiments carried out by *all, always and everywhere* that will come about when national armed forces transform their weapons into instruments for the regulation of atmospheric phenomena.

All that is good in the *Critique of Pure Reason* — that is

God — is an ideal ; and in the *Critique of Practical Reason*, is a reality beyond this world. So reality consists of (1) a soulless world, an irrational, unfeeling force which it would be more appropriate to call chaos than cosmos, and its study *chaosography* rather than cosmology, and (2) a helpless soul, a knowledge of which can be called psychology (in the sense of *psychocracy*) only because of its potentialities, since a soul, separated from God and from the Universe, is merely a *capacity* to feel, know and act, while deprived of energy and will. The union of reason, feeling and will could result in a project, a grand plan, but this is not to be found in Kant. For spiritualists peace can be found only in the world beyond ; for materialists there is no peace either here or in the world beyond ; and in critical philosophy (Kant) peace is merely our thought, not a reality. When the separation of the intelligentsia from the people is recognised as illegitimate, thought will become planning. Are we not justified in saying that both positive and critical philosophy are schools and belong, therefore, to the age of immaturity ?

Like the positivists, Kant doomed knowledge to permanent childhood. Constrained within the boundaries of artificial, toy-sized experiments, science is kept aloof from the unknowable, from metaphysics and agnosticism. Similarly the *Critique of Practical Reason* (the critique of action), by denying humans a common task, forces them into illusory activities like hypnotism, spiritualism, and so on.

Happiness in life is dearly bought by Kant. Forget about perfection — it is unattainable (for God is but an ideal) ; therefore your imperfection should not worry you. Do not think about death, and you will not fall into the paralogism of immortality. Attend to your business and do not think about what lies beyond — whether the world is finite or infinite, eternal or temporary, you cannot know. So says Kant in his *Critique of Pure Reason*. However, all the negation of the *Critique of Pure Reason* is based solely on the assumption that human dissension is inevitable and that union in a common task is impossible. This assumption is but prejudice, of which

Kant was not conscious, and which he did not perceive because he was a great philosopher and, consequently, could not imagine anything superior to thought. What Kant regarded as unattainable to knowledge is the object of action, an action achievable only by humanity as a whole, in the communion of individuals and not in disunion and separateness. The *Critique of Practical Reason* is similarly based on the unconscious assumption of inevitable disunity. The vice of disunity (though not recognised as such) is also the basis of Kant's moral system. This philosopher, who lived in the days of so-called enlightened despotism, projected the principle of absolutism into the field of morality, as if God had said, 'All for men but nothing through men.'

The principle of disunion and inactivity informs all three Critiques. The philosophy of art which he embodies in his *Critique of Judgement* does not teach how to create, but only how to judge the aesthetic aspects of works of art and of nature. It is a philosophy for art critics, not for artists and poets. In the *Critique of Judgement*, nature is regarded not as an object to be acted upon and transformed from a blind force into one governed by reason, but merely as an object of contemplation to be judged on its aesthetic merits ; not from the point of view of morality, which would recognise it as destructive and death-bearing...

§ 15

Since first and last causes are outside of its investigations, positivism considers it impossible to know the meaning and purpose of life. For positivists resurrection is neither possible nor desirable. Does not their reluctance to restore life prove that, to them, this life is not worth restoring ? For the progressives the present is bad and the past was even worse. Only the least thoughtful of them imagine that the future is good, though it, too, will become the present and then the past, that is, the bad. Therefore a true progressive must be a pessimist. A well known professor[4] has said :

4. Nikolai Ivanovich Kareev was professor of history at Warsaw University

Progress is a gradual ascent in the level of general human development. In this sense the prototype of progress is individual psychic development which is both an objectively observable fact and a subjective fact of our consciousness ; the inner experience of our development appears as the recognition of a gradual increase in knowledge and lucidity of thought, and these processes represent an improvement of our thinking being — its ascent. This fact of individual psychology is repeated in collective psychology, when members of a whole society recognise their superiority over their predecessors in the same society.

However, a society consists of an older and a younger generation, of parents and children. Apparently, the author had in mind both old and young without regard to differences in age, assuming that members progress equally (neither ageing nor weakening), so that their superiority is only over the deceased. Remembrance and history are necessary solely to have someone to outclass. Can one overlook the sinfulness of this claim to superiority of the living over the dead, and fail to notice the egotism of the present generation ? Yet the life of a society consists in the ageing of the old and the growing up of the young. Growing up and realising its superiority over the deceased, the younger generation cannot, according to the law of progress, fail to recognise its superiority over the ageing and the dying. When an old man says to the young man, 'It's for you to grow and for me to decline', this is a laudable wish, showing fatherly affection. If, however, the young man says, 'It's for me to grow and for you to get off to the grave', this is not progress, but the voice of hate, the obvious hate of prodigal sons.

Progress without internal union and without an external

and, later, at the University of St Petersburg. The quotations are taken from vol. 2, part 4 of his 3-volume work *Basic Problems of the Philosophy of History* (*Osnovnye voprosy filosofii istorii*), Moscow, 1886-90.

task shared by all humanity is a natural phenomenon. So long as there is no uniting for the purpose of transforming a death-bearing force into a life-giving one, man will be dominated by the blind force of nature, on a par with cattle, other beasts and soulless matter.

Progress is a sense of superiority, (1) of an entire generation of the living over their ancestors, and (2) of the younger over the old. This superiority — a point of pride among the young — consists of an increase in knowledge, of improvement and advance in the thinking process ; even the formation of moral convictions is seen as a reason to extol the younger generation over the older. 'He (every member of the younger generation) feels his superiority over his elders whenever he enriches himself with knowledge, perceives a new idea, comes to appreciate his environment from a new angle or when, in a collision of duty with habit and emotion, duty is the victor.'

All this is the subjective aspect of the consciousness of intellectual superiority over one's predecessors. In what way will this consciousness become manifest externally ? How will it be expressed as an objective fact observable by those progenitors who are still alive ? The professor does not say. However, the haughty attitude of sons and daughters towards their parents as a necessary expression of their sense of superiority is all too well known, and has even found a mouthpiece in the author of *Fathers and Sons*,[5] although in a watered down form.

While there are young people in Western Europe — in France, in Germany — nowhere is the antagonism of the young towards the old so extreme as it is with us. That is why it is easier for us to appreciate fully the doctrine of progress. Biologically, it is the replacement of love by presumptuousness, contempt and the moral, or rather immoral, displacement of fathers by sons. Sociologically, progress is the achievement of the greatest possible individual freedom accessible to man — but not the broadest participation of all in

---

5. I.S. Turgenev, *Fathers and Sons* (*Otsy i deti*), 1861.

a common task. Yet society — an unbrotherly association — limits the freedom of individuals. Therefore, sociology demands at the same time the greatest possible individual freedom and the minimum of community feeling. Consequently, it is a science not of association but of dissociation and even subjugation, insofar as it admits the absorption of the individual by society. As a science of dissociation for some and of subjugation for others, sociology sins against the Holy Trinity, the indivisible and unconfused Triune God. Progress is precisely the form of life in which the human race may come to taste the greatest sum of suffering while striving for the greatest sum of enjoyment. Progress is not satisfied with the recognition of the reality of evil ; it wants the reality of evil to be fully represented, and revels in realistic art. As to ideal art, it strives to convince people that good is unreal and impossible, and revels in nirvana. Although stagnation is death and regression no paradise, progress is truly hell, and the truly divine, truly human task is to save the victims of progress, to lead them out of hell.

Progress involves superiority not only over the fathers (still alive) and ancestors (already dead) but also over animals. 'The ability to conceive general principles is a purely human ability which sets us above animals and makes possible the development of knowledge, ideals and convictions.' However, this purely mental development is not sufficient to unite us in shared convictions, to lead us to accept common ideals and become of one mind. While placing human nature above animal nature, the advocates of progress deny any importance to humanity in the face of the blind force of nature. While recognising our superiority over fathers and ancestors and, to a lesser degree, over animals, they accept humanity's utter insignificance before blind, insensate nature.

Progress makes fathers and ancestors into the accused and the sons and descendants into judges ; historians are judges over the deceased, that is, those who have already endured capital punishment (the death penalty), while the sons sit in judgement over those who have not yet died. Scholars may argue that whereas in ancient times old people were put to death, now they are only despised. Does not replacing physical by spiritual death constitute progress ?! In the future, with the march of progress, contempt will decrease, but not even the withering away of contempt will engender love and respect for one's predecessors, that is to say, the feelings which really ennoble the descendants. Therefore, can progress give any meaning to life, let alone any purpose ? Only that which can express the loftiest forms of love and veneration gives meaning and purpose to life. 'The aim of progress is a developed and developing individuality and the greatest degree of freedom attainable by man' : such an aim entails not fraternal feelings but disunity and, consequently, the zenith of progress is the nadir of brotherhood.

Resurrection is not progress, but it requires actual improvement, true perfection. A spontaneous happening like giving birth requires neither wisdom nor willpower unless the latter is confused with lust, whereas resuscitation is the replacement of the lust of birth by conscious recreation. The notion of progress in the sense of development, evolution, has been borrowed from blind nature and applied to human life. It recognises an advance from the worse to the better and places articulate man above the dumb beast, but is it right that progress should follow nature's example, taking for its model an unconscious force and applying it to a conscious, sensate being ? Insofar as progress is regarded as a movement from the worse to the better, it obviously requires that the shortcomings of blind nature be corrected by a nature which perceives these shortcomings — that is, by the combined power of the human race. It demands that improvement should arise not through struggle and mutual annihilation but by the return of the victims of this struggle. Then progress will mean the improvement of means as well as ends. Such an improvement would be more than correction ; it would be the elimination of evil and the introduction of good. Progress itself demands resuscitation, but this involves progress not only in knowledge but also in activity ; and progress in knowledge means a knowledge not only of *what is*, but above all of *what should be*. Only with the passage of the learned class from knowledge to action will progress move from a knowledge of *what is* to one of *what should be*...

The ideal of progress, according to the learned, is to enable everybody to participate in the production and consumption of objects for sensual pleasure, whereas the aim of true progress can and must be the participation in a common task, the work of studying the blind force that brings hunger, disease and death in order to transform it into a life-giving force.

§ 16

The doctrine of resurrection could also be called positivism, but a positivism of action. According to this doctrine it would not be mythical knowledge that would be replaced by positive knowledge, but mythical, symbolic actions that would be replaced by actual, effective ones. The doctrine of resurrection sets no arbitrary limits to action performed in common, as opposed to action by separate individuals. This positivism of action derives not from mythology, which was a fabrication of pagan priests, but from mythological art forms, popular rituals and sacrifices. Resuscitation changes symbolic acts into reality. The positivism of action is not class-bound but popular positivism. For the people, science will be a method, whereas the positivism of science is merely a philosophy for scholars as a separate class or estate.

§ 17

Positivism was right in its critical attitude to knowledge, in considering it incapable of solving fundamental problems. However, the knowledge it envisaged critically was one divorced from action, but which cannot and must not be divorced from action. Aristotle may be regarded as the father of the learned, yet he is reported to have said, 'We know only what we can do ourselves', a statement which obviously does not allow for the separation of knowledge from action and, consequently, the segregation of the learned into a special estate. Yet, although two thousand years or more have elapsed since Aristotle, no thinker has made this principle, this criterion for proving knowledge by action, into the corner-stone of his philosophy. Otherwise, a knowledge of the self and of the external world — of nature, past and present — would have become a project to transform that which is born or given gratis into that which is earned through labour, entailing the restitution of strength and life to the procreators. It would have become a plan to transform a blind force into a rational one and prove that life is not 'a fortuitous and futile gift'.[6]

Positivism is also partially justified in its critical attitude to personal, individual wisdom, or that of people in general taken individually. But this criticism would be fully justified only if it included a demand for the transition from class knowledge (consisting of a clash of ideas from which truth is expected to emerge) to universal knowledge, uniting all individual abilities in a single common task. Instead, scholarly positivism, ignoring the necessity for universal cooperation, has resulted merely in splitting the learned estate itself into positivists and metaphysicians. Scholars are right to say that for them the world is a representation because, insofar as they are scholars, they have no other approach but the cognitive. However, this approach is only that of scholars and not that of mankind in general. Therefore, scholars are wrong to substitute knowledge for action and even to resist the possibility of action. In their subjective approach they fail to perceive the projective.

Contemporary monism claims 'to reconcile within a superior unity mind and matter as manifestations of a single mysterious essence, perceived as spirit subjectively through inner experience and objectively through external experience as matter'. But, surely, such a reconciliation is spurious and ineffective ? 'The anthropopathic monism of primitive man

6. First line of Pushkin's poem *Dar naprasny, dar sluchainy...*, 1828.

and the mechanistic monism of modern science — such are the first and last word in the history of human philosophy."[7] Yet a mechanistic world view can be the last word only for soulless people, scholars and positivists. The admission that the world is a soulless mechanism inevitably provokes attempts to make this mechanism into an instrument of will, reason and feeling. Primitive mankind persistently spiritualised matter and materialised spirit, whereas the new humanity should strive no less perseveringly to control the blind forces effectively. Therein lies the true transformation of the mythical into the positive.

If positivism and science in general are, linguistically, actions, it is not because the development of language lags behind the progress of thought (is inactivity perfection ?), but because man is active by nature *(homo factor)*. The savage imagines himself and the world as they should be, that is, himself as active and the world as alive, whereas the error of positivists is that, while considering themselves superior to savages in every respect, they accept themselves and the world as they should *not* be. This is why they cannot overcome even the contradiction between their language and their thought. (When scholars of all convictions speak of their mental processes and perceptions as actions, or when they describe their imaginary reconstructions of the past as resurrecting it, they speak metaphorically of knowledge as if it were action.) Yet the primary meaning of words is not to deceive but to express what should be.

§ 18

So long as scientists and philosophers remain a caste, even the problem of morality, that is, of behaviour, will remain for them one of cognition and not of activity, a subject for study and not for practical application, something that just happens rather than something that must be done and, furthermore, done not by individuals but collectively. So long as scholars

---

7. Both quotations are free renderings from a speech by Haeckel on monism as a link between science and religion, 1892.

are not prepared to become a Commission for the elaboration of a plan of common action (and without this mankind cannot act according to a single plan as a single being, which is to say, attain adulthood), the contradiction between the reflective and the instinctive cannot be resolved. Failure to accept action as their duty confines the learned class to reflection, while the rest of the human race, uncommitted to any single task, continues to act instinctively and remains the tool of a blind force. Reflection can have only a destructive effect, since it does not restore what is being destroyed. 'To be a conscious agent of the evolution of the universe' means to be the conscious tool of mutual constraint (struggle) and elimination (death). It means subjecting the moral to the physical, whereas even in the present state of disunity and inactive knowledge men still express, one way or another, moral aspirations, though they yield to necessity because of their physical weakness. Only when discord and inaction are recognised as temporary will we be able to imagine the magnitude and meaning of supreme bliss.

As to the state which Spencer,[8] and his followers in particular, promise humanity in the future, it cannot be regarded as a higher nor yet as the lowest good. On the contrary, when conscious actions become instinctive and automatic, and man is reduced to a machine (the ideal of fatalistic blind progress), such a state must be regarded as evil — even the greatest evil. The day will come, says Spencer, when altruistic inclination will be so well embodied in our organism itself that people will compete for opportunities of self-sacrifice and immolation. When altruistic inclinations are implanted in everyone, how will opportunities arise to apply them ? Either such a state presupposes the existence of

8. The references to Herbert Spencer (1820-1903) are not actual quotations but summaries of Spencer's arguments elaborated in the chapters on Egoism *versus* Altruism and Altruism *versus* Egoism and, especially, the appendix to these two chapters, entitled 'Conciliation', in *The Principles of Ethics*, vol. 1, pp. 289-303, included in his *A System of Synthetic Philosophy*, vol. IX, London, 1892.

persecutors, tormentors and tyrants, or else the general urge to sacrifice oneself will engender benefactors who will turn into tormentors and persecutors merely to satisfy this passionate craving for martyrdom. Or will nature itself remain a blind force, and fulfil the role of executioner?

If life is good, to sacrifice it is a loss to those who do so in order to save the lives of others. But will life be good for those who accept the sacrifice and retain their life at the price of the death of others? How is altruism possible without egotism? Those who sacrifice their lives are altruists, but what are those who accept this sacrifice? If, however, life is not a blessing, then those who sacrifice it are neither making a sacrifice nor committing any meritorious act. If knowledge is divorced from action as it is in class knowledge, learned knowledge, then the instinctive, by becoming conscious, leads to destruction. If morality is an instinct which motivates the sacrifice of the individual for the sake of the species, Spencer argues, it will disintegrate by discovering its origin. If, however, morality is the love of the begotten for those who have given them life, then the consciousness of their origin, which is linked to the death of the parents, instead of stopping short at knowledge, will become the task of resuscitation.

§ 19

The question of lack of brotherhood, that is, disunity, and that of how to restore kinship in all its fullness and force (visibly and evidently), and the question of uniting the sons (brothers) for resurrecting the fathers (complete and full kinship), are obviously one and the same. Both are contrary to progress, which is perennial puerility, that is, the inability to restore life. One should add that the union of sons for the resuscitation of the fathers is the fulfilment not merely of their own will but of that of the God of our fathers — which is not alien to us and gives a true purpose and sense to life. It expresses the duty of the sons of man and is the result of 'knowledge of all by all', not of class knowledge. In re-creation, in substituting resurrection for birth and creativity for nutrition, we achieve the purest eternal beatitude as opposed to mere material comfort.

Thus posed, the problem of unbrotherliness can oppose socialism, which uses and abuses the word brotherhood while rejecting fatherhood. Socialism has no opponent. Religions, with their transcendental content, being 'not of this world', with the Kingdom of God only within us, cannot stand up to socialism. Socialism may even seem to be an implementation of Christian ethics. Only the union of sons in the name of the fathers, as a counterweight to union for the sake of progress and comfort at the expense of the fathers, exposes the immorality of socialism. To unite for the sake of one's own comfort and pleasure is the worst way of wasting one's life — intellectually, aesthetically and morally.

The forgetting of the fathers by their sons transforms art, from the purest enjoyment felt in the restoration of life to the fathers, into a pornographic pleasure ; while science, instead of being the knowledge of all things inanimate aimed at the restoration of life to the deceased, becomes sterile speculation or a procurer of pleasure. Socialism triumphs over the state, religion and science. The appearance of state socialism, Catholic, Protestant or academic socialism, is a proof of this triumph. Socialism has no opponent, and even denies the possibility of having one. Socialism is deception ; it applies the words 'kinship' and 'brotherhood' to associations of people alien to each other and linked only by common interests, whereas real blood kinship unites through inner feeling. The feeling of kinship cannot be limited to representatives ; it demands real presence. Death transforms real presence into representation (memories). Therefore kinship demands the return of the deceased, each one being irreplaceable, whereas in an association death brings about an easily replaceable loss.

Union, not for the sake of material comfort and affluence for the living but for the resurrection of the dead, requires universal compulsory education which would bring to light the abilities and character of everyone, and would indicate to everyone *what* he should do and with *whom* — starting with marriage — thus contributing everyone's labour to help transform the blind force of nature into one governed by reason, and to change it from a death-bearing into a life-giving force.

Is it possible to limit 'humanity's task' to ensuring a fair distribution of the fruits of production, obliging everyone to ascertain without acrimony or passion that no one should appropriate more than the next man, or give up something to others and deprive himself ? Although socialism is an artificial conception, socialists have touched upon the natural weaknesses of man. Thus in Germany they rebuked the German workers for their limited needs, pointing out that the English are more demanding. They also reproached them for excessive diligence and urged them to demand shorter working hours. Socialists, who are solely bent on self-promotion and not the welfare of the people, fail to perceive that even a cooperative state requires not the vices which they awaken, but virtues, the acceptance of duties and even sacrifice.

In modern industrial societies factory work is usually fairly light, but the very existence of factories is based on the inhuman work of the miners who extract the coal and iron which are the very foundation of manufacturing industry. Under the circumstances, what is needed is not economic reform but a radical technical revolution bound up with a moral one. To impose inhuman labour for the sake of material comfort, even if it were shared by all, is an anomaly. With the control of the meteorological process, energy would be derived from the atmosphere — that is, coal would be replaced by the energy that once produced the coal deposits. In any case, the atmosphere will have to be tapped because coal deposits are being continually depleted. We might hope that energy obtained from atmospheric currents would produce a revolution in the production of iron. Moreover, regulation is necessary to bring industry nearer to agriculture, because the excess of solar heat which affects air currents, winds and destructive hurricanes could be used to power

cottage industries and enable manufacture to spread all over the earth, instead of being concentrated in industrial centres. Regulation would also transform agriculture from individual into collective work. What is needed is :
1. To eliminate wars.
2. To replace the back-breaking, inhuman work of miners.
3. To link agriculture with cottage industries.
4. To transform agriculture from an individual into a collective form of work.
5. To transform agriculture from a means of obtaining maximum incomes — with the ensuing crises and overproduction — into a means of obtaining *reliable* incomes.

The call for regulation comes from all quarters.

The nineteenth century is nearing its sad and gloomy end. It does not advance towards light and joy. Already it can be given a name. In contradistinction to the eighteenth century, the so-called age of enlightenment and philanthropy, and to the earlier centuries from the Renaissance onwards, it can be termed the age of superstition and prejudice, of the negation of philanthropy and humanism. However, the superstitions it brings back are not those which lightened life and awakened hopes in the Middle Ages, but those which made life unbearable. The nineteenth century brought back faith in evil and rejected faith in good ; it abdicated both the Kingdom of Heaven and faith in earthly happiness — that is, that earthly paradise that the Renaissance and the eighteenth century believed in. The nineteenth century is not only an age of superstition ; it also denies philanthropy and humanism as reflected in particular in the doctrines of modern criminologists. In rejecting philanthropy and accepting Darwinism, the present century has accepted struggle as a legitimate occupation, thus endowing a blind tool of nature with a conscious purpose. The armaments of today are in complete harmony with its convictions, and only the backward — who wish to be regarded as progressives — reject war.

At the same time the nineteenth century is the direct result and true stirp of the preceding centuries, the direct consequence of that separation of the heavenly from the earthly which is a complete distortion of Christianity, whose precept is to unite the heavenly with the earthly, the divine with the human. General resurrection, immanent resuscitation carried out with all the heart, thought and actions — that is, by all the power and abilities — of all the sons of man, is the implementation of the precept of Christ, Son of God and also Son of Man.

Part II [1]

A memorandum from the 'unlearned' to the 'learned' Russian secular scholars, written with the war fought against Islam (1877-8) and the expected war against the West in mind, and ending with the approaching 500th jubilee of St Sergius

This part of the memorandum is addressed to Russian scholars, the scholars of an agricultural, patriarchal, continental country, that is to say, one of climatic extremes; moreover, a country suffering from soil exhaustion and subject to periodic and increasingly frequent crop failures. It is addressed to the learned of a country where the need to regulate natural phenomena is so obvious that it is incomprehensible how they could have overlooked it.

§ 1

True religion is the cult of ancestors, the cult of all the fathers as one father inseparable from the Triune God, yet not merged with Him. In Him the indissoluble union of all sons and daughters with the fathers is divinised, while they still

---

1. Only excerpts are given from Part II, since much of it is a restatement of Fedorov's views on the Holy Trinity as a model for the transfiguration of humanity, a model not provided by either Islam or Buddhism; moreover, the original Part II also deals at length with matters relevant only to some aspects of Russian medieval history, in particular to the spiritual influence of St Sergius of Radonezh (d. 1392), founder of a monastery consecrated to the Holy Trinity (now Zagorsk). Fedorov compiled Part II of *FOD* in 1891, on the eve of St Sergius's fifth centenary.

retain their individuality. To abdicate universality is to distort religion ; it is characteristic of pagan religions which venerated only the gods and ancestors of their own nations... and even of those Christian denominations which restrict salvation to those of their ancestors who were baptised. Separating our forefathers from the Triune God is a distortion of religion, as is the limitation of its universality.

God Himself confirms the truth that religion is the cult of ancestors by calling Himself the God of the fathers. We have no right to separate our fathers from God, or God from our fathers ; neither have we the right to merge them with Him, that is to say, to permit their absorption (which would mean merging God and nature), nor to limit the circle of fathers to our own tribe or race. The doctrine of the Trinity divinises the universality of religion and its catholicity, as well as the indivisibility of the fathers and God (while remaining unmerged). Therefore it condemns not only segregation and division, but also deism which separates God from the fathers and pantheism which merges them with God. Both deism and pantheism lead to atheism, that is, to the acceptance of a blind force and its veneration and submission to it. Venerating a blind force means deifying it, assuming it to be alive. Such worship and deification are not religion but mere distortion, while the present subservience to the blind force is a negation of religion ; it engenders either practical technology (manufactures) or its diabolical (military) application to destruction. The negation of religion consists in using the blind force not for true and good purposes, but for evil ones ; to submit to it (under the guise of mastering it) is to submit to sexual selection (through manufactures) and to natural selection (through all types of destruction). Serving God entails transforming the blind, death-bearing force into a life-giving one, by controlling it. Contrary to the exploitation and utilisation of nature — that is, its plundering by prodigal sons to pander to women's caprice — which only leads to exhaustion and death, regulation brings about the restoration of life.

If religion is the cult of ancestors or the universal prayer of all the living for all the dead, then nowadays there is no religion because there are no cemeteries adjoining churches. And in these sacred places reigns the abomination of desolation... [To overcome such neglect] museums, especially natural science museums, and schools should be built in the vicinity of cemeteries... To save cemeteries, a radical change is necessary : society's centre of gravity should be moved to the countryside... Such a relocation would also be conducive to union with other nations, starting with the French. In view of the present (1891) relations among nations, union should start with France rather than with the Slavonic peoples. However, neither exhibitions nor naval visits can be regarded as the beginnings of unification.[2] Unification could be started only by an exchange of the products of the mind and by congresses concerned with the study (helped by armies) of the effect of explosives on atmospheric phenomena, or any other means of affecting those phenomena, and by founding a joint institution for such research that would promote and develop a rapprochement. It would be both immoral and unwise to expect such a rapprochement to come about automatically in the course of history.

Having recognised that an exchange of the products of the mind is more essential than an exchange of handicrafts (even those made by artistic French hands, as shown at the exhibition), one must admit that even intellectual exchanges do not suffice for closer cooperation. What is needed is action — joint action — but this action must not be war,[3] even with scholarly Germany, that representative of inactive pure knowledge and of knowledge applied to militarism... The

2. A reference to the official visit of a French naval squadron to Kronstadt (St Petersburg's naval base) as a preliminary to the signing of the 1891 Franco-Russian Alliance. In 1889 a French Exhibition had been held in Moscow.

3. Relations between Russia and Germany had been strained since the Berlin Treaty of 1878, which had thwarted Russia of the fruits of her hard-won victories over Turkey and accorded only a limited independence to the Slavs in the Balkans.

union of all nations will obviate the need for forcible annexations or continued domination of some over others. This is the meaning of the inscription over the Moscow Rumyantsev Museum, 'non solum armis'.[4] This task requires not only intelligence but also feeling ; so the educated class will become the organ not merely of thought but of feeling too — that is, it will cease being a class indifferent to common human suffering.

...As long as history was limited to the shores of seas and oceans, that is to say, to territories influenced by them, where the benevolent sky inflicted neither scorching heat nor excessive cold, nor downpours nor droughts, human labour was confined to the earth and, furthermore, to certain parts of the earth, and not to the planet as a whole ; and it certainly did not extend as far as the sky. Then dissension dominated, because unity is possible only in heaven, where solar energy affects meteorological processes, and when it is controlled by humans. When the continental countries free themselves from the influence of the maritime ones and become active and independent — when they emerge on to the historical scene — being so liable to scorching heat, extremely hard frosts, floods and droughts, they will understand the need for weather control and will find unity in a task common to all. With soil exhaustion exacerbating the unfavourable weather conditions, people will realise the importance of the Earth as a celestial body and the importance of celestial bodies as terrestrial forces ; they will realise where the exhausted Earth can and

---

4. The Rumyantsev Museum was founded in 1826 to house the collections of Count Nikolai Petrovich Rumyantsev, eldest son of the famous general and statesman Pyotr Alexandrovich Rumyantsev-Zadunaisky. In 1861 this collection of books and artefacts was moved to Moscow, and in 1867 its library (where Fedorov worked) was further enriched by the addition of the Chertkov collection of ancient Russian and Slavonic books and manuscripts. After the Revolution, the museum's exhibits were allocated to other museums and the library renamed after Lenin. Modern books are now kept in the new building, but the old one (sometimes referred to as Pashkov House, after the name of its first owner) still houses the collections of ancient books and manuscripts.

must draw its energy, and that the Earth, separated from other celestial bodies, can bear only mortals and, therefore, will increasingly become a cemetery. They will come to see that the knowledge of the Earth as a celestial body and that of celestial bodies as earths cannot remain idle knowledge...

So long as no direct communication links the most continental country with its outlying territories, either from the west (St Petersburg-Odessa) to the east (Nikolaevsk-Vladivostok) or from north-west to south-east (from the far northern ice-free harbour of Rybachi peninsula to a point on the Pacific), and so long as communications depend on sea routes, maritime countries will predominate. However, as soon as these outlying territories become linked by direct overland railways, the continental countries will come into their own. Despite such names as *Vladi*vostok and *Vladi*kavkaz,[5] this should not lead to domination over other nations but to their unification. Indeed, centres of unification such as Constantinople and the Pamir lie not in any continental country but between the continental and oceanic belts. Moreover, there might arise the possibility of global cooperation, because a transcontinental railway will require a trans-Pacific telegraph, which together with the existing transcontinental lines will form the first electric ring around the globe.

Could this ring be electrified by the magnetism of the Earth ? Could a spiral of such rings have effect on the Earth, which is a natural magnet ? Could they affect clouds and thunderstorms (belts of dead calm and gales) as a kind of meteoric equator ? Could such rings shift those belts ? Could they be used as an apparatus encircling the Earth to regulate the meteoric processes affecting the Earth ? Could globe-encircling cables supported by aerostats with lightning conductors be lifted into the thunderstorm belt ? And, finally, could there be any wars when every country's harvest would depend

---

5. The phoneme *vlad* in Vladivostok and Vladikavkaz (now Ordzhonikidze) is the root of the verb *vladet'*, meaning 'to possess'.

on an apparatus encircling the whole planet and managed by all ?[6] Such specialised problems would be part of joint activities, uniting the human race the world over. We presume that the use of a world network of telegraph cables for such a purpose is undoubtedly more important than the transmission of commercial telegrams.

Global communications by land and sea, rail and ship, require energy. Past energy received by the planet and embodied in coal, peat, and the like, is insufficient to maintain unifying communications among the inhabitants of the Earth ; so use will have to be made of the force which gives rise to storms, hurricanes, and so on. A united humanity will become the consciousness of the planet Earth and of its relationships with other heavenly bodies.

§ 4

By recognising ourselves, according to Christian criteria, as the mortal sons of all the deceased fathers, we would recognise the transcendence of God (His externality to the world), but this could only be the case if we, the living sons of deceased fathers, failed to consider ourselves to be the instruments of God in the task of returning our fathers to life (the immanence of God). One should not remove the Immortal Being from the world and leave it mortal and imperfect, nor should one confuse God with a world where reign blindness and death. Our task is to make nature, the forces of nature, into an instrument of universal resuscitation and to become a union of immortal beings. The problem of

---

6. Telephone cables obviously have not affected the magnetism of the Earth. However, in the late 1970s there was some talk in the USSR of siting all nuclear power stations beyond the Arctic Circle, away from densely populated regions. In this connection the question was raised whether high-tension transmission lines radiating southwards from the vicinity of the magnetic pole could perhaps in some way affect the Earth's magnetism ; see N. Dollezhal and Yu. Koryakin, 'Yadernaya energetika : dostigeniya i problemy', *Kommunist*, 1979, n° 14, pp. 19-28, and N.M. Mamedov, 'Ekologicheskaya problema i tekhnicheskie nauki', *Voprosy filosofii*, 1980, n° 5, pp. 111-20.

God's transcendence or immanence will only be solved when humans in their togetherness become an instrument of universal resuscitation, when the divine word becomes our divine action. If it is true that Semites tend to deism and Aryan tribes to pantheism, then in the doctrine of the Trinity as a commandment both will find pacification, for this commandment prescribes peace to all tribes.

§ 5

The Divine Being, which is itself the perfect model for society, a unity of independent, immortal persons, in full possession of feeling and knowledge, whose unbreakable unity excludes death — such is the Christian idea of God. In other words, in the Divine Being is revealed what humanity needs to become immortal. The Trinity is the Church of the Immortals and its human image can only be a church of the resurrected. Within the Trinity there are no causes for death, and all the conditions for immortality. An understanding of the Divine Trinity can be attained only by achieving universal human multi-unity. So long as in actual life the independence of individuals is expressed in their disunity, and their unity in enslavement, universal human multi-unity modelled on the Trinity will be only a mental image, an ideal. If, however, we reject the separation of thought from action, then the Three-in-One will be not merely an ideal but a project, not merely a hope but a commandment.

One learns to understand only by doing. Our understanding of God increases with unity and, conversely, decreases with discord. If our thought processes result from experience, and experience shows only enmity and enslavement, and if in life we witness only either fragmentation into individuals hostile to one another (manifest in paganism) or the Muslim absorption of many by a single personality, it becomes obvious that only the victory of the moral law, its complete triumph, can make us understand the Triune Being : that is to say, we will understand Him only when we (humanity as a whole) become the union of many or, better still, when in our togetherness we become like a single being. Then unity will not manifest itself in domination, and the will to individual independence not in discord, but there will be complete mutual understanding and trust.

Will the realisation by humanity of the Christian idea of God be also that of the law of love ? External authority can impose silence, but not conviction and truth ; and disunity leads directly to the negation of truth and justice. Truth requires the same conditions as good : namely, the absence of oppression (by any external authority) in the search for truth, and the absence of discord. There is no truth or justice in the West because of disunity, and none in the East because of oppression.

§ 7

The man who, out of feelings of love — and not of self-interest, as nineteenth-century people would assume, projecting their attitudes into the past — the first man who, although he was capable of living separately and independently, yet did not leave his parents even after their death, can be said to have been the first son of man ; and with him began tribal life, tribal religion (ancestor worship) and our human society. If at different times and in different places there arose other progenitors, the possibility of there having been several does not invalidate the unity of humankind, because the unity of the Common Cause — that of resuscitation — is the highest form of unity.

§ 8

The grief of a son mourning the death of his father is truly universal, because death as a law (or, rather, an inevitable hazard) of blind nature could not fail to arouse intense pain in a being who has attained consciousness, and who can and must achieve the transition from a world dominated by this blind force of nature to a world governed by consciousness, and where there is no place for death. This universal grief is both objective because of the universality of death and subjective because mourning a father's death is common to all. Truly universal grief is the regret for having been lacking in love for the fathers, and for one's own excessive self-love. It is sorrowing for a distorted world, for its fall, for the estrangement of sons from fathers and of consequences from causes.

However, we cannot speak of universal grief if we grieve over the death of our fathers not because we have survived them, that is, failed in our love for them, but merely because their death implies our own. Nor can we regard as universal grief that manifested by our intelligentsia, for it is universal neither in volume nor in content. To demand happiness, unearned in any way, to demand all good things without labour, to desire for one person what should belong to all and to grieve that this is not possible, is merely selfish world-weariness which excludes others from happiness. Obermann[7] admits that he was not unhappy, merely not happy. This is an offence on the part of God and the world against him. Why was the world not created solely to be at his service ? This is what Obermann complains about. René,[8] who shuns all activity, especially that of earning his daily bread, does not question his right to live, only his failure to enjoy it.

In general, grieving about the impossibility of happiness in oniness or even of happiness limited to one generation cannot be called universal grief. Nor can one regard as universal the so-called civic grief, such as that displayed over the failure of the French Revolution or the failed ideals of the Renaissance which, incidentally, were very limited. Universal Christian grief is the sorrowing over disunity (that is, over enmity and hatred and their ensuing consequences such as suffering and death), and this sorrow is repentance ; it is something active that includes hope, expectation and trust. Repentance is the recognition of one's guilt over disunity and of one's duty to

7. Obermann : the principal character of the French novel of the same name by Senancour (1804).

8. René : a similar character in a story by Chateaubriand, first included in his *Génie du Christianisme* (1802).

work for unification in universal love in order to eliminate the consequences of disunity.

Buddhism, negative and passive, grieves also over evil, but does not see disunity, hate and enmity as the greatest evil ; nor does it see unification and universal love as the greatest good. On the contrary, Buddhism hopes to destroy evil by abdicating love and affection. It encourages life in isolation, in separateness, in the desert ; a life of constant meditation and inaction ; and then laments the illusoriness of the world. As if not only thoughts and day-dreams but also the manifestations of the forces of nature — uncontrolled by us — are nothing but ghostly, elusive, transient phenomena indistinguishable from visions and mirages ! Therefore life itself becomes either a pleasant but delusory dream or an oppressive nightmare. Indeed, natural phenomena will remain visions until they become the product of the general will and activity of all humans, acting as God's tools. And notions will remain ghostly and dream-like until they become projects, blueprints for the works to be achieved by the general human will and that of God manifested in it.

§ 9

Implicitly the doctrine of the Son of Man embraces also the daughter, because with the son she shares not only a common birth but also a common knowledge. When speaking of the Son of Man as the Word, that is, as the knowledge which leads to divine likeness, the daughter too must partake of the knowledge of the fathers (seen as one father) and in the knowledge of nature, to transform it from a death-bearing into a life-giving force. The daughter of man is especially called to repentance, to self-knowledge, to the knowledge of being the daughter of all the deceased fathers, to the rank of myrrh-bearing woman (bringing life), thus rising far above any woman physician who is capable merely of healing. Moreover the parable of the prodigal son concerns not only sons. Our forgetting brotherhood and God — the perfect Being — highlights our imperfection, our unworthiness. This in turn leads to self-knowledge and a conscious recognition of our superiority over other creatures, since the sons of man should always keep in their mind's eye the image of the Son, and the daughters that of the Holy Spirit.[9] In this sense the former should always strive for a likeness to the Son of God, and the latter to a likeness to the Holy Spirit.

Do we conform to the criteria of the Gospels when we take the Holy Spirit as a model for the daughter of man ? It would show our indifference, insincerity and dead faith not to take as model for both individuals and society the One God, venerated in three Persons. The model of the children — to whom belongs the Kingdom of God — implies that filial love is not only the love of sons but also, obviously, that of daughters. If the kingdom of God is an image of the Deity, then the Deity is the spiritualised Son and Daughter imbued with boundless love for the Father.

§ 11

...The state has arisen as an exceptional measure against the danger of mutual tribal extermination, or for the defence of one group of tribes against another group that had formed an alliance to destroy or enslave the former. The state will be necessary until worldwide brotherhood is achieved. Unconsciously, universal kinship is beginning to come about but in a distorted way.

The minorship of the human race is nowhere more evident than in the superstitious veneration of everything natural, the acceptance of the supremacy of blind nature over intelligent beings (natural morality). It is not the savages who are in this state of childishness and minority, not young nations, but the ageing ones which do not notice their superstitions and even pride themselves on being free from superstition. This happened in ancient history, it is happening now, and this

---

9. In ancient Syriac, the Holy Spirit is referred to as *she*. In many languages, including Church Slavonic, the dove — symbol of the Holy Spirit — is a feminine noun. Fedorov refers to book 2, article 26, of the *Apostolic Rules*, where the bishop is compared to the Father, the deacon to the Son, and the deaconess to the Holy Spirit.

state of childishness usually begins during the era of a nation's decline, though the nation believes itself to be at the zenith of its civilisation. The present puerility of Western Europe is a form of paganism, though secularised since the era of the so-called Renaissance. Death is venerated too, as being natural. The fear of death leads to regarding death itself as a liberation from this agonising fear, to writing laudatory hymns and glorifying it (the bards of death — Leopardi, [the nineteenth-century French poetess Louise Victorine] Schéquet, Ackermann and others).

Nature is regarded as a death-bearing, self-destructive force, but not because of its blindness. Yet where can a blind force lead except to death ? Humans admit nature to be a blind force even when they regard themselves as part of it and accept death as a kind of law and not as a mere accident which has permeated nature and become its organic vice. Yet death is merely the result or manifestation of our infantilism, lack of independence and self-reliance, and of our incapacity for mutual support and the restoration of life. People are still minors, half-beings, whereas the fulness of personal existence, personal perfection, is possible. However, it is possible only within general perfection. Coming of age will bring perfect health and immortality, but for the living immortality is impossible without the resurrection of the dead.

§ 24

...The deepest and fullest assimilation of the idea of duty is needed in order not to fall into despair and lose hope, and in order to remain always faithful to God and the ancestors, because humanity will have to overcome difficulties of such magnitude as may frighten away the most daring imaginations. Only hard and prolonged labour will purify us in the fulfilment of our duty, bring us to resurrection and the communion with the Triune Being, while we remain, like Him, independent, immortal persons, capable of feeling and conscious of our oneness. Only then will we have the ultimate proof of the existence of God and behold Him face to face.

Part III [1]

What is history ?

What is history for the uneducated ?

1. History as fact.
2. History as a project for resuscitation, which is a demand of human nature and of life.

In order to avoid any arbitrariness in defining history or siding with any party (learned or unlearned — that is to say, popular) and, above all, in order not to fraudulently appropriate the right to set limits to the scope of human work, it must be said that history is always resuscitation and not judgement, because the subjects of history are not *the living*

---

1. Only excerpts are given from Part III, since Fedorov's views on historical events are obsolete, biased and of little interest to modern readers, apart from his definition of history as a chronicle of mutual extermination and the despoliation by humans of their natural environment. Fedorov attributes much importance to the struggle between Asia and Europe, from the Graeco-Persian wars right up until his own day with the domination by Western maritime powers of India and South-East Asia and also, in some ways, of China ; and to the West's hostility to Russia. He stresses the role of Constantinople — 'Tsargrad' for the Russians — as a link between the continents and therefore as a centre for human reunification. The failure of Byzantium to achieve the mission of universal unification through the spread of Christianity is attributed to its losing the pristine purity of the Christian faith. This leads him to criticise Catholicism for its authoritarianism, Protestantism for individualism and dissension, and even Orthodoxy for replacing action by symbolism. The fall of Byzantium, which triggered the Renaissance in Western Europe, is seen as a return to paganism, which was further promoted by the French Revolution and the ensuing rise of Communism, and the general loss of the sense of kinship.

but *the dead*. So in order to judge it is necessary to resuscitate, even if not literally, those who have died, that is, those who have already suffered the supreme penalty — capital punishment. For thoughtful people history is merely a verbal resuscitation, a metaphor ; for those endowed with imagination, it is artistic resuscitation ; for those in whom feeling is stronger than thought, history will be sorrowful remembrance, lamentation or a representation mistaken for reality — that is, self-deception.

What is history for the learned, is prayerful remembrance for the uneducated. History as resuscitation embraces the learned as well as 'the lower classes', and even savages who write history as remembrance on their own skin (tattooing). History as a purely objective account or tale amounts to recalling the deceased out of idle curiosity, while history as propaganda — that is to say, when the dead are called up as witnesses in favour of some particular idea, political or economic (for example, in support of a federation or a constitution) — is profanation, the work of people living an artificial life who have lost any natural sense or goal ; it is no longer the work of worthy sons, but rather of sons who have forgotten their fathers — of prodigals.

One should not take the name of God *in vain*, nor should one use that of the dead *in vain*, either. Therefore, history as propaganda should be rejected as an infringement of that commandment ; it is not history itself that should be rejected, but vanity. Lastly, there is history as a search for a sense, a meaning, to life. This is another philosophy of history that is open to vilification or subjectivism. The philosophy of history has itself a long history, although it has not yet found the meaning of life and has even despaired of finding it. Indeed, history cannot make sense as long as humanity fails to attain true wisdom. So if there is no sense, inanities are bound to occur. Inanities may show a certain constancy or frequency, which will give them the appearance of laws and are the subject of statistical history. There will be no sense in history so long as it is an unconscious and involuntary phenomenon.

History cannot be *our* action, the result of *our* activity, as long as we live in discord. Even when we are united our tribal life cannot be ruled by reason, as long as man depends on the blind forces of nature and fails to make it into a tool of his collective reason and single collective will.

The search for meaning is the search for a goal, a cause, a common task. Those who do not accept this must either assume an external, transcendental existence (the religious philosophy of history) or become zoomorphists (the secular philosophy of history), whether they admit the evolution of species (progress) or reject it. The former are partisans of transformism, evolution or development, the latter of the doctrine of cultural-historical types or castes. Only a goal gives meaning to human life. Man need not search for the meaning of life if he recognises that he is a son and mortal, that is, the son of deceased fathers. History itself will tell him that, being an account of the past, history is merely an imaginary resuscitation and, therefore, pointless until it becomes real...

What is history for the unlearned ?

1. History as fact is mutual extermination, the extermination of people like ourselves, the pillage and plunder of nature (that is, the Earth) through its exploitation and utilisation, leading to degeneration and dying (culture). History as fact is always mutual extermination, either overt in times of barbarism or covert in times of civilisation, when cruelty is merely more refined and even more evil. This situation raises the question : must man be the exterminator of his own species and the predator of nature, or must he be its regulator, its manager, and the restorer to life of his own kin, victims of his blind unruly youth, of his past — that is, of history as fact ?...

2. What should the project be ?

If the life of the human race is unconscious, what should it be if it were conscious ?

Meditation for most people is a temporary, exceptional state of the soul, transitory even for the soul of a scholar ; whereas thinking about a task, that is, planning, is for most people a constant state of mind, even among the learned class. The value of a thought is determined by the larger or smaller number of people it concerns ; the most general evil affecting all — a crime, in fact — is death, and therefore the supreme good, the supreme task, is resuscitation.

...If we consider history as the 'Good News', it is clear that the reason why the Resurrection of Christ was not followed by general resurrection is that the Resurrection of Christ was the beginning and history is the continuation. General resurrection could not immediately follow that of Christ because it has to be the conscious work of the human race uniting the length and breadth of the globe — indeed, the field of action is not limited to planet Earth. By using the mass of Earth and transforming it into conscious force, the united human race will give to the telluric force, controlled by reason and feeling — that is, by a life-giving force — domination over the blind force of other celestial bodies, and will involve them in a single life-giving force of resuscitation.

Humanity has not yet begun this task consciously, though the necessary preliminary unification of the human race has begun and is continuing, albeit in a distorted way... The great Common Task which constitutes the essence of Christianity has come to be replaced by competition in the production of trifles, which has brought conflict and war. An investigation into the causes of this distortion (loss of kinship) would be the turning-point towards conscious unification for the purpose of resuscitation. Such an investigation would entail not only knowledge : its aim would be to discover the life purpose of mortals — not that of one, or of several, but of all.

For scholars, history is judgement, judicial sentences passed by them on the deceased, but for the unlearned (among whom the scholars are a drop in the ocean), history is a prayer for the departed. If this prayer is sincere it cannot remain a prayer only, a lament, but must become a general task of resuscitation, the only task which enables men to feel brothers and not merely participants or shareholders in some enterprise. Only then will history become universal...

...However, our account of history begins with that of the disunion among people who had forgotten their kinship ; it begins with the history of a campaign waged by the West against the East, which can be seen as an ever-expanding battlefield spreading over the whole globe, and taking both direct and indirect routes along natural pathways, transforming them into artificial roads, straightened and smoothed. They bring together West and East, continental and coastal countries, in an accelerating movement, the direct routes leading to Tsargrad, the circuitous to the Pamir.

Will the coming together be peaceful, or not ?

With its inventions, its improved means of communication, science enables both the Far East and the Far West to join in the battle for mutual annihilation, in the 'scientific' struggle, applying all its knowledge to rapid-action and long-range guns, to smokeless gunpowder with melanite and roburite ; in battles fought on land and at sea, under ground and under water, in the air, night and day, by the light of electric suns. The most fantastic apocalypse pales before reality. The West, having provided a scientific organisation for the disorganised masses of the Far and Near East, will lead the maritime nations against the continentals.

It is for scientific strategy to determine the last focal point of the scientific battle. However, Constantinople and the Pamir are bound to be the focus of confrontation for the continental and maritime forces. In the event of a peaceful outcome to their encounter, it is easy to understand the Christian significance of these two centres, if one represents the Pamir (the hypothetical grave of the ancestors) as a skull over crossed bones, and Constantinople (the first place to be blessed by the cross) as the centre for the transformation of the destructive force into a life-giving one...

...Our history is a saga of confrontation as well as a dirge for all those who fell under the walls of Troy and were lamented by Homer (and those who still read Homer), and for those who fell under Plevna[2] and on the Shipka Pass... Our history is both secular and sacred. As a history of struggles it is secular. As that of the preaching of 'Thou shalt not kill, nor make war, nor battle' it is not yet sacred, nor Christian, but remains ancient history. Man does not cease to kill, to make war, to battle. On the contrary, he improves and invents ever more lethal weapons (modern history begins with the invention of gunpowder) to defend his accumulated riches which are increasing in the wake of progress. History will become sacred only when remembrance — which is love — replaces the superfluous by the necessary, mass production by handicrafts, and death-bearing armaments by life-giving tools to unite all in a single task. To become sacred, Christian, history must cease to be the saga of men's struggles against each other, of East against West — which has become nowadays the struggle of maritime countries against continental ones. History must become the chronicle of the struggle for each other and against the blind force of nature acting both outside and within us ; not a struggle to the finish against each other, but a struggle to the finish for union against death, for resuscitation and life.

The learned consider their work completed when they have explained to their own satisfaction the causes of conflict by the influence of external and internal natural factors (temperament and character). However, for the unlearned it is only here that the solution to the problem begins. Universal military service is a preparation for the common sacred struggle not against but for each other, against the force of nature acting outside and within us.

2. Plevna : a Turkish fortress in Bulgaria, which during the Russo-Turkish war withstood 3 assaults and inflicted heavy casualties on the Russian and Romanian armies, before its garrison of 50,000 men surrendered in Dec. 1877. The Russians captured the Balkan mountain pass of Shipka in July 1877 and held it till Jan. 1878, eventually allowing a Russian breakthrough into the Bulgarian plain.

The present part of our memorandum is designed to explain their obligations to those called up for service. It is a catechism not in form but in essence, and sets out *what a human being ought to do*. It teaches the sons of man, who are the participants in history, how to solve the problem of lack of kinship and how to redirect their arms...

...The Common Task is a response to catastrophes affecting all humans — that is, death and all that leads to it — whereas social problems concern not all but a greater or lesser part of society and are a response to phenomena such as poverty. However, considered at a deeper level than the superficial and frivolous one which informed the French Revolution, it becomes apparent that phenomena like poverty will exist as long as death exists. As Christ said, 'The poor always ye have with you.' The Common Task knows no compromises even with death, because there is nothing arbitrary about it, whereas social objectives are essentially compromises.

Participation in a common task makes understandable the Christian idea of God as a perfect Triune Being. However, if we consider social tasks as ultimate goals, we distort the idea of God, we deprive Him of perfection, we perceive Him as Ruler and Judge, we admit that we are incapable of being brothers and have no Father, that we need a Ruler and Judge ; and the lower we fall morally, the sterner is the Ruler we need. In ascribing to God our own characteristics of domination and justice, we do not mean to reduce the greatness of God but, rather, we exalt the importance of these features because we prefer that society be organised so that everyone, however temporarily, has some power to dominate others, the right to judge and to punish. So we take as an ideal arrangement the principle of the [French] Revolution, that everyone periodically, temporarily, can exercise supreme power.

We appear to prefer such an organisation of society to one where a common task opens up to all a wide field of activity, and eliminates dissension, superfluous power and law courts. Which society is better : the one where justice (power and law) dominates, and is exercised and belongs in turn to everyone, and where no one is deprived of this power to judge and punish — that is to say, it is a power that cannot belong to a kinsman, since a father is not made to judge his son nor the obverse (though such cases have happened and are signalled as cases where love was sacrificed to justice and kinship to the public good) — or a society founded on parental, filial and brotherly love ?

Even if, through the good economic organisation of society, the impossible were to be achieved and criminality were eliminated, the outcome would still not be brotherhood, because even when people are not battering each other they do not necessarily love each other. Even to achieve that much is hardly possible, not because people are bad but because man cannot live without interacting with others in some great common task ; he cannot be content with trifles...

...Equality itself cannot be regarded as Good, so long as people are insignificant — that is, mortal. For the sake of equality any superiority, any higher abilities, must be driven out, whereas among those united in brotherhood for the sake of a common cause, any talent arouses not envy but joy. The same applies to liberty. The freedom to live only for oneself is a great evil, even when it does not impinge on the rights of others and when justice would prevent conflict. The highest degree of equity can only demand that those capable of working should not be deprived of work, and that those incapable of working should not be deprived of means of existence. Yet that which in a society that has no common cause or purpose, a society of legality, of law and order, is the highest, is the lowest in a society of paternal and filial love and brotherhood.

A common cause enables all to take part in religion, science and art, the object of which is to achieve rehabilitation and a secure existence for *all*. In such a society there can be no question of the right to work, because it is the duty of all, without exception, to participate in it ; nor can there be any question of those incapable of working merely receiving the means of subsistence, because part of the Common Task is to rehabilitate them or endow them with the abilities of which they are deprived. If at last we become participants in the Common Task, we will be able to thank fate for having been saved, for not having wasted our forces, by being able to apply them to the Common Task...

...Now we can see how right is the view that the French Revolution was, in fact, two quite different revolutions, one of which benefited individualism (starting in 1789), the other being a noisy attempt at fraternity (ending on 9 Thermidor). Both were forms of anti-Christianity, with which we have already met — pagan individualism and Semitic socialism, that is, the subjugation of individuality. For the sake of fraternity, noisy or, rather, bloody action was taken by those who strove for it and failed, because they mistook for fraternity (identified with liberty and equality) what are in fact the consequences of fraternity. Moreover, they wanted to achieve it through violence — that is to say, in an unbrotherly way. So even the little they wanted to achieve could not be achieved, and even placed obstacles to its achievement in the future. Only love liberates, making duty towards others desirable and the implementation of that duty pleasant, something that is not a burden but ardently longed for. Only love equalises, making those more richly endowed with abilities and strength sincerely anxious to serve the less fortunate.

Therefore, love alone leads to brotherhood, whereas neither the liberty to satisfy one's own whims nor envious equality can lead to fraternity. According to the Christian doctrine of original sin, to popular belief and even to prevailing modern views, heredity is an incontrovertible fact. It follows that no sinful, vicious feeling that prompts enmity or the like can disappear without leaving traces. It will find an outlet ; it will manifest itself even when the object that aroused it has passed away. Therefore, it is quite impossible to create fraternity when hate and bitterness are aroused in the generation that originally experienced these feelings, nor among their descendants, even in the narrow sense of fraternity as understood by the men of the Revolution and their forerunners, the *philosophes*. No external organisation can annihilate inherent characteristics. Sins are material, they are diseases which need to be cured... All the peoples of Western Asia bordering on the Mediterranian, as well as India and China, have been subjected to the invasions of barbarians. All strove, without realising it, to transform those nomads into settled tillers of the soil, and to persuade the country whence these 'scourges of God' came to adopt agriculture. That country was known to the Aryans of Iran by the name of Turan, the kingdom of darkness and evil ; Ezekiel spoke of Magog, the kingdom of Gog, whose invasion was to be so terrible as to signal the end of the world. Byzantium shared the wishes of the peoples of Western Asia, having experienced 'the sufferings of Tantalus', in the words of Polybius,[3] as a result of the devastations caused by the nearby barbarians and even by the more distant ones, for whom the renamed Constantinople had become the most coveted prize.

The West, in the fifth century, had similar experiences, though it attributed its disasters to its having abjured its gods while it was pagan, and to its sins in general when it became Christian. What the prophets had hoped for in the fifth century — namely the rout of the 'scourges of God' — came about not in the way they expected, not in a transcendental way, but in a natural, human way when the Slavs and Russia in particular formed a bulwark against the invaders...

...Europe sees Russia as an enemy. But should this enemy, these pseudo-Turanians — incidentally, we do not despise this relationship — perish, Europe would witness the visit of real Turanians. Can it be possible, now that a thousand years of working towards the expansion of agriculture is nearing completion, now that our borders are approaching the Indian

---

3. Polybius : Greek historian (204-124 BC). Even before the Emperor Constantine made Byzantium a capital of the Roman Empire and renamed it Constantinople, the city, founded probably in the seventh century BC, had been of some importance because of its geographical position.

Caucasus, now that we can stretch out our hand to England and thus close the Christian circle surrounding Islam... can it be possible that all that work will be destroyed by the moral short-sightedness of the West ?

...The project that sets the doctrine of the Trinity as a model and comprises that of resuscitation should consist of the following :

1. The object of the action, namely, the Earth in its relation to the Sun and nature in general.
2. The method of the action, that is, via various professions, in particular agriculture, being transformed by experimentation and research work.
3. The coordination of these activities towards a common goal, that is, towards a focal point...

...All human endeavours have tended to concentrate in two such focal points : Constantinople and India. The latter was the centre of seduction and temptation which, however, pointed to the Pamir, the centre of atonement. These centres promoted the improvement of routes and the discovery of new ones. Although they contributed to closer relations, these were purely superficial and all too often were pretexts for further conflict. So the unconscious activity which could have worked out a means of resuscitation directed people to the destruction towards which the world is veering. That the world is approaching its end is believed by the faithful, while science comes to the same conclusion on the basis of the classification of worlds, that is, stars, according to their age as determined by spectral analysis. According to this classification our solar world has already passed its youth ; it no longer belongs to the stars of the first class, although it has not yet reached the degree of cooling and eventual extinction of third-class stars.

If in any one of these stars consciousness emerged (which is very doubtful), it failed to become the governing, creative reason of that world undoubtedly because those conscious beings limited themselves to the procreation of similar ones, to laboratory experiments (experimental science), and wasted their time in internecine squabbles, in local government and constitutional intrigues (politics and social work) or in idle contemplation (philosophy). Meanwhile the energies of that world became diffused and spent themselves into extinction. Our sun is dimming, however slowly, and we are right to say that the hour will come when it will no longer give light, that 'the time is at hand'. The extinction of stars (sudden or slow) is an instructive example, a terrifying warning. The growing exhaustion of the soil, the destruction of forests, distortions of the meteorological process manifested in floods and droughts — all this forebodes 'famines and plagues' and prompts us to heed the warning. Apart from a slowly advancing end, we cannot be certain whether a sudden catastrophe may not befall the Earth, this tiny grain of sand in the vastness of the Universe.

And yet, planet Earth is perhaps the only bearer of salvation, and the other millions of worlds merely nature's unsuccessful attempts. Do we not hear the awe-inspiring 'Ye know not the place, nor the day, nor the hour', and does this not spur us to even greater watchfulness and work in order to resolve this agonising uncertainty ? So the world is nearing its end and man contributes to this by his activities, because civilisation and exploitation without restoration can have no other result than that of accelerating the end.

Part IV

What should we do ?

Resuscitation as an ongoing act unites all religions and denominations ; it unites in a common filial love and a single activity both believers and doubters, the learned and the unlearned, all classes, both urban and rural. The age of disputation comes to an end, because words and thoughts are no proof. And when a dogma becomes an assignment, a filial duty, we move from the field of theory — the most controversial — to the field of morals and action — the least controversial. The doubters are in the position of the apostle Thomas : his doubts did not impede him from being a follower of Christ. The other apostles, too, had been unwilling to believe a rumour, and were convinced only when they saw with their own eyes. For Thomas the testimony of even ten eyewitnesses was not enough. Doubt in his case was the manifestation of a most profound love, the longing to hear and see the beloved Teacher and be convinced by the most tangible proofs. Love is above faith or hope ; even with faith, but without charity, we are nothing (I Cor., 13:1).

The union of faith and charity, the union of the three so-called theological virtues, is faithfulness to God as to the one Father, just as the faithfulness to the fathers is unthinkable without faithfulness to the brothers. All evil is betrayal, or to use the expression of our common people, a misfortune. Yet even the most unfortunate of all, whose name has become synonymous with the supreme degree of criminal betrayal and whom the West in the words of Dante placed in the depths of hell without issue, can be cursed only by him who is without sin ('He that is without sin among you, let him first cast a stone')...

Food and sanitary problems

The interests of past generations are not contrary to those of present and future ones, provided the overriding concern is the assured existence of humanity, and not mere enjoyment. But an assured existence is impossible so long as our earth remains isolated from other worlds. Because of its very isolation it cannot provide for immortal beings. On every planet the means of subsistence are limited, and not inexhaustible even if they are very great. Consequently starvation may set in even if, for other fortuitous reasons, death does not appear. A greater or lesser shortage of food results in a quicker or slower death. Shortages lead to struggles which shorten life, limiting living beings in both time and space. Death comes also through sickness caused by the more or less harmful influences of death-bearing nature (death as decomposition, contagion, and so on). Generally speaking, death is the consequence of our being at the mercy of the blind force of nature, acting without and within us and not subject to our control. Yet we accept this dependence and submit to it.

Hunger and death are due to the same causes. Therefore the problem of resuscitation is bound up with that of freedom from hunger. To achieve freedom from hunger man must know himself and the world so as to produce himself out of the very basic elements into which the human body can be decomposed. In this way he will acquire the possibility, indeed the necessity, to recompose himself and all deceased beings. In other words, the living must submit themselves and those already dead to the process of resuscitation, and only through the resuscitation of the dead can they re-create in themselves life everlasting.

Alongside the problem of nutrition — of hunger and food

— comes the sanitary problem. Again, because of the isolation of our Earth the process of decomposition is necessary for the life of successive generations, but it results in epidemics that may hasten the end of the human race, if it remains inactive. Methods of burial are a part of global sanitary measures. The systematic burning of corpses, the destruction of all rotting substances by fire, could lead to soil exhaustion and eventually to death through starvation. The problems of famines and epidemics impel us to transcend the confines of the globe. Human labour must not be limited by the boundaries of the planet, particularly since no such boundaries or frontiers exist. The planet Earth is open from every side. Means of transportation, and methods of living in different environments, can and must be changed.

A radical solution of the sanitary problem consists in the return of the particles (molecules) of decomposition to the creatures to whom they belonged in the first place. Thus the sanitary problem, like that of food supply, leads us to general resuscitation. By transforming the unconscious processes of eating and procreating into one of conscious resurrection, humanity re-creates generations and discovers in other worlds means of subsistence. This solves the Malthusian equation of balancing population growth with food production. Herein lies the only way to eliminate general mortality, a fortuitous event due to ignorance, and the ensuing impotence that heredity has made into an epidemic disease, compared to which other epidemics are mere sporadic outbreaks. Death has become a general organic evil, a monstrosity, which we no longer notice and no longer regard as an evil and a monstrosity.

Both the food and the sanitary problems can obviously be solved only by the agricultural class. The urban population contributes nothing — it merely refines what is produced in the countryside. For town dwellers the food problem is merely one of distribution : they ignore how dependent humanity is on nature. They are equally indifferent to a bumper harvest or to a crop failure ; they do not imagine, and do not even wish to know, that in the latter case it is impossible to divide 100 lb. of bread among a hundred persons so that each gets 2 lb. of bread. This explains the strangeness of the socio-economic solutions that are proposed. The split between town and country, the independent existence and even domination of manufacturing industry over agriculture, are a root cause of proletarianisation. Apart from mutual insurance, the city has invented nothing and, since nature has no part in its obligation, the validity of such insurance is questionable.

While civilisation is capable of making considerable profits for some, it is incapable of ensuring the necessary minimum, always, for all. Considering the indifference of town dwellers to good or bad harvests, one might think that they believe, literally, that 'any trade feeds the worker'. Yet large-scale crop failures remind them of their dependence on the countryside, which provides the essentials for the very existence of humanity. A minute aphis, beetle or fly can bring to an end the life of mankind. What is the place of these insects in the general destiny of the Universe ? Insect control based on the use of certain fungi which cause epidemics among beetles is not the same as forestalling their proliferation or distorting a natural process, one which endows an organic force with an entomological form. Yet the very production of cereals (which has transformed the steppe into an endless wheatfield) has contributed to the increase in cereal-eating insects. Will the advocates of natural progress (as opposed to rational labour) consider this phenomenon — the spread of a fauna which lives off the work of others — a progressive one ? For them, bugs have the same right to exist as humans. The struggle for survival decides who has the greater right to exist. For them, the means of pest control used by man are unnatural and hence unlawful. If, however, progress is the transformation of the spontaneous (procreation) into conscious work, we must regard parasites as an inherent evil. The control method used is undoubtedly immoral, since it takes advantage of the natural evil of an epidemic. Nor can the annihilation of any insect be considered moral. Only the complete transfiguration of a blind force (procreation) into a conscious act can be called moral.

Another method of pest control (used against the Hessian fly) is to alter the time of sowing. This can be done within fairly narrow limits and still gives a chance of survival to those individual flies which hatch later. Methods of tilling, better soil cultivation, crop rotation, and so on, may reduce but not destroy parasitic populations. As virgin lands are brought under cultivation, so will the cereal-eating species proliferate and adapt to the crop rotation of cultivated plants. The fundamental biological problem is to discover the conditions which cause an organic force to take on an entomological form.

With the growth of towns, food and sanitary problems become more acute and urgent. The very existence of towns is a proof that man prefers luxury and momentary enjoyment to a secure existence. The growth of towns and their domination over the countryside has occurred mainly among maritime nations. In continental countries, in their backwoods, another form of life has prevailed. Here the emphasis has been on agriculture, and here industry could become an ancillary occupation. In these backward areas communal land tenure persists. The death of the father involves the loss of the land holding (which reverts to the community). This heightens the sense of loss and fosters the feeling that is at the basis of the duty of resuscitation. Moreover, the community provides new holdings, not for each new-born child but for those who come of age, and this encourages chastity, which is also required by the duty of resuscitation. But the greatest advantage of communal land ownership is that it prevents agriculture from becoming an industry designed to achieve higher rather than stable incomes — that is, regular, reliable harvests. Thus the commune promotes the desire to achieve a secure existence, the highest form of which is immortality, rather than temporary pleasure and enjoyment.

In industrialised countries science cannot come to full fruition because it cannot find applications momentous enough to match the breadth of knowledge. There, reality does not coincide with knowledge because whereas reality is limited to the production of trifles and frippery, knowledge tends to encompass nature as a whole. Clearly, science has outgrown its cradle. Factory and workshop are too constricting ; science needs more space. Admittedly, some scientists hope that science will make possible the industrial production of foodstuffs (the ideal of the urbanised West), but the varied activities of the farmer would then be reduced to the monotonous motions of a valve, a lever, and so on. A factory prison instead of fields and sky !!! In any case, these measures are doomed to failure because the resources of the planet are finite. Besides, how mean and even nasty they are (and what a moral and intellectual threat to our people), compared with the boundless scope of discovering the conditions that affect harvest and plant life and are not limited to our planet. For, as peasants say, 'It is not the earth that feeds us but the sky'.

The regulation of natural meteorological processes by means of lightning conductors raised on aerostats seems to have been invented specifically for the agricultural commune. Fortunately for the human race, the latter has not been killed by modern civilisation in its present form. The common folk in the majority of countries, even those whose upper classes have been europeanised, still live in communes. It is not beyond belief that the nations of Western Europe and America may re-establish such communes if the majority of the human race retains this way of life, not out of backwardness, as is the case today, but because people will have realised its advantages over other forms of civilised life. When the instruments proposed by Karazin[1] become available to all communes, the entire terrestrial meteorological process will be regulated ; wind and rain will become the ventilation and irrigation of the earth, worked as a unified economy.

From clouds and rain it is a natural step to showers of shooting stars and clouds of meteorites : 'When we see

1. See note 19 to the Introduction.

showers of shooting stars, we cross the path of some comet and, observing it in the sky, we actually observe at a distance a cloud of meteorites.'* Those who have not lost all sense of kinship seek, and will continue to seek, in every discovery a way of re-establishing and securing life. This is contrary to the theories of Laplace and Kant, who only seek to explain the systems of the Universe without participating in or acting on these worlds with the creative power of reason. The first approach seeks to revitalise decaying worlds by using the power of active reason ; only in this manner will the formation of the systems of the Universe be understood, for without the ability to reconstitute them we are reduced to mere supposition.

Just for the sake of argument, let us develop Karazin's idea and assume that electrical currents have been sent in certain directions, perhaps with the help of telegraph cables encircling the Earth in a spiral formation or in some other way — then our huge siderolite, our natural magnet, becomes an electromagnet. This might enlarge the magnetic field of the Earth, and bring in the small siderolites that are said to move in Earth's orbit (and manifest themselves as zodiacal light). These could be condensed like vapour or diffused to affect the intensity of solar radiation ; they could be made to increase the mass of the Earth, or to form rings or spirals in the path of the Earth or around the sun. They could control the magnetic field of the sun itself. Experimentation would no longer be confined to laboratories — it would become literally infinite. And however incredible and impossible such assumptions may sound from the point of view of present-day science, to reject them out of hand would be criminal. It would mean rejecting the elimination of crime — the crimes of revolution, disorder, turmoil and war. It would also mean rejecting the criminals, who in this case would be not the worst but the best people, the most gifted, whose strengths, nurtured by the expanse of

---

* Quotation abridged from Sir J. Norman Lockyer's *Elementary Lessons in Astronomy* (first publ. 1868, Macmillan, London), Lesson XXIV, § 299.

continents and oceans, need greater scope.

A classless agricultural commune, where the intellectuals would be the teachers and where cottage industries would be carried on during the winter months, would end competition, speculation, social unrest, revolutions and even international wars, because all those vital forces now squandered on quarrelling would find a boundless field of application. In the worldwide activity of the classless rural communes there would be scope for peaceful labour and also for daring courage, the spirit of adventure, the thirst for sacrifice, novelty and exploits. And any commune is likely to have a percentage of such innate abilities. Out of such stuff were made knights errant, the ascetics who opened up the forests of the far north, Cossacks, runaway serfs, and the like. Now they would be the explorers, the new explorers of celestial space.

The prejudice that the celestial expanse is unattainable to man has grown gradually over the centuries, but cannot have existed *ab initio*. Only the loss of tradition and the separation of men of thought from men of action gave birth to this prejudice. However, for the sons of man the celestial worlds are the future homes of the ancestors, since the skies will be attainable only to the resurrected and the resurrecting. The exploration of outer space is only the preparation for these future dwelling places.

The spread of humanity over the planet was accompanied by the creation of new (artificial) organs and coverings. The purpose of humanity is to change all that is natural, a free gift of nature, into what is created by work. Outer space, expansion beyond the limits of the planet, demands precisely such radical change. The great feat of courage now confronting humanity requires the highest martial virtues such as daring and self-sacrifice, while excluding that which is most horrible in war — taking the lives of people like oneself.

The destiny of the Earth convinces us that human activity cannot be bounded by the limits of the planet. We must ask whether our knowledge of its likely fate, its inevitable extinction, obliges us to do something or not. Can knowledge be useful, or is it a useless frill ? *In the first case* we can say that Earth itself has become conscious of its fate through man, and this consciousness is evidently active — the path of salvation. The mechanic has appeared just as the mechanism has started to deteriorate. It is absurd to say that nature created both the mechanism and the mechanic ; one must admit that God is educating man through his own human experience. God is the king who does everything *for man* but also *through man*. There is no purposefulness in nature — it is for man to introduce it, and this is his supreme *raison d'être*. The Creator restores the world through us and brings back to life all that has perished. That is why nature has been left to its blindness, and mankind to its lusts. Through the labour of resuscitation, man as an independent, self-created, free creature freely responds to the call of divine love. Therefore humanity must not be idle passengers, but the crew of its terrestrial craft propelled by forces the nature of which we do not even know — is it photo-, thermo- or electro-powered ? We will remain unable to discover what force propels it until we are able to control it. *In the second case*, that is to say, if the knowledge of the final destiny of our Earth is unnatural, alien and useless to it, then there is nothing else to do than to become passively fossilised in contemplating the slow destruction of our home and graveyard.

The possibility of a real transcendence from one world to another only *seems* fantastic. The necessity of such movements is self-evident to those who dare take a sober look at the difficulties of creating a truly moral society, in order to remedy all social ills and evils, because to forgo the possession of celestial space is to forgo the solution of the economic problem posed by Malthus and, more generally, of a moral human existence. What is more of a fantasy — to think how to realise a moral ideal while closing one's eyes to the tremendous obstacles in the way, or to boldly recognise these obstacles ? Of course, one can give up morality, but that implies giving up being human. What is more fantastic — to create a moral society by postulating the existence of other beings in other worlds and envisioning the emigration thither of souls, the existence of which cannot be proven, or to transform this transcendental migration into an immanent one — that is, to make such a migration the goal of human activity ?

The obstacle to the building of a moral society is the absence of a cause or task great enough to absorb all the energies of those who spend them at present on discord. In world history we know of no event which, although threatening the end of the society in question, could unite all its forces and stop all quarrels and hostilities within that society. All periods of history have witnessed aspirations that reveal humanity as unwilling to remain confined within the narrow limits of our Earth. The so-called states of ecstasy and ravishments into heaven were manifestations of such aspirations. Is this not a proof that unless mankind finds a wider field of activity, eras of common sense, or rather of fatigue and disillusionment with fruitless longings, will be succeeded by eras of enthusiasm, ecstatic visions, and so on ? Throughout history these moods have alternated. Our era confirms all this, for we see alongside 'the kingdom of this world', with its filthy reality, a 'Kingdom of God' in the form of revivalist movements, spiritualistic table-turning, and the like. So long as there are no real translations to other worlds, people will resort to fantasies, ecstatic rapture and drug abuse. Even common drunkenness is apparently caused by the absence of a wider, purer, all-absorbing activity.

The three particular problems — the regulation of atmospheric phenomena, the control of the motion of the Earth and the search for 'new lands' (to colonise) form one general problem, that of survival or, more precisely, the return to life of our ancestors. Death can be called real only when all means of restoring life, at least all those that exist in nature and have been discovered by the human race, have been tried and have failed. It should not be assumed that we hope that a special force will be discovered for this purpose. What we should assume is that the transformation of the blind force of nature into a conscious force will be that agent. Mortality is an inductive conclusion. We know that we are the offspring of a multitude of deceased ancestors. But however great the number of the deceased, this cannot be the basis for an incontrovertible acceptance of death because it would entail an abdication of our filial duty. Death is a property, a state conditioned by causes ; it is not a quality which determines *what a human being is and must be.*

We know no more about the essence of death, actual death, than about actual life. Yet by limiting our knowledge to the phenomena of life we narrow our field of action ; whereas by rejecting the proud right to decide what death is in reality, we widen our field of action, we become the executors of God's will and the tools of Christ in the cause of general resurrection.

In discussing the immortality of the soul, the intellectual class display scepticism and distrust ; they demand convincing proof. Yet their credulity borders on philosophical superstition when it comes to discussing death. This is far from innocuous, for such childishly superstitious credulity narrows their field of research. Decomposition is regarded as a sign which admits of no further experimentation. However, one should remind them that decomposition is not a supernatural phenomenon and that the dispersed particles do not scatter beyond finite space. The organism is a machine and consciousness relates to it like bile to the liver — so reassemble the machine and consciousness will return to it. These are your own words, and they should impel you to start at last on the job... Thus posed, the problem of death obliges us to transform burial places and actual tombs into objects of active research.

Natural science and medicine (in its applied form) should abandon their pharmaceutical and therapeutical laboratory experiments carried out in hospitals and clinics, and endeavour to utilise the telluric-solar and psychophysiological force brought under control by knowledge. They should seek to eliminate sickness in general, and not limit themselves to the treatment of individuals. Could the instrument designed by Karazin be used on corpses for the sake of research, and possibly even of reanimation, as a first step towards resuscitation ?

The study of the molecular structure of particles is not sufficient for resuscitation because they are scattered throughout the solar system, perhaps even beyond. Gathering them would make the problem of resuscitation a telluric-solar one — and possibly telluric-cosmic.

To ensure good harvests, agriculture must extend beyond the boundaries of the Earth, since the conditions which determine harvests and, in general, plant and animal life do not depend on soil alone. If the hypotheses are correct that the solar system is a galaxy with an eleven-year electromagnetic cycle during which the quantity of sunspots and magnetic (the Northern Lights) and electric storms reach in turn their maximum and minimum, and that the meteorological process depends on these fluctuations, it follows that good and bad harvests do so too. Consequently, the entire telluric-solar process must be brought into the field of agriculture. If, moreover, it is true that interactions between phenomena are of an electrical nature and that this force is akin to or even identical with that of the nervous impulses which serve will and consciousness, then it follows that the present state of the solar system can be compared to an organism in which the nervous system has not yet fully developed and has not yet become differentiated from its muscular and other systems.

Man's economic needs require the organisation of just such a regulatory apparatus, without which the solar system would remain a blind, untrammelled, death-bearing entity. The problem consists, on the one hand, in elaborating the paths which would transmit to human consciousness everything going on in the solar system and, on the other, in establishing the conductors by means of which all that is happening in it, all that is procreating, could become an activity of restoration. So long as no such paths for informing consciousness exist, so long as we have no more than conductors directing activity —

mere revolutions and upheavals — the world will present a strange, distorted order, which could better be described as disorder. 'Indifferent nature', unfeeling and unconscious, will continue 'to shine with eternal beauty',[2] while a being conscious of the beauty of incorruption will feel both excluded and excluding. Could a Being which is neither excluded nor excluding be the Creator of what is a chaos rather than a cosmos ?

Of course we cannot know what the world was like in the beginning because we only know it as it is. However, judging by the Creator, we can to some extent presume or imagine what a world of innocence and purity could have been. Could we not envision, too, that the relations of the first humans with the world were similar to those of an infant not yet in control of his organs, who has not yet learned to manage them — in other words, could the first humans have been beings who should (and could, without suffering or pain) have created such organs as would have been capable of living in other worlds, in all environments ? But man preferred pleasure and failed to develop, to create organs adapted to all environments, and these organs (namely, cosmic forces) became atrophied and paralysed, and the Earth became an isolated planet. Thought and being became distinct. Man's creative activity of developing organs corresponding to various environments was reduced to feeding and then to devouring.

Man placed himself at the mercy of fate (that is to say, the annual rotation of the Earth), he submitted to the Earth ; childbirth replaced the artistry of reproducing oneself in other beings, a process comparable to the birth of the Son from the Father, or the procession of the Holy Ghost. Later, proliferation increased the struggle, which was fostered by an unbridled surge of procreation ; and with the increase in births, mortality increased too. The conditions which could have regulated this concatenation of phenomena disappeared,

2. From Pushkin's poem 'Brozhu li ya vdol' ulits shumnykh...', 1829.

and gradually there came revolutions, storms, drought and earthquakes ; the solar system became an uncontrolled world, a star with an eleven-year cycle or some other periodicity of various catastrophes. Such is the system we know. One way or another, to confirm us in our knowledge, the solar system must be transformed into a controlled economic entity.

The immensity of the solar system is sufficient to inspire awe and, naturally, objectors will stress our smallness. When we turn our attention to small particles which consist of an enormous number of even smaller ones and which should also be brought within human economic management, then the objection will be our own size ; indeed, for infusoria these tiny particles seem very great, and yet they are more accessible to them than to us.

The problem is obviously not one of size, and our relative smallness or bigness only indicates the difficulty — a severe difficulty, but not an impossibility. For a vast intellect able to encompass in one formula the motions both of the largest celestial bodies in the Universe and of the tiniest atoms, nothing would remain unknown ; the future as well as the past would be accessible to him. The collective mind of all humans working for many generations together would of course be vast enough — all that is needed is concord, multi-unity.

ESSAYS AND
OTHER WRITINGS

Supramoralism or general synthesis (universal union)

The synthesis of the two reasons (the theoretical and the practical) and of the three subjects of knowledge and action (God, man and nature, when man becomes both the instrument of divine wisdom and the rational principle of the universe) *is also the synthesis of science and art within religion, which is identified with Easter, the great feast and the great deed.*

Supramoralism is the duty to return life to our ancestors; it is the highest and incontrovertibly universal morality, the morality of rational and sensate beings; on the fulfilment of this duty of resuscitation depends the destiny of the human race...

Supramoralism is not only the highest Christian morality, it is Christianity itself; for it transforms dogmatics into ethics (that is, dogmas become commandments) — an ethics inseparable from knowledge and art, from science and aesthetics, all of which merge into ethics. Divine services become acts of atonement, that is to say, of resuscitation. Supramoralism is not based on the Beatitudes, which are elementary morality. It is based on the supreme commandment given before the first Easter and the last commandment given after the Resurrection by the First of the risen, as the necessary condition for continuing the task of resurrection. In essence, supramoralism is the synonym or translation of the greatest commandment, and leads us through the fulfilment of the last commandment ('Go ye into all the world, and preach the gospel to every creature'), to become perfect like our

Father who is in heaven ; it calls for re-creation and resuscitation to liken us to the Creator, for this is what Christ prayed for in his last prayer ('that they may be one, that they too may be one in us, as Thou, Father, art in me and I in Thee'). Immediately after His resurrection, Christ indicated the way to such unity, which would endow us with the likeness of God and make us perfect like our heavenly Father, when He said, 'Go out all over the world preaching to all nations and baptising them in the name of the Father, the Son and the Holy Spirit.' Baptism washes away original sin, the cause of death, and implies resurrection for the dead and immortality for the living.

Supramoralism is the problem of the two unions and the two divisions, that is, the external division into rich and poor and the internal division into learned and unlearned (the two reasons). This is solved by replacing the problem of the universal striving for wealth by the striving for a universal return to life — that is to say, by replacing our artificial life, our artificial tasks, by a natural task achieved in us by nature itself which — through us — becomes rational. Of course, owing to our urban way of life, which is extremely artificial and burdensome to all, the natural task of man, universal resurrection, must seem unnatural — one might even say very unnatural — but that does not mean that the task of universal resurrection is in fact unnatural, only that we have ourselves become too unnatural ; we have distorted ourselves, our very nature. For nature, transcending its state of unconsciousness to that of consciousness, resuscitation is as necessary and natural as birth and death are for blind nature.

Nature has attained consciousness in the sons of man, the sons of deceased fathers, and this consciousness can be regarded as natural in nations living a rural way of life near the graves of their fathers ; whereas in town dwellers who have, like prodigal sons, left the land and separated themselves from their fathers, the naturalness of consciousness has been lost. The greatest remoteness from naturalness, the greatest degree of artificiality, is reached by the learned ; for them *the God of the fathers* has become the abstract *god of deism*, and the *Son of Man* an indeterminate *human* ; there is complete freedom, but no sense or goal in life ; there is division into two classes and two reasons, and a sense of rupture ; yet at the same time there is a yearning for the restoration of unity. Only when the unification of the human race (namely, nature achieving consciousness, coming to an understanding of itself) is attained, will there be further progress both in this consciousness and in the control of nature itself by the human race — which is also part of nature, that part which has attained consciousness.

What will nature — which, in its present, unconscious state, is a force that procreates and kills — become when it achieves consciousness, if not a force restoring what it has destroyed in its blindness ? How senseless are statements about the incommensurability of the forces of man, that is, of nature striving towards consciousness and control, and the forces of the same blind nature. And should one term 'human force' merely that of man's own hand, or include what he can achieve through nature ? And are human force and human activity to be limited to what man achieves *now* by using the forces of nature ? Why, the true, the natural task has not even begun...

An organism with its sensory and motor nerves leading to the brain centre is a model for a government of the Universe ; all the heavenly bodies should be connected by two sets of conductors, one transmitting the force of feeling, the other that of motion. If such a unification of the Universe is not achieved through us, through the generations of resurrected fathers and ancestors, and if the Universe does not achieve full self-consciousness and self-government in the likeness of God the Creator, this will not be because we are insufficiently gifted but perhaps because we are too gifted — and the most gifted are the least inclined to work for self-organisation and self-creation. Yet only this work can lead to self-consciousness and self-improvement, or adulthood, which entails living a self-determined life. To hope that a blind force would produce stronger beings with more perfect organs which would displace and oust mankind is a complete betrayal of reason. For reason would become an unnecessary appendix if it was not through reason that further improvement and the creation of organs were brought about, to replace those produced by the blind method of birth.

To carry out the natural task two unifications are necessary : an external one, which can be achieved by [the Russian] Autocracy, and an inner one to be achieved in Orthodoxy ; it would be the union of all rational beings in the task of comprehending and controlling the irrational force which procreates and murders.

Supramoralism is expressed in the form of paschal questions addressed to all the living, to all sons endowed with the ability to comprehend — that is, an ability which gives the power to replace the freely given by that obtained through labour. These questions demand that all those who have been born should come to understand, and to feel, that birth means receiving, or rather taking, life from the fathers ; and from this follows the consequent duty of the resuscitation of the fathers, a duty which gives immortality to the sons. These questions are raised at a time when the history of mutual extermination, committed unconsciously, becomes the history of the fulfilment of the project of resurrection unconditionally demanded by consciousness ; these questions are called 'paschal' because, when they are put into effect, they lead to the return of life and to atonement for sin and death.

Since the duty to return life is an unconditionally universal one, the paschal questions are addressed to all. Though few in number, they embrace the manifold diversity of contemporary life, and in accordance with their goal and purpose lead to the union of all. Moreover, they alone can give meaning and purpose to the already existing but uncertain longing for the countryside and for a simpler way of life.

Question I

Concerning *two problems* : the *social* (about wealth and

poverty, or general enrichment) and the *natural* (about life and death, or the universal return to life), not merely in the theoretical sense, trying to answer the question 'Why does the existing exist ?', but in the practical sense, demanding an answer to 'Why do the living suffer and die ?'

It should be borne in mind that the problem of wealth merely refers to industrial toys and entertainments, and not to the essentials, the needed ; the solution of this problem is unthinkable without the radical elimination of crop failures and famines, of epidemics and sickness in general (the sanitary and food problem) ; therefore the problem of essentials is part of that concerning the general return of life. 'Whilst there is death, there will be poverty.' What is more precious — gold, which is at the source of mutual extermination, or the dust of the fathers, as a means towards the reunification of the sons ? What should have priority ? The solution of the problem of wealth and poverty (the social problem), or the solution of the problem of life and death (the natural problem) ? What is more important — social disasters (artificial pauperism) or common natural disasters (natural pauperism) ? Is wealth a good thing and poverty evil, or is life, eternal life, the true good, and death the true evil ? And what should be our task ?

The problem of poverty and illusory wealth is also a problem of the two classes or estates (the poor and the rich), an insoluble one. However, the problem of life and death is the problem of the common calling which unites rich and poor in the Common Task of returning life, and this life — earned by labour — will be inalienable and eternal. So the first paschal question is how to replace the problem of poverty and wealth by that of death and life, which is the same for rich and for poor. The object of the problem is the whole of nature, namely, the blind force that procreates and kills ; its solution requires the union of the two forms of knowledge and of the two classes — the learned and the unlearned — so that it becomes for both an object of knowledge and action. Only the substitution of the problem of life and death (natural pauperism) for that of poverty and wealth (artificial pauperism) can provide so vast a subject for study and action (the whole of nature) that it can unite the two reasons in the Common Task of understanding and governing the blind force that procreates and kills. And in this task of understanding and governing lies the fulfilment of God's will. So the first paschal question becomes a project whose purpose is to make everybody the subject and everything the object of knowledge and action.

The problem of wealth and poverty becomes identified with that of universal happiness, which is impossible in the face of death, while the problem of death and life should be identified with that of complete and universal salvation, instead of an incomplete and partial salvation whereby some (the sinners) are condemned to eternal suffering and the others (the righteous) to an eternal contemplation of this suffering. Replacing the problem of poverty and wealth by that of death and life does not exclude the problem of adequate nutrition, that is, of the basic needs, because wealth as excess and poverty as malnutrition and deprivation conducive to death are part of the problem of death, while the problem of nourishment as a precondition for work and life falls within the problem of life, of sustaining life in the living and returning life to those who have lost it ; it is the food and sanitary problem.

As mentioned earlier, the problem of wealth is one of industrial toys and entertainment, as testified by those exhibitions where one constantly hears the enthusiastic exclamation, 'It's like a little toy !' The problem of wealth and poverty is, so to speak, a problem for minors, because apart from being insoluble it does not remove the problem of death, and this deprives wealth of its value. Therefore after an era characterised by the pursuit of wealth comes an era of renunciation, of asceticism. However, neither general enrichment nor general impoverishment (asceticism) can be the goal of life, nor can they give meaning to it, since neither is able to remove the problem of death — so beautifully expressed in the Indian legend about the king who surrounded his son with every possible luxury and tried to conceal from him the existence of illness, old age and death. Only a universal return to life can give meaning and purpose to life. The possibility of achieving this purpose cannot be proved or disproved by words alone — only action can provide proof.

Question II

Concerning *two dead religions and a living one* :
1. The inner, hypocritical, inactive, lifeless religion — 'ideolatry', deism, which does not demand any union or impose any action, and humanism, which actually postulates disunion under the guise of freedom.
2. The external, ritualistic and similarly lifeless or dead religion (idolatry).
3. The sole living, active religion for which the problem of life and death is a religious problem, that of resurrection ; when every Friday asks, 'Why do the living suffer ?', each Saturday asks, 'Why do the living die?' and every Sunday, 'Why do the dead not come to life again ? Why are those in their tombs not resurrected ?'

'I am the God of thy fathers, the God not of the dead but of the living', and 'thou (son of man) shalt have no other gods' (that is, thou shalt not worship the dead god of deism, nor the lifeless god of humanism). Nature is not God and God is not in (blind and fallen) nature. God is with us. The rational force should govern the blind one, not the reverse. The rational force will govern when amongst us, rational beings, there shall be no discord, that is, when God is with us. 'Thou madest him (man) to have dominion over the works of thy hands ; thou hast put all things under his feet' (Ps. 8:6). 'Thou hast put all things in subjection under his feet. For in that he put all in subjection under him, he left nothing that is not put under him' (Heb. 2:8).

The God of the fathers — not the dead but the living — created man in his likeness, and the *living* sons, the sons of the *deceased* fathers for whom the fathers are *dead, incontroverti-*

bly dead, dead for ever, are evidently not in the likeness of God. Likeness to God is attainable only by re-creating life, by actual re-creation. A living religion is simply the 'religionisation', that is to say, the making into a religion, of the problem of life and death, of the return of life, of resurrection. Rural paganism is a living religion which not only buries the grain and sows the dead, but believes that its ring-dances symbolising the course of the sun bring it back from winter to summer,* and the life-giving force of this heavenly body revives the grain and resurrects the dead — resurrects them at least in the imagination of the people. Nor can the living Christian faith consider the sons of the deceased fathers other than as the instruments of the God of the fathers, His instruments in the task of returning life to the fathers ; that is what religion should be.

The greater the place in life accorded to wealth, to enrichment, the less room is left for religion, and the more it becomes lifeless, abstract, internalised, personal and idle, demanding no action — to put it briefly, a mere ghost... The art of concealing death is a characteristic feature of a dead religion : in fact, it constitutes the negation of religion. Indeed, the art of concealing death makes any religion a dead one. So what should be our faith and where should our duty lie ? In lifeless deism, requiring no action and imposing no divine duty, or in the abstract indeterminism of humanism ? Or should we seek for a cause, a duty to the God of our fathers (not dead but living) and to the sons of the fathers, both dead and dying (not yet dead), the 'morituri' ? Must we, the sons of deceased fathers, be the instruments of God's will that they and we should live, or shall we remain for ever the opponents of the divine will, failing to unite in this common task and continuing to oust our fathers and exterminate each other as we do today ?

---

* *Khorovod* from Khor or Khors, the name of the sun-god among the ancient Slavs, and *vod*, the root of the verb *vodit'*, to lead. Hence also Khorosan — the land of the sun.

Question III

Concerning *the two types of relations of rational beings to the irrational force : the present one* (exploiting and exhausting nature), or *as it should be* (regulating and re-creating it).

The present exploitation, exhaustion and utilisation of nature oblige us to ask : what for ? And it turns out to be for the production of toys and trifles, for entertainment and fun. This should not arouse our anger ; we must remember that we deal with minors, even though they may be called professors, lawyers, and the like. Not 'with blind nature should our life be at one', but with our own kin, in order that rational beings may govern the irrational force.

Contrary to Schopenhauer's 'world as will and representation', it should be 'world as slavery and the project of liberation from enslavement', from dependence, from subordination to a blind force ; for us the world has no will, and for beings endowed with feeling and capable of action and not mere contemplation, the world is not solely a representation but a project of liberation from bondage. The expression 'the world as will and representation' could be justifiably replaced by the expression 'the world as lust', for lust procreates and kills, giving birth to sons and destroying the fathers. For us the world is not a representation but a project, moreover one that does not oppose lust (the opposite of lust is asceticism) but transforms the procreating force into a re-creating one, the lethal into a vivifying. Then the world can no longer remain a representation but becomes a project of the restoration of the predecessors by the offspring, that is, a project of resuscitation. That is how it should be, but at the present time the world is as it is — lust and representation.

These are the two attitudes of rational beings to the irrational force :

1. The theoretical or illusory domination of nature entails a theoretical superiority of the rational beings over the natural force, but in practice accepts dependence on and subservience to the irrational force. The superiority over the irrational force

is not put into effect, and this leads to complete submission. Similarly inactive — in other words, wrong — is the attitude of those who limit themselves to laboratory experiments and their application to manufacturing industry, to the exploitation and utilisation of natural resources.

2. Only the regulation of natural processes, that is, of the blind force, is the right attitude of a rational being to the irrational force. Regulation means the transformation of a procreating and annihilating force into one that restores and vivifies. Regulation is not self-indulgence (that is to say, not subjection to arbitrary caprice) and not self-will (exploitation), but the endowing of nature with will and reason. Man will govern nature when discord among people ends, when they bring into the world not selfishness but good will and, consequently, become instruments of God's will. Man as a rational being has but one enemy — the blind force of nature — and even that enemy will become an eternal friend when discord ceases among people, when they unite in order to understand and govern the blind force of nature, which punishes us for our ignorance as it punished Martinique this year (1902) for the scientists' incorrect understanding of the volcanic processes.

So what should be the attitude of rational beings living not in discord but in concord, of beings both rational and sensitive to bereavement ? What should be their attitude to an irrational force which is both life-giving and lethal ? Is it right for a rational being endowed with willpower and already possessing not only natural innate gifts but the fruits of his labour, created by himself, to submit to a blind, spontaneous force ? What indeed should be the common task of rational, sensate beings ? Is it merely to exploit and utilise nature and exhaust it (exhaust its freely given, freely procreated gifts), or else to regulate nature, by transforming the freely given into the fruits of labour, the procreated into the created, the being born into the restored, the lethal into the vivifying ? For a rational being to obey nature means to govern it, because in the rational being nature has acquired a leader and a governor ; whereas for submission, subservience, servility and ignorance, nature, as already said, imposes the death penalty, and this year has sentenced to death over 40,000 people for poor progress in the study of volcanic forces. For man as the *consciousness* of nature, the natural problem, the problem of nature as a force which procreates and kills, constitutes his natural task because it solves the problem of hunger, epidemics and sickness in general — that is, of old age and death. Both believers and unbelievers can unite in this natural task, and by uniting and carrying out the task they will attain oneness of mind. In taking part in this task the believers will not oppose God's will, but carry it into effect, while for unbelievers it will be their liberation from enslavement to the blind force, and submission to the will of God, instead of that persistent denial of divine will on which philosophy squanders its powers.

Question IV
Concerning the *two reasons* (the theoretical and the practical) and the *two classes* (the learned, the intelligentsia ; and the unlearned, the people) ; and concerning philosophy as an infantile babbling of humanity, or thought without action, and the sole true reason that unites everybody in common knowledge and in the government of the blind, irrational force by regulation ; resulting eventually in the knowledge and ever-expanding government of all the worlds, of all world systems, till the ultimate spiritualisation of the universe, regulated by the resurrected generations, comes to pass. This will be in its cosmic fullness what — in a much shortened form — each being goes through in its prenatal state.

Know thyself (in other words, do not believe your fathers, that is, tradition ; do not believe the testimony of others or of your brothers ; know only thyself, says the demon (of Delphi, or Socrates). *I know, therefore I exist*, answers Descartes, and Fichte comments : *I — the knowing — am the existing ; all the rest is only what I know, namely, my mental image and, therefore, non-existing.* Hence, *Love thyself with all thy soul and all thy heart*, conclude Stirner and Nietzsche, *find thyself in thyself, be the only one and recognise nothing except thyself.*

Or *Know yourselves in the fathers and the fathers in yourselves, and you will be a brotherhood of sons.* Then condemnation (critique) will be replaced by atonement — an atonement not in words only but in action, in resuscitation — and then we will become truly the disciples of Christ.

The two reasons The contemplative (theoretical) reason sees both God and the deceased fathers as mental images, and each other as things, not as thinking beings. It recognises the regulation of nature (cosmology), yet only in the field of knowledge (representation), not in reality. The practical reason that does not transform thought into action but leaves it as imagery — that is superstition. Neither the critique of pure reason nor that of practical reason explains the basic causes for the division into two reasons and two classes (the learned and the unlearned), those basic causes which result in two ignorances.

The two classes One of them admits being benighted and the other (philosophers and intellectuals) does not recognise the possibility of actual (objective) knowledge ; the result is two forms of ignorance, the inevitable consequence of a divided reason. The theoretical reason is incapable of distinguishing between hallucination and reality, while the practical remains passive and submissive to the lethal force, and even transforms its life-giving force into sterile lust (deliberately childless marriages), which leads to the extinction of the race and makes eternal life impossible.

The one reason is that 'true' reason to which all are called so that none should perish but all should unite in the task of 'the sons of man', *so that all be one.*

When the theoretical reason which studies death and life, and the practical one which returns life and thus defeats death (in the task of universal resuscitation), together carry out the will of the Son, who gave the commandment for all to come together, and the will of the Holy Spirit, who acts (and not only speaks) within those who unite, then in working on the Common Task they will learn to make a reality of 'the hoped for' ; the task will unite faith with reason, for such is the true natural relationship of the two reasons ; it is the relationship as it should be, but fails to be at the present time. Now the theoretical reason divorced from the practical — that of the people, the believers (Christians and peasants) — replaces the problem of life and death with the urban problem of wealth and poverty, making it a problem either of general enrichment or of impoverishment, thus condemning the human race to remain perennial minors.

To establish a correct, adequate relationship between the two reasons, priority should be given to practical reason, that of the common people who believe in resurrection and in participating in the task of resurrection. Indeed, the people believe that they participate in this task as the instruments of the will of the God of the fathers and, in their paganism, ascribe to their ring-dances the power of bringing back the sun from winter to summer, of returning the buried grain and bringing back to life the bodies of their fathers sown in the earth ; or else the people attribute a similar effect to the sole *power of prayer*, because they do not know of any work or endeavour which would enable them to influence nature in cases of drought, flood and other disasters. The people, who live close to nature and are completely dependent on it, will not give up their superstitions and superstitious activities, whatever they are told, unless they are shown effective means of governing those forces on which they are dependent today. The task of theoretical reason should consist in the discovery of such means, and not in the denial of a rational cause of all being and a rational purpose for existence. Therefore, to allocate pride of place to theoretical reason is usurpation, a betrayal of its begetter — the practical reason from which theoretical reason originated in the first place, just as the town developed from the village and town dwellers from villagers. Therefore the return of theoretical reason to the practical, in other words, to the village, will be an expression of repentance for this betrayal and usurpation.

In distancing themselves from the countryside, the town dwellers have forgotten the fathers and the God of the fathers; God has become for them an unattainable ideal, an idea, and the question has even arisen of how this idea of God originated. Town dwellers have begun to ask how this idea of a god ever entered their heads. Upon returning to the countryside, they are bound to repent the oblivion of the fathers and of the God of their fathers; they will come to understand that one can speak of the sins of desertion, of forgetting and of alienation, but not about the origin of the idea of God, which always existed and arose with consciousness...

When separated, the theoretical and practical reasons are two forms of ignorance, of darkness, but when theoretical reason unites with the practical, believing, peasant Christian reason, together they will shine with double radiance; there will be none of the former mutual accusations by the believers of the unbelievers of gloomy doubt, nor of the believers by the unbelievers of obscurantism and retrograde fanaticism. It should be noted that in accusing the believers of obscurantism the *unbelievers* do not consider their own light as true, since they admit themselves that *their knowledge*, that of theoretical reason, *is merely subjective.*

Question V

Concerning *the two passions* : sexual sensuousness and a child's love for its parents or, what amounts to the same, universal enmity and universal love.

'There is no eternal hate — to eliminate temporary hate is our task.' 'Become as little children.'

The two passions are sexual sensuousness and the ensuing asceticism as a rejection of sensuousness, and *the one feeling of universal love for the parents*, which is inseparable from the one reason.

Has hostility no cause, or are there *real* causes for the *unbrotherly* relations between people and *the lack of kinship* between blind nature and rational beings ? And how can kinship be restored ?

The attraction of external beauty for the sensuous force is *a ploy to mislead individuals for the sake of preserving the species* ; attraction which neither sees nor wishes to see in the sensuous force also a lethal force fails to see the connection between birth and death, and leads to *industrialism* which serves to excite the sexual instinct. To protect itself industrialism creates militarism and exacerbates wealth and poverty, and the two latter engender socialism and the problems arising from the pursuit of wealth.

A *sentient* but not sensuous force arises in the souls of children. With the onset of old age and the death of the parents, it is transformed into one of *compassion*, of *co-dying* ; it unites all sons and daughters in knowledge and government, that is, in the regulation of nature ; it becomes a mighty force re-creating those who have died. As the generations come back to life, this regulation gradually expands to all the worlds. Out of the child's love, the son's and particularly the daughter's love, arises universal love, which develops and is strengthened by participation in the filial task common to all and close to the hearts of all.

Question VI

Concerning *the two wills and the two moralities*.

1. *The two wills : the will to procreate*, that is to say, will in the sense of lust or the denial of lust (asceticism), life for oneself (egotism) and life for others (altruism), and *the will to resuscitate and live with all the living for the raising of the dead.*

'Know thyself, for the kingdom of the world is at hand.'

'Repent, those who know only themselves, for the Kingdom of God, the Kingdom of all, is at hand.'

In contradistinction to the one will to procreate and its negation, asceticism, the one will to resuscitate is inseparable from the one reason and the one passion.

2. *The two moralities*. What is preferable : *the morality of disunion*, that is, the freedom of the individual expressed in

the struggle for an illusory personal *dignity* and illusory *goods*, among sons who have forgotten their fathers and replaced love for the fathers by lust ; or *the morality of union*, the morality of sons conscious of their loss, sensitive to their orphanhood and finding their happiness in the task of fulfilling their duty towards their fathers ?

The will to procreate, as lust, engenders wealth and leads the human race to *demoralisation* (of which the Universal Exhibition is a striking expression), whereas the will to resuscitate, when the problem of returning life is seen as the purpose of conscious beings, *moralises* all the worlds of the Universe, because then all the worlds that are moved by insensate forces will be governed by the brotherly feelings of all the resurrected generations. This involves both their *moralisation* and their *rationalisation*, because then the worlds of the Universe will no longer be moved by blind insensate forces but will be governed by the feelings and reason of the resurrected generations.

Question VII

Concerning the *two styles*, the *two ways of life*, or rather the one rural life (that is, that of the sons who have not deserted the graves of their fathers), the immature form of which is nomadism and the obsolescent one the urban, the civilised.

The fact that the urban, industrial way of life gives pride of place to *luxury industry*, which is even termed *scientific industry*, shows that all industry and technology are doomed to serve the sexual instinct ; this is deeply humiliating and shameful for the human intellect, and highlights the close affinity of humans to animals as well as the increasing moral degradation of the city. It can be said that all urban culture is the worship, the divinisation, the cult, of woman.

What path to choose ? The urban cult of things and of woman, of the splendour of putrefaction, or the countryside and the dust of the fathers ? Will we choose the countryside, in the hope that it will attain a state when the dust of the fathers will no longer be transformed into food for their offspring but into the blood and flesh of the fathers, so that they become alive for us, beings of flesh, as they are alive for God ? Will we choose the cult of graveyards, of the deceased awaiting revival, or the Universal Exhibition, the fruit of industrialisation — an institution which has already reached maturity and is becoming obsolescent, an institution allegedly hostile but in fact friendly to militarism, which is displacing graveyards, churches and universities, which scorns the museum (where the relics of the ancestors are preserved) — in brief, an institution which admits life only in itself ?

Rural life as it is now, although superior to the two others (the nomadic and the urban), is not yet a perfect life. Rural life will achieve the conditions necessary to attain perfection, will become capable of perfection, only when town dwellers return to the graves of their fathers and nomads become settled — that is to say, when no one deserts the tombs of the ancestors, when cemeteries become centres for the gathering together of sons, when, united in their filial task, they become brothers. The conditions for attaining perfection will be acquired only when the problem of the two types of people is solved — those who are the sons of deceased fathers, who remember and pray for them, and those who have forgotten their fathers, the prodigals for whom the highest title is 'man', man in general, complete man and finally superman (the most abstract philosophical definition, which contains nothing definite ; when we see the solution to problems of the peasants, who retain the cult of their fathers, and the town dwellers, with their cult of woman and sexual passion in its various manifestations ; when it is recognised that the truly loftiest definition is *son of man*, for it epitomises the duty of all sons, as one son, to all the fathers as one father, that is, the duty of resuscitation, the duty of rational beings, united in the image of the Triune Being in whom is revealed for us the prime cause of immortality and man's guilt, which has brought death on us.

Question VIII

Concerning *science as it is and as it should be*, class science or science based on universal observations and experimentation, on conclusions drawn from observations carried out everywhere, always and by all, on experiments carried out by nature itself ; the experience of the regulation of meteorological, volcanic or plutonic and cosmic phenomena, and not experiments carried out in academic and industrial laboratories ; conclusions drawn from the experimentation carried out by all the living together, over the whole earth as a single unit seen as the cemetery of innumerable generations, gradually returning to life and joining those who learn and govern in expanding control from one planet, our Earth, to others, to the solar system as a whole and eventually to other systems, to all the Universe.

Is present-day science adequate ? Is the university an obsolete institution ? For it is a slave to industrialism, unaware that the latter produces merely toys and trifles and recognises nothing higher than the goods it provides. The university is 'the enemy of throne and altar', the enemy of 'autocracy, orthodoxy and nationality' ; it sets itself up as judge over ancestors, prophets, Christ and even God himself ; it is the enemy of all authority, exciting sons against fathers, ranking discord above unity, leading to monism and solipsism, enjoining everyone to consider himself as the only one and transforming the whole world into a representation. Such are the principles basic to the university and its existence. This makes it into an obsolescent institution where the voice of the professors is drowned in the clamour of demands from student-pupils on strike.

Can a class science be called true science whilst it is based on observations carried out here and there, sometimes and by some people, and on deductions limited to laboratory experiments and applied to industrial activities ? Or should it be based on deductions from observations carried out everywhere, always and by everybody, and be applied to the regulation and government of the blind, insensate force of nature ? Has pure science, university science, the right to remain indifferent to human disasters ? In other words, must it be knowledge just for the sake of knowledge, a knowledge of why the existing exists and not why the living suffers and dies ?! And is not applied science criminal in creating objects of contention — industrial toys — and arming those contending for these toys with ever more destructive and pain-producing weapons, which powerfully contribute to making the Earth into a cemetery ?

Science, as it is, could merge all branches of knowledge in astronomy, or else in history. If all knowledge is merged in astronomy, history becomes a minor chapter of zoology ; whereas if all branches of knowledge are brought together in history, astronomy becomes just a short page in the history of human thought. However, science as it should be, in order to be true and active, must open up to history, that is, to the generations who were confined to, suffered and died within our small planet ; and history must open up to them, as a field of activity, all the Universe and all the heavenly worlds.

Question IX

Concerning *art as it is*, that is, a game or the creation of dead likenesses, and *art as it should be*, that is, art as re-creation, through the labour of all, of the life that has passed away — real, authentic life.

Humanity is not a product of nature, but a creation of God mediated by ourselves, and including the resurrected generations for the rational government of the universe.

Art as it should be, how it was and what it has become

Must art, for the sons of deceased fathers, be limited to the creation of dead semblances of what has passed away, or else simulations of the Universe symbolically represented in church buildings ? Or should it be the actual creation of the past and of the Universe, a task both divine and human ? Has not this second purpose of art been obvious from its very inception ? For it began with the rising up of the living to a vertical posture and the raising of the fallen, the dead ; indeed, if living man, having adopted a vertical posture, looked up to heaven, the dead were symbolically raised by the erection of memorials. Later, art sought to re-create earth and heaven in church architecture, and only latterly did it fall to the level of the Universal Exhibition, where sons who had forgotten their fathers gathered what merely serves to stimulate sexual selection.

All arts can be combined in the German way as in opera or the theatre, or, as we assume, in the Slav or the Russian way, in architecture at its loftiest — in the church and its services. The church building is a representation of the Universe, infinitely superior because of the idea embodied in it ; for the church is a projection of the world as it should be. The church is a representation of heaven, of the heavenly vault, and on its walls are representations of deceased generations as if already risen. On iconostases such as the one in Moscow's Cathedral of the Assumption and in other temples, we see, however much compressed, a picture of all history beginning with Adam, then the forefathers who lived before and after the flood, kings, prophets, the Forerunner, Christ, the apostles and so on to the end of time. During the divine service these celestial beings join in worship with clergy and congregation, so that both the living and the dead constitute one church.

However, church buildings are representations of the world according to the Ptolemaic world view, and so long as this was accepted there was no contradiction between knowledge and art. When the Ptolemaic world view was superseded by that of Copernicus, there arose a contradiction between art and knowledge because art had remained Ptolemaic and knowledge had become Copernican. The Ptolemaic world view as expressed in art, in church buildings and services was a pseudo*patrification* in heaven, whereas the Copernican should lead to real patrification — resuscitation — and this will solve the contradiction between knowledge and art.

Could the museum, that repository of relics of the past, be the institution to carry out this task ? It is still immature, and uncertain to what purpose it preserves the obsolete, and has not yet asked, 'Will these bones come to life ?' Nor does it yet understand its closeness to the church of the God of the fathers, or that it is the complete opposite of industrialism and militarism. Nor does it notice its enemies either in the university itself, the devotee of the blind force of nature which kills the fathers, or in the master of the university, industrialism, which openly despises the museum and, though less openly, the university itself.

Question X

Concerning *faith and knowledge*, or Easter as a feast and the act of resuscitation. In Christianity art and knowledge are reunited in Easter, and even in paganism the ancestor cult can bring religion to perfection, reality and implementation. Religion as a symbiosis of knowledge and action is the cult of the dead, or the Easter of suffering and resurrection. Religion is the universal prayer of all the living in the face of suffering and death, a prayer for the return of life to all the deceased. To carry this out is the duty and task of all those at prayer, and in it lies the fulfilment of truth, good, beauty and the magnificence of incorruptibility. The suffering and risen Christ is the prototype of all human sons of man. Two weeks in the year are devoted to Him, but the other fifty are only the repetition of these two.

Must faith and knowledge always be opposed and hostile to each other, or should they unite, and if so how ? Will this problem be solved in the city, which is increasingly dominated by the fourth estate, a class solely concerned with utilitarianism and secularism, a class which considers maximum enjoyment and minimum work as the greatest good and rejects as rubbish anything, even science, that fails to promote this goal directly ?! Or can the solution be found in the countryside, where everything that has been squeezed out of the city will come together in order to enter into direct, immediate relations with the land (that is, the dust of the fathers) and the sky — the force that kills and vivifies — and transform it into a governable entity ? In the task of governing the blind force, which is also the task of resuscitation, all knowledge and art will serve as tools in the great cause ; and only in this way can faith and knowledge be united.

Easter begins with the creation of man by God, mediated by man himself. It is expressed in the rising up of the sons (vertical posture) and in the restoration (in upright memorial stones) of the deceased fathers ; it is expressed in the spring ring-dances symbolising the course of the sun on All Saints' Day, [celebrated by the orthodox on the ninth day after Easter] performed at cemeteries, symbolising the return of the sun from winter to summer to bestow life...

The celebration of Easter, which has practically disappeared in the West, especially the far West, is kept in Russia, and above all in the Kremlin, in the vicinity of the graves of those who gathered and united the sons for the purpose of resurrecting the fathers. And when unbrotherliness ceases, the Kremlin, the citadel which defended the ashes of the fathers, will change its purpose from guarding to reviving those ashes. The Coronation, which entrusts Him who stands for all the fathers with the common task of resuscitation, would have no meaning if it took place elsewhere than in the Kremlin. The Coronation would be even more meaningful if it took place on Easter Day. The manifesto of 12 August 1898, the 'manifesto on disarmament', as it is called,[1] could take on its full meaning only on Easter Day, which replaces the day of retribution, judgement and punishment by universal pardon, amnesty. The well known homily of John Chrysostom, read usually at the end of Easter matins, is an amnesty. The same is expressed by the kiss of peace exchanged among parishioners, which shows that all wrongs and offences are forgotten. At its place of origin, Old Jerusalem, and its copy, [the monastery

---

1. This is a reference to the First Hague Peace Conference convened on the initiative of Emperor Nicholas II of Russia in 1899. Its wide scope was eventually reduced to the setting up of what has become the Hague International Court of Justice ; see note 1 to 'Disarmament', p. 144, and Appendix IV.

of] New Jerusalem, built by Patriarch Nikon, Easter is particularly tangible and palpable and in these places it is ever present, constant, all the year round ; there the identification of Easter and Orthodoxy is particularly evident and comprehensible.[2]

The sons who venerate their fathers have not only preserved and defended the dust of their fathers with the utmost valour, but have seen their fathers in heaven and their churches represented in heaven — that is, the world as it appears to our senses. However, when the scholars rejected the Ptolemaic world view, which made patrification possible, and rejoiced that all was dead, that there was no heaven and that patrification was impossible, it became apparent that the Copernican view required, as proof, actual patrification, that is to say, the regulation of all the worlds by past generations not born but re-created, because any proposition (and the Copernican view was and remains a proposition), unless substantiated by tangible proof, ceases to be a hypothesis and becomes superstition. How can the Copernican world view be tangibly proven, if we do not acquire the faculty to live beyond the Earth, all over the Universe ? Without the ability not only to visit but also to inhabit all heavenly bodies, we cannot be convinced that they are as posited by the Copernican view and not as they appear to our senses.

The ability to live all over the Universe, enabling the human race to colonise all the worlds, will give us the power to unite all the worlds of the Universe into an artistic whole, a work of art, the innumerable artists of which, in the image of the Triune Creator, will be the entire human race, the totality of the risen and re-created generations inspired by God, by the Holy Spirit, who will no longer speak through certain individuals, the prophets, but will act through all the sons of

2. The Voskresensky Monastery (the Monastery of the Resurrection), some forty kilometres from Moscow, was built in the 1650s by Patriarch Nikon. It was known as the New Jerusalem because its main church was a copy of that of the Holy Sepulchre in Jerusalem.

man in their ethical or brotherly (supramoral) totality, through the sons of man attaining divine perfection ('Be ye therefore perfect, even as your Father which is in heaven is perfect') in the cause, the work of restoring the world to the sublime incorruptibility it had before the Fall. Then, united, science and art will become ethics and aesthetics ; they will become a natural universal technology of their work of art — the cosmos. United, science and art will become an ethico-aesthetic theurgy, no longer mystical but real.

If the church building in Ptolemaic art was a reflection of the Universe as it appears to *our external senses*, if this insignificantly small building *inspired by inner feeling*, by its profound meaning, was spiritually incomparably greater than the Universe, then in Copernican art the inner and outer expressions must achieve complete congruity. *This is what man was created for* ; herein lies the answer to the question regarding sense and purpose, about which rational beings, sons forgetful of their fathers and who have lost faith in the God of their father, have never ceased to ponder and torment themselves.

Our ancient Russia did not forget her fathers, nor did she lose faith in the God of the fathers. Yet we look upon her as the Jews did upon Galilee, on Nazareth, expecting no good to come therefrom, nothing outstanding intellectually or morally. Our ancient Russia never doubted that the answer to the question 'What has man been created for ?' is that humans were created to be the heavenly powers replacing the fallen angels, God's divine instruments for governing the Universe and restoring it to the incorruptible magnificence it had before the Fall.

Question XI

Concerning *minority* and *the coming of age*.

Be perfect as God your Father is perfect, God the Father of the living, not of the dead. Where should we look for models of living ? In the world of the animals, of blind nature, or in a world that is superior to the human race ? Should the model for our society be an organism and the blind evolution of life, or should the model for our unity-in-pluralism be the Divine Trinity, within which unity is not a yoke and independence not discord ? Would not then Divine creativeness, replacing our present destruction of life, serve us as a model for its re-creation ?

The problem of minority and the coming of age is one of crisis, and this crisis is a necessary consequence of our minority. An amnesty is the precondition of our coming of age, an amnesty to eliminate the Last Judgement, world war, catastrophe and the end of the world.

Wealth, and the craving for industrial toys, doom mankind to perennial minority, make of a son and brother a citizen needing constant supervision and the threat of punishment, and lead to diplomatic intrigues and military adventurism. Does not minority consist in submission to blind evolution, leading to the revolt of sons against fathers and conflict among brothers, that is, to *depatrification* and *defraternisation*, and eventually to degeneration and extinction ? Does not adulthood consist in all becoming brothers for the re-creation of the parents, the victims of struggle and progress ? And will this not be made manifest by the transfiguration of the Kremlin from a fortress protecting the dust of the fathers and a church for funerals into a centre for extra-ecclesiastical liturgy or resuscitation ?

The human race, persisting in its infantilism, a state of discord, failing to unite in order to study the blind force and submitting to its will in a *natural* way, drifts towards degeneration and extinction. In a *supernatural* way it can only expect transcendental resurrection, achieved not by us but by an external force and even contrary to our will ; this would be a Last Judgement resurrection of wrath, condemning some (the sinners) to eternal suffering and others (the righteous) to the contemplation of this suffering. We who venerate God, *Who wants all men to be saved*, to come to true wisdom so that none shall perish, cannot but find such an end extremely sad, extremely distressing. Therefore we dare to think that the prophecy of the Last Judgement is conditional, like that of the prophet Jonah and like all prophecies, because every prophecy has an educational purpose — the purpose of reforming those to whom it is addressed ; it cannot sentence to irrevocable perdition those who have not even been born yet. If that were the case, what sense, what purpose, could such a prophecy have, and could it accord with the will of a God who, as already stated, wishes all to be saved, all to come to true reason and none to perish ? Jonah was rebuked for his disappointment when his prophecy did not come true, and his disappointment was held against him ; we dare to think the author of the Apocalypse, who was also the apostle of love, would thank the Lord for his prophecy failing to be fulfilled.

Question XII

Concerning *despotism* (bondage) and *constitutions* (self-will), or overt domination (despotism) and covert yoke (constitution), and *autocracy*, when power over humans is replaced by power over the blind force, which leads to adulthood, true pacification and good will — good will being the essence of autocracy.*

Render to God what is God's and to Caesar what is Caesar's is the scriptural law under pagan power. *The people exist not for the Tsar, nor the Tsar for the people, but the Tsar and the people together are the executors of God's cause*, the all-human cause — such is the scriptural law of a Christian Orthodox power. It is *the solution to the antinomies of God and Caesar, the spiritual and the secular, and the solution of the two reasons.*

Constitution means entertainment in Austria, a boxing match in Italy, 'a game not worth the candle' in France, and

---

* Fedorov held the view that in a constitutional monarchy or republic different political parties fight for the sectional interests of their electors, turning parliamentary debates into institutionalised discord which was not conducive to brotherhood. Similarly, brotherhood could not be enforced by a despot upon unwilling subjects.

idle verbiage everywhere, whereas *autocracy* means sonship and fatherhood ; it means the task of sons directed by *him who stands in place of the fathers and forefathers*, anointed by the God of the fathers (living, not dead) for the protection of the land (the dust of the fathers) from those who fail to recognise the brotherhood of sons ; autocracy is the task of the sons which becomes, with the full union of those sons, the return of life to the dust of the fathers — that is to say, struggle not against members of our own species but against the dark force which procreates and destroys life.

Will not the fulfilment of the task of autocracy put an end to all divisions — division in religion, division into two reasons, into two classes (the learned and the unlearned) — and will this not put an end to the division of power, the power of God and of Caesar, so that Caesar becomes an instrument of God ? The Tsar together with the people will become the executor of God's cause ; the problem of life and death will replace that of wealth and poverty ; the moral will supersede the legal, economic and social ; the obligatory will be replaced by the voluntary, and the poverty of the human being — his natural poverty, not to mention his artificial poverty — will become *a wealth indestructible* and the life of all, for all and with all, a treasure to which we should devote our minds, hearts and will.

The paschal question is the question of whether humans will remain perennial minors or achieve true adulthood. Will the human race remain at the first stage of nature's transition from blindness to consciousness, which, at the present time, it has reached through us, or will it achieve full consciousness and the government of all the worlds by resuscitated generations ?

To abdicate the task of resuscitation leaves the human race only the choice between constitutional debating and despotism. To retain Easter as a feast only and the liturgy as a church service, an expression of an as yet incomplete love for the fathers which does not entail actual resuscitation, or, by abdicating completely brotherhood and filial love, to indulge on the graves of the fathers in bestial orgies followed by savage mutual extermination ; to retain the art of dead likenesses or to annihilate any true likenesses ; not merely to censure parents for giving life to their offspring without their consent, but to curse one's procreators ; to retain academic class science or, rejecting all knowledge, to descend into the hopeless darkness of obscurantism ; to remain in the perennial city of brides and bridegrooms, surrounded by toys and trifles, indulging in pleasures and entertainments, or else, rejecting not only fathers and forebears but even progeny, sons (artificially childless marriages), in order to indulge in boundless lechery ; to retain will as either lust or mortification of the flesh ; to retain sensuousness or to be satisfied by mere grieving for the dead or — the last and greatest evil — to plunge into nirvana, the product of total evil negation — such are the fruits of abdicating the task of resuscitation.

Quite different are the good tidings of Christianity. Just as Buddhism is contrary to Christianity, so the hoped-for future promised by Christianity is the opposite of nirvana. In contradistinction to the Buddhist nirvana, which is non-existence, supramoralism demands from rational beings the fullest development of existence — of all that was, is and can be. Rational beings are in possession of the present, of all that is, and resurrect all that was, transfigured, made perfect. Supramoralism postulates paradise, the Kingdom of God, not in the world beyond but here and now ; it demands the transfiguration of this earthly reality, a transfiguration which extends to all heavenly bodies and brings us close to the unknown world beyond. Paradise, or the Kingdom of God, is not only within us ; it is not only a mental and spiritual kingdom, but a visible, tangible one, perceptible to our organs as developed by psychophysiological regulation (by the control of spiritual and bodily phenomena), organs capable of sensing not just the growing of the grass but the motion of atoms and molecules throughout the Universe, thus making possible the restoration of life and the transfiguration of the entire Universe.

Therefore the Kingdom of God, or paradise, is the product of all the forces, all the abilities of all the people in their totality ; the result of positive, not negative, virtues. Such is the paradise of adults. It can only be the product of humans themselves, the result of a fullness of knowledge, a depth of feeling and the might of willpower. Paradise can be created only by the people themselves in fulfilment of God's will, not by individuals but by the power of all humans in their totality. Moreover, it cannot consist in inactivity, in eternal rest, which is nirvana ; perfection lies in life and activity. 'My Father has never ceased working, and I too must be at work' — this is perfection. There can be no paradise for *the imperfect* or for minors. Therefore all attempts to depict such a paradise by Dante, Milton, Chenavard[3] and many others have been quite fruitless. To describe a paradise not created by humans and without their participation, simply bestowed on them as a reward, is rightly considered to be a thankless task. Perfection, adulthood, is paradise, just as the state of minority expressed in bestial orgies, brutal mutual extermination and boundless, insatiable lechery is hell indeed.

The first shortcoming of Dante's paradise, this paradise for minors, for those who consider immortality and bliss to be theirs by birthright and not as the result of work, is that this paradise is not created by them ; it exists already, it has been created for but not by them. This negation of work, this contempt for it as shown by Byron's Cain, an aristocrat like his author, prove his immaturity and childishness. Yet bliss resides first and foremost in the work of creation, and the

---

3. Paul Joseph Chenavard (1808-95) was a French painter. In 1848 the French Republican government commissioned him to paint murals in the Paris Pantheon representing the history of humanity and including symbols and legends of all religions. Five mosaics on the floor of the building were to depict hell, purgatory, paradise, the Elysian fields and palingenesis. This grandiose scheme foundered with the establishment of the Second Empire under Napoleon III, who returned the Pantheon to the Roman Catholic Church in 1852. However, Chenavard's sketches had been described by his friend, the writer Théophile Gautier, in a series of articles (*La Presse*, 5-11 September 1848) later included in his *L'Art moderne*, Paris, 1852. Fedorov wrote a scathing analysis of their symbolism, completely rejecting Chenavard's syncretic religion : *FOD*, pp. 541-9, 585-8.

regulation of the meteorological process is the first stage of the celestial task — the creation of paradise.

The second shortcoming of Dante's paradise — its vice, even — consists in his transporting into heaven humanity with all its present moral limitations; consequently contemplatives, regarded as creators of such a paradisiac life, are placed at the highest of the planetary heavens. Yet contemplation, because it is mere contemplation, cannot find room in a real paradise, for its wings are illusory, mental; they cannot raise it up into paradise. Only contemplation which becomes action could create paradise and transform its imaginary into bodily wings.

All the heavenly space and heavenly bodies will become accessible to man only when he is able to re-create himself from primordial substances, atoms and molecules, because only then will he be able to live in any environment, take on any form and visit all generations in all the worlds, from the most ancient to the most recent, the most remote as well as the nearest. Governed by all the resurrected generations, these worlds will be, in their wholeness, the creative work of all generations in their totality, as if of a single artist.

Dante's paradise as depicted by him is a kingdom of pagan virtues — these do not create their paradise and hence cannot dwell therein. The Roman eagle, that is to say, the Western Emperor, arbitrarily elevated to that rank by the Pope, has also given birth to the present-day German Black Tsar, as he might be described, in contradistinction to the Russian White Tsar. The Roman eagle, which introduced discord into Christendom, has risen to the heaven of Mercury but has not cleansed himself of that ambition and lust for power which are able to create a state but neither a paradise nor a paradisiac society in which, instead of legal and economic relations, there is only kinship. Solely the Emperor of the undivided Empire, leading his army to confront not humans but the dark, blind force, can enter with his comrades-in-arms into the paradise they will be creating.

Theology has risen as high as the sun but has remained a

discourse about God — the word, not the act, of God ; only divine action (not mystical theurgy), only our transforming ourselves into instruments of the Divine work, will transfigure all suns, all heavenly worlds, into the Kingdom of God, paradise. Negative virginity is not yet a celestial virtue ; chastity is not yet active wisdom ; not to beget is not yet liberation from death — resurrection. It is essential that unconscious procreation be replaced by the task of resuscitation. Placing virgins on Venus could be interpreted as a bitter irony, because Earth itself is not yet free from the power of Venus, and negative virginity cannot liberate from this power. A similar irony can be seen in Dante's placing of warriors and crusaders under the protection of the pagan god Mars. Contrary to the opinion of some Roman Catholics, war cannot create paradise ; war merely destroys and exterminates, and only the transformation of instruments of destruction into instruments of salvation can create paradise. The warriors on Mars could also be transformed on Earth into an army for salvation from hunger, disease and death — in other words, even on earth they could free themselves from the power of Mars, the god of war. Nor was there any point in sending lawyers to Jupiter, considering the great demand for them on Earth, a demand which is on the increase ; indeed, the Earth groans under their yoke, and even recently lawyers who took part in the Peace Conference aborted it by transforming it into a court of arbitration. To transport to heaven the shortcomings of this Earth, which consist of the failure to live by moral law and therefore to need juridical laws, does not create paradise, and we must thank God that all this is not reality, but merely the dreams of a poet.

But the greatest sin of Dante, the poet of paradise for minors, is committed when he reaches the highest level of his paradise and sees the Holy Trinity as eternal light, that is, as dormant (inactive) knowledge that understands only itself, knows only itself, loves only itself. Thus Dante replaces the Holy Trinity — a model of unanimity and harmony — by self-love ; thus heaven turns out to be no better than Earth.

Dante's paradise is based on Ptolemaic superstition, but the Copernican world view has not yet emerged from superstition either, because so far it has been an intellectual concept only ; so long as we cannot govern the motion of the Earth we cannot be certain of the reality of this motion — we merely assume it. Of course, we can believe that the Earth is a tiny star and the sun a large star, but we merely believe it, for we cannot actually see it and consequently we do not know.

Ways of solving the paschal questions, or the course of a natural task

'Go and teach all nations, baptising...'

The proposal to replace the problem of poverty and wealth by that of death and life (the problem of luxury by that of essentials) is addressed to both believers and unbelievers. The believers must give up their resistance to God's will, which is manifested in our continuing worship of other gods and our constantly breaking all commandments, particularly the first five which form together but one — the supreme commandment. What is required from the believers is to replace our present enslavement to the blind force by its regulation and control. Incidentally, the demand to control and subjugate the irrational blind force to reason is directed not only to the unbelievers but also to believers, as a Divine command for all to unite in one task, even though *in thought* initially they disagreed. Such control of the blind force and its subjugation to the rational will of all the sons of man would be tantamount to the subordination of all the sons of man to the will of the God of the fathers, and would render them *of one mind* ; in other words, the participating in one common task would bring both believers and unbelievers to unanimity.

Unification must begin with the intelligentsia becoming a united educational force ; the intelligentsia will unite all nations in the task of governing blind, irrational nature. It will transmute all nations into a single scientific force and thus, through the educational power of the intelligentsia, everyone will become *a naturalist-experimenter*. The people's *practical reason* will unite with *the theoretical reason*, the reason of the intelligentsia, the learned. In other words, the ideal of the latter will become a duty for practical reason, a duty demanding implementation, and man will become an instrument of the Divine will in carrying out this duty. Thus will be solved the problem of the two reasons, their antinomy ; then will be solved, too, the problem of the two feelings, two wills and two moralities, and the cult of woman will be replaced by that of the ancestors, in conformity with the will of the God of the fathers, the God of *the living and not of the dead*. The transformation of all peoples, with the help of the intelligentsia, into a scientific force entails the union of all the abilities and energies of all humans in the Common Task of transforming a procreating and death-bearing force into a re-creating and vivifying one, and this will be achieved through science and art united in religion, which is identified with Easter, the great and holy deed.

The union of all the abilities and energies of all nations can be achieved through the school : the school-church (in the name of the Trinity and the Resurrection uniting for resuscitation), the school-museum (the shrine of the ancestors) and the school-camp (serving the transition from nomadic to settled life, from urban to rural — to life alongside the dust of the fathers, near their graves). And all these schools will come together in kremlins, that is to say, citadels protecting the ashes of the fathers. As the nations come together in a peace conference, the representatives of all the peoples of the Earth will not institute an arbitration court but will accept universal compulsory military service and universal compulsory education — that is, the study of the force that promotes hostility among people, causes wars and makes it necessary to defend even the dust of the fathers ; then the instruments of annihilation will be transformed into instruments controlling the enmity-bearing force. Governing the procreating and destroying force will not only eliminate the causes of war but will return life to the victims of war. The Autocrat, *as godfather to all who are born*, takes upon himself the duty to provide universal education with the help of all scholars and intellectuals, and he can then introduce, via this education, the Common Task, which he directs as *the executor of all the deceased*. Thus the Autocrat carries into effect the commandment of the First risen from the dead — the commandment to teach — and acts as his successor in the task of resuscitation.

The Russian Autocrat who, at his coronation, receives the *akakia* (the dust destined to be revived) will transform the *temporary* paschal movement from the city to the countryside, as happens in the West and also in Russia in imitation of the West, into a *permanent* resettlement. At the same time, because military service and study have become universal and obligatory the celestial energy arising from thunderstorms will become available to any village or hamlet, enabling crafts and cottage industries to supersede and displace urban manufacturing industry.

When external regulation has been achieved, the inner psychophysiological force will tilt the balance away from sexual drive and lust towards love for the parents, and will even replace them, thus transforming the force of procreation into one of re-creation, the lethal into a vivifying force ; in other words, childbirth will be replaced by patrification, in fulfilment of the will of the God of the fathers. The antinomy of the two reasons will obviously be solved ; the unbelievers joining with the believers in one task will become of one mind, unified in one faith ; the problem of wealth and poverty will become irrelevant, because there has been poverty only so long as there has been death, whereas when — through toil — life immortal is achieved, there can no longer be any question of poverty.

Summarising the above, it should be said that *the proposal to replace the problem of wealth and poverty by that of life and death, of the universal return of life*, as stated in the first paschal question, points to *the object* demanding action — the force that begets and kills — that is, nature, which procreates and kills, creates and destroys ; so the object for action is the entire Universe, which submits now to blind force — what a tremendous object !! The last paschal question speaks of the Autocrat, the pacifier, the gatherer of all the forces of all humans for the understanding and control of the object indicated in the first question. The XIth question refers to minority and to schools, that is, institutions designed to make all minors into adults — in other words, into people who understand and who are, therefore, capable of controlling the object designated in the first question. The Xth question makes sacred the knowledge of how to control and to return life — sacred to the supreme degree : it makes it into Easter, an act and a feast — which is to say, the victory of that act. Questions IX and VIII involve science and art in the task of studying and regulating with a view to the return of life, thereby deflecting science and art from serving industrialism and militarism. Question VII brings all those who have become alienated from their fathers back to their fathers' graves, to their dust ; and this is the first step in the task of returning life. Questions VI and V counsel against the worship of women, an urban cult, and replace it with ancestor worship. For this it is necessary that all intellectuals, both believers and unbelievers, should unite for the education of the people, as explained in questions II and III, thus transforming the people into a nature-studying force, and thus solving the contradiction of the two reasons, the theoretical and the practical (question IV). This will unite the intelligentsia and the people, under the leadership of the Autocrat, into *one subject* acting on *the object* indicated in the first paschal question.

Thus *the subject* of the natural task, of the problem posed by nature itself, which through the human race comes to consciousness and feeling aroused by death, will be the totality of all those living and acting upon the lethal force in order to return life to all those who have died, under the leadership of the executor of all the dead. It will be the totality of the living, the sons and daughters of deceased parents or of parents destined to die, united by him who stands in the place of all the fathers, that is to say, all *rational* beings united in the study of the irrational force and in its control by the Autocrat, the godfather present at the baptismal fonts of all those being born. Thus the tools of destruction will be transformed into instruments of salvation. The *object* of this action will be the procreating and death-bearing force, the ashes of the fathers or the molecules and atoms from the decomposition of their bodies, for these are blind and irrational forces which must be understood and controlled.

Only supramoralism, involving a common natural task, that of the universal return of life, can eliminate the external (wealth and poverty) and the internal (learned and unlearned) discords and unite both internally (in feeling and in thought) and externally (in a common task of transforming the life- and death-bearing force into a re-creating one). Supramoralism is a natural problem for all the living, a problem posed by nature itself reaching a state of consciousness and feeling ; and this problem is posed not so much by love of life — that life that we know only as poisoned by the constant prospect of death — as by revulsion for death and the natural sorrow for the dead and the dying.

Supramoralism is a natural and sacred problem for all sons, and especially for those who believe in the God of their fathers. Lastly, supramoralism is the most natural problem for rational beings, since death is caused by an irrational force. Therefore *all the living, all sons and daughters, all rational beings, must take part in the solution of the problem*, or the task of returning life. It is indeed a natural moral duty to transform the abstract 'Why does the existing exist ?' into living knowledge and living art, not into dead reproductions but into living reality and a knowledge of the life of all the past, all that has existed.

The project of a common action by the subject, in its totality, on the object in its totality (that is, on the entire planet Earth and not just part of it, on the entire solar system and eventually the Universe) is as follows :

1. The transformation of the procreating force into a re-creating one and of the lethal into a vivifying one.

2. The gathering of the scattered dust and its reconstitution into bodies, using radiation or outlines left by the waves caused by the vibration of molecules.
3. The regulation of the Earth, that is, the management of the Earth as a cemetery, a management comprising the consecutive resuscitation or re-creation of numerous generations, and the extension through them of the regulation of all the uninhabited worlds. Such a project is the full expression of supramoralism, or the answer to the question, 'What has Man been created for ?' ; it indicates that the human race, all the sons of man, through the regulation of the celestial worlds, will themselves become heavenly forces governing the worlds of the Universe.

So how should the supramoral commandment of unification, 'Go out and teach all nations, baptising them...' — that is to say, cleansing them from sin, the cause of death — be expressed ? In what way should this commandment differ outwardly (for in substance it is unalterable and eternal), in this era when means of transport and communication make walking unnecessary, while the press removes the need for preaching ?

Without quite penetrating the profound yet simple meaning of this commandment, one has the impression that it does not adequately indicate the purpose of unification. It says, 'teach...', but it does not say what is to be taught. However, bearing in mind that the commandment was given immediately after His Resurrection by the First risen from the dead — and whose Resurrection was to be followed by a succession of resurrections — we come to understand that the command to teach implies universal compulsory education in the sense of coming to an understanding of that original sin which has made us mortal, of being aware that such knowledge entails the task of cleansing ourselves of original sin as the cause of death. Then we will come to understand that in our day education can be carried out only in a school-church adjoining a school-museum in winter, and a school-camp in summer, the supreme expression of all of which is the Kremlin, that is, a cemetery-fortress where the instruments used to defend the dust of the fathers are transformed into instruments for the return of life. Then the sacrament of baptism, that cleansing from original sin which, as already stated, made the human race mortal, will become the universal task of all the people in control of all the natural forces, and it is for this task that they are chrismated. From being invisible, this cleansing will become visible, no longer a mystery but a reality, and there will no longer be any need to repeat baptism, now replaced by confession and penance. Then will become clear and evident the mystery of the bread and wine, obtained from the dust of the fathers and transfigured into their flesh and blood. And all this will be done in the name of the Triune God, and those partaking will attain a likeness to the Trinity, which exists in boundless love of the Son and the Holy Spirit for the Father, a love that excludes death.

Disarmament :
How to transform
an instrument of destruction
into one of salvation [1]

Our simple folk explained the lack of rainfall and snow in 1897 as a punishment for our sins. Our intelligentsia saw in this popular view mere prejudice and superstition. Was it mere superstition, or is there a causal link between wars — these international sins — and meteorological disasters like our drought of 1891 and the rainstorms of 1897, which prevented the Turks from pursuing the retreating Greeks at a time when up to four hundred artillery guns were firing simultaneously ? Could there be any connection between the heavy downpours

---

1. First published in *Novoe vremya*, St Petersburg, 14 October 1898, pp. 2-3, unsigned ; reprinted in *FOD*, vol. I, pp. 656-68. Its publication was connected with the peace initiative of Emperor Nicholas II of Russia. On his instructions Count M.N. Murav'ev (Mouravieff), his Minister of Foreign Affairs, handed out a circular letter to the diplomatic representatives accredited to Russia on 12 August 1898 (see Appendix IV). This peace initiative was warmly welcomed by the general public, especially the pacifist movements in Western Europe, but it was less welcome to their governments. Kaiser Wilhelm II wrote back, 'Can we picture a monarch, a Supreme Commander-in-Chief, disbanding his illustrious historic regiments, consigning their glorious flags to arsenals and museums, and thus delivering his cities over to anarchists and democrats ?' (Quoted by Emil Ludwig, *Kaiser Wilhelm II*, London, 1927 ; Ludwig uses the expression 'War-Lord', not 'Commander-in-Chief', which is probably a mistranslation of *Kriegsherr*.) The second circular letter contained more precise proposals. The Conference met in May 1899, but the proposals on arms limitation were opposed by Germany and France, while those on obligatory arbitration were reduced to the setting up of a Permanent Court of Arbitration. Moreover, on the insistence of Germany the submission of disputes was voluntary and the Court findings not binding. Fedorov's high hopes were disappointed — for him any court of justice was merely the institutionalising of discord.

over the war zone and our drought ? Did the Graeco-Turkish war of 1897, which was fought in a country with a long coastline and peculiar vertical and horizontal landlines, trigger off the floods which spread further north into Turkey and Austria, and did these floods cause a lack of precipitation in Russia ?

While in 1891 Russia went short of bread, in 1897 she went short even of water. 'The Volga is a huge waterless sandbank', said newspaper reports. Water transport came to a standstill. The Ministry of Transport was unable to maintain communications. Indifferently, scientists recorded increases in precipitation in some regions and decreases in others, without even asking whether there was any link between these phenomena and the cannonade on the battlefields. Yet this was not a new question. It had been raised in 1891 in Russia in connection with the famine caused by drought, and in connection with the rain-making experiments in America. Even earlier, Powers had listed in his book[2] a number of battles accompanied by storms and rain since the introduction of firearms.

In 1891 this problem was debated by several learned societies ; it was written about and then, unsolved, it was shelved and consigned to oblivion. Yet in 1891, at a meeting of the Odessa Technological Society, one of its members had spoken of the 'experiments in artificial rain-making in America'. This was followed by a pessimistic debate about the likelihood of such attempts being successful in combating drought. By their attitude to the possibility of deliverance from famine, the learned technologists showed that there was no way of overcoming their indifference and lack of understanding of the people's needs, even when bare, parched, unsown fields reached practically to the very outskirts of their town. The technologists simply rejected the American method of rain-making. Experimental data were dismissed by meaningless verbiage, although the failure of the

2. Edward Powers, *War and the Weather*, Chicago, 1871, 2nd rev. edn 1890. See also note 18 to the Introduction, p. 27.

experiment merely showed the inadequacy of one method and the need to seek others, to constantly try out new ones, because of the very predicament we were in then and still are today.

A society of technologists which in that terrible year of 1891 could fail to form a commission for the investigation of methods of preventing drought and storm, proved its alienation from the land, the people and agriculture in other countries too. Meanwhile, there are signs that a natural worldwide crisis is disrupting the meteorological process so much that efforts will need to be made in order to right what was formerly harmless and could be left to right itself. Therefore, a new technology becomes necessary. The meeting of the Odessa Technological Society that rejected rain-making may prove fatal to the old technology, the daughter of leisure and not of necessity, of artificial, not vital, needs... The new technology should not be town-based, for only town dwellers can call artificial a rainfall produced by conscious action and see in it a breach of order. The experiments effected in America should have become the starting point for the introduction of regulation, that is, the introduction of order into disorder, of harmony into blind chaos — provided, naturally, that these experiments were not regarded as a private affair of individual farmers but as the common task of mankind, a task both morally and physically natural, because there can be nothing more unnatural for a rational being than to submit to a blind force. The regulation of atmospheric phenomena is an attempt at the natural action, the common action, of replacing a blind process by a conscious one.

Even today science remains indifferent to the regulation of atmospheric phenomena, despite the depletion of rivers, their transformation into waterless beds as happened in 1897, when regulation should have become not merely a national but a universal issue. Scientists have not bothered to gather information, either, about the number of shells fired by both sides in the Graeco-Turkish war (something that could be done even today) or about the weather conditions during that war (something that can no longer be done), because meteorological observations are not carried out on battlefields nor even during manœuvres and artillery practice in peacetime.

...It would be too superficial to lay the blame for the natural disasters of 1897-8 on international politics such as the Graeco-Turkish war, or on the present state of the Eastern Question. The responsibility rests on our entire culture and civilisation, where the aim of existence is for each individual to live for himself, where obligations and service to the community are accepted only as unavoidable evils, while the common cause of fathers and sons is entirely and deliberately overlooked, because people fear the loss of freedom and of seductive variety. Yet true freedom lies not in disunity (the right to ignore the existence of others) ; it lies in the true fullness of life attained through the common task of generations. The drought would not have reached such proportions had it not been for deforestation and soil exhaustion — the very consequences of civilisation and, in general, of that climate in which each individual lives for himself alone.

At the present time steam power is being replaced by electrical energy obtained from waterfalls. Even in Russia there is a project to supply electricity to St Petersburg from Lake Saimen, which is fed partly by waters from Finland and partly from the Narva waterfall, which drains the Pskov-Chud basin. Soon the waterfalls of the Alps will become sources of energy for Western Europe ; those of the Caucasus will serve the same purpose for Eastern Europe ; the Pamir and Tibet for Asia, and Abyssinia for Africa. Then not only agriculture but industry and transport too will cry out for the regulation of the meteorological process, because the power generated will depend on the volume of precipitation. The latter can be kept constant if regulation is achieved ; but otherwise, sudden cloudbursts may prove destructive, while drought may result in factories and railways coming to a standstill. Then Western Europe will also have to turn its attention to the control of atmospheric phenomena. But must Russia, once again, await instructions from the West ? Weather control has always been desperately needed in agricultural Russia, but our intelligentsia, incapable of independent thought since the 1840s and even more so since the 1860s, has been busy saving Russia from a proletarianisation that did not even exist then, and it was distressed not to find the pauperisation that it wished to see in its beloved homeland.

Yet weather control is not a daydream or fantasy but a task which, had our intelligentsia turned its attention to it, could have prevented the emergence of a proletariat in Russia and shown other countries, where a proletariat did exist in the 1840s, how to eliminate it without violence or bloodshed. As proof that rain control is not just a wish but a feasible task, here is a quotation from the well known scientist Mendeleev[3], according to whom, 'it is certainly not impossible to produce rain by means of explosions carried out at a certain altitude in the atmosphere.' However, he adds : 'This subject, like all phenomena associated with rain formation, requires much further research directed towards the control of the forces involved, for the benefit of mankind.'

Another, less famous, scientist who is evidently concerned with the problem of inducing rainfall by means of explosions, A. Starkov, the editor of *The Transactions of the Odessa Branch of the Imperial Russian Technological Society* and a member of many other Russian and foreign learned associations, whose testimony is therefore reliable, published two papers in Odessa in 1892 under the titles 'Can rain be artificially induced ?' and 'Experiments in artificial rainmaking in America'. He comes to the conclusion that :

> The problem regarding the possibility of artificially producing rain presents nothing that is impossible or

3. Dmitri Ivanovich Mendeleev (1834-1907), Russian scientist, best remembered for his Table of Elements. In his appendix to the article on Explosives in *Entsiklopedichesky slovar'*, Brockhaus & Efron, St Petersburg, vol. 11, pp. 206-7, Mendeleev argues that the destructiveness of modern firearms will in itself be a deterrent against future wars.

supernatural, or that exceeds the limits of human powers... it is a most urgent problem of modern science and technology. It is so bold and grandiose that it appears at first as unattainable and beyond human capacity. Many reject it because they are stunned by the boldness and magnitude of the endeavour. But this is contrary to the spirit of science and technology. For the more difficult the problem, the more effort should be directed to its solution.

It is difficult to imagine even approximately, says Starkov in his other work, what tremendous consequences would result from the discovery of how to distribute (according to a general plan) the moisture stored in the atmosphere, because once in the possession of such a method we could regulate our agriculture and thus avoid crop failures. 'Atmospheric moisture is sufficient, but often its distribution does not favour the tiller and can even do harm. When he needs rain, it does not come. Then, when the tiller needs fine weather, it pours.' Discussing the reasons why the American experiments allegedly produced no results, Starkov asks :

But did these experiments prove the opposite, that is, the impossibility of causing rainfall artificially ? Not at all ! On the contrary, eyewitnesses and others, both scientists and laymen, in their various papers agree on one point only, namely that these experiments did not prove the sterility of the endeavour ; on the contrary, they offered hope that rain could be artificially induced... The American experiments in rain-making have given a real fillip to this task. Let us hope it will give rise to a new and sustained research effort into this exciting and tremendously important problem. Its successful solution would, on the one hand, be a momentous achievement of modern science and technology and, on the other, it would bring about an extremely significant and beneficial revolution in the economic life of the tiller, and consequently in society as a whole.

Starkov adds that, apparently, public opinion in America got so enthusiastic about this experiment that the timid approaches to Congress for a few tens of thousands of dollars have now grown into demands for millions to promote further research... However, Mr Starkov's hopes have so far not materialised, for no millions of dollars, and not even more modest sums, have yet been allocated to research in rain-making. Yet we would like to point out that if the problem is adequately posed, this research would not require millions — which might even prove an impediment (large sums are inseparable from misappropriation) — provided the problem of rain-making is understood as the overall regulation of the meteorological process and the management of natural forces.

Experiments in producing rain artificially — or, rather, by rational human intervention — deal only with one aspect of the problem. For regulation, here used in its full meaning of the prevention of drought in some areas and of destructive rainstorms in others, cannot be confined within one region, however large : it is needed everywhere and always ; and it is not artificial, but as natural as reason itself. What is unnatural is the continuation of the blind process in the face of reason, because it shows the inactivity of that reason.

It is the force acting in the meteorological process that is blind — if one does not confuse it with God, who created both the blind force and Reason to control it. However, mankind, the bearer of Reason, instead of controlling this blind force in accordance with the divine commandment given at Creation and enjoining common, shared human labour, has replaced toil by prayer, whereas prayer in common should initiate and accompany work in common. Praying for our daily bread does not abolish the need to sow and till the earth, nor can it eliminate the need to manage (regulate) meteorological phenomena, including rainfall. Praying to God for daily bread together with working to control nature's blind force — such is the task entrusted by God to man. To carry it out is to fulfil the prayers, 'Thy will be done on earth as it is in heaven', 'Thy kingdom come' and 'Hallowed be Thy name'.

Methods of rain-making can be tested with the help of armies, without vast expenditure or any special allocations for the experiments. The government has but to order all artillery and other units carrying firearms to record meteorological observations, both in wartime and during manœuvres, before, during and after firing their weapons ; in other words, to transform artillery into instruments of research and soldiers into researchers recording the effects of explosions on atmospheric phenomena. These activities would not reduce the army's military power, if it came to the worst ; and it would be unnecessary to continue with them if the results of the research proved successful, that is, if explosions did turn out to be a means of controlling atmospheric phenomena. Only thus, with the help of armies, can one discover the effects of gunfire and explosions in general on atmospheric phenomena. Do they disperse clouds, as some argue, or do they condense them into rain ? Possibly — even undoubtedly — results will vary, and these variations will probably be explicable in terms of shells fired, the state of the atmosphere, the lie of the land, and so on. If different results could be traced to specific conditions, firing could be carried out in precise experiments capable of being quantified (by number, volume and weight), replacing the present passive and rather meaningless meteorological observations.

Moreover, of overriding importance will be the transformation of military activity into the study of nature ; a new purpose will be given to armies — that of scientific research. Thus will begin the transition from an unnatural, unbrotherly activity — the struggle against one's own kin — to the natural, rational action upon the blind, irrational forces of nature, which inflict upon us droughts, floods, earthquakes and other catastrophes, and reduce us, rational beings that we are, to an unnatural dependence on them.

Should gunfire prove inadequate to produce the rarefaction of the air, that is, a reduction in atmospheric pressure sufficient to alter air currents (winds),* one could resort to the method proposed by V.N. Karazin (well known for his role in the foundation of the University of Kharkov and the setting up of the Ministry of Education). This consisted in raising lightning conductors into the upper layers of the atmosphere by means of fixed balloons so as to provoke an electrical discharge which would affect the motion of the clouds and might offer a way of directing their movement in the sky. The possibility of this has been corroborated by Baudouin and Lodge,[4] and the latter considered it not impossible that the electrical tension of the atmosphere, and consequently weather conditions, might be controlled. Experiments with such devices would not require special expenditure if they were made mandatory for armies, since balloons, though not yet used as weaponry, are moving in that direction...

The transformation of military activity into a study of atmospheric phenomena would solve, incidentally, the question of the need for and the usefulness of manœuvres. Short-sighted pacifists and detractors of the armed forces — those Pharisees who do not even bother to ask whether it is better to down arms or to use them to save mankind from natural disasters — would protest against what they call 'war games'. Yet manœuvres combined with meteorological observations — later to develop into experiments — would help solve the question of the effects of explosions on the meteorological process. Therefore it would be desirable for numerous manœuvres to be carried out, as far as possible

---

* Even the simplest of explosives, gunpowder, can have an effect on meteorological processes, as shown by the explosion in the Moscow Kremlin ordered in 1812 by Napoleon. The Kremlin suffered little damage because only some of the mines went off, but the atmospheric phenomena were extraordinary. It began to rain so hard that the fire started by the explosion was extinguished ; then the temperature fell to $-29°C$, a real January frost, though it happened in the first half of October, the beginning of autumn. When experiments in rain-making have been discussed in various learned societies and meetings, no one has mentioned the 1812 Kremlin explosion.

4. Sir Oliver Lodge (1851-1940), *Lightning Conductors and Lightning Guards*, London, 1892, chap. 1.

simultaneously and in as many places as possible, by mutual agreement, in all countries...

Since the cost of maintaining armed forces is so great, governments should maximise the usefulness of this expensive form of defence. According to a contributor to the journal *Russky Invalid (Russian Invalid)* for 1896, the expenditure incurred by our armies is already justified at the present time, not only by their defence of king and country but also by their self-sacrificing help in times of natural disaster...

Pettiness and philistinism are the hallmark of our positivistic industrial era. But no Gogol has yet arisen to denounce the philistinism of the European, and particularly the American, nineteenth century. This philistinism and cupidity, this absence of true greatness, were displayed also in the American attempt at rain-making. It merely proved that the Americans are not worthy of the great cause of saving mankind from starvation — a possibility they apparently did not even consider, being merely bent on profit. Indeed, it is even desirable that such small-scale private American experiments should fail because of the evil that American individualism could do if rainfall could be produced just by a few shots and explosions.

The distribution of rainfall should not be the responsibility of a few farmers, but of armies operating over vast territories or, better still, over the entire Earth. To patent the artificial production of rain, as attempted by the Americans, is worse than perverse : it is a profanation, a manifestation of ultimate moral and religious degeneration. They wished to emulate gods while remaining in a disunity inspired by Satan and failing to seek total unity in the likeness of the Triune God ; nor did they wish to become perfect like God the Father in accordance with the words of the Saviour, the Victor over the spirit of discord and pride. The task of transforming the blind force which directs both dry and moist currents into a consciously regulated one can be given only to a commonwealth of all peoples and nations.

To justify its existence, the diabolical armaments technology asserts that the very destructiveness of its weapons is a deterrent to war, forgetting or concealing the fact that armaments and the expectation of war are hardly better than war itself. This justification is satanic sophistry. The Spanish-American war[5] is a case in point. 'No sooner has it come to an end, than a new war is looming on the horizon', writes a correspondent from Buenos-Aires. The war season is ending in our hemisphere, only to begin in the other. Two of the largest and wealthiest republics of Latin America 'are arming with febrile haste'. Although neither of these blood-related states has the overwhelming superiority in weapons that the USA had over Spain, nevertheless both ignore Mendeleev's law according to which the inclination to wage war is in inverse ratio to the might of a nation raised to the second, third and even higher power, the might of armaments being measured by their range and speed of firing. Much dynamite has been used for the peaceful purpose of building strategic roads, which are no worse than the commercial ones and have themselves been built in order to expand and protect commercial interests. The Chileans have mined their mountain passes. 'The armaments of both contending parties are up to the latest standards of military science.' Despite logic, common sense and such glaring facts as the struggle of the terrifyingly armed USA against one so poorly armed as Spain, Mendeleev continues to assert that wars will cease because of the destructiveness of weapons — so nothing needs to be done. True wisdom demands that we should not lull ourselves with such sophistry, but call a worldwide scientific congress to discuss the possibility of transforming armies — bearing in mind present-day compulsory military service, this means whole nations under arms — to combat famine. This would render unnecessary the various military draft exemptions and deferments.

A successful solution to the problems of drought and

5. The Spanish-American war of 1898 for the possession of the Philippines, which had been colonised by the Spanish since the sixteenth century.

rainfall, the control of weather conditions and, more generally, of all the forces of nature, will radically change the economic conditions of our social order. This will affect fundamentally our views on society, on nature, on intelligence itself and its limits, and these changes will have beneficial consequences. They will be fatal only to those who take out patents and who sign contracts for the supply of rain, who are ready to expand financial speculation right up into heaven and make atmospheric phenomena into a source of profit.

When war has been transformed into research, and military service accepted by all nations, coordinated experiments will become universal and acquire a unity which will make induction equal to deduction.

Once armies go over from observation to action — a worldwide, telluric action — and harvests are made dependent on a system of regulation that embraces the entire Earth, then both international wars and internal ones, whether open or covert, will become impossible, for both tyranny and rebellion will become unthinkable. The critique of pure, theoretical reason, that of practical reason and all other critiques, will lose their present importance. Kant, the king of philosophers, as well as Comte, will be discredited, and Russia will free herself from these alien influences. Without such an intellectual and moral victory, Russia cannot hope to succeed even in a material struggle against Germany or France or Japan — or perhaps all of them together — unless the struggle is forestalled by the transformation of military action into scientific research and the regulation of natural forces.

Regulation and its consequences will not merely free Russia from foreign influences, but will mean the coming of age of all mankind, united in the common cause of transforming a blind, death-bearing force into one directed by reason. Humanity will come to see its ideal organisation not in an animal organism[6] — which justifies the existence of upper and lower

---

6. Implicit reference to Herbert Spencer (1820-1903), who in his *Principles of Sociology*, part 2, had likened societies to animal organisms, comparing

classes, as now — but in the Trinity, indivisible and unmerged, which is the true model of a society where union is not a constraint and the autonomy of the individual is not discord, a society free of the extremes of both oriental fatalism and Western individualism. The adoption of regulation will solve the social problem, put an end to proletarianisation without recourse to violence and do away with the miseries of our time.

The change in the use of arms would be of greater consequence than one in the digestive systems of animals, which determine their predatory or peaceful character. War would become an impossibility because harvests, humanity's food supply, would depend on the implementation by the armies of a coordinated plan. Of course, the proposed method of deliverance from war would not be immediate. To use armies for a new purpose straightaway is not possible, though an immediate start could be made by enjoining them to carry out meteorological observations or by using the Karazin method of lightning conductors described above... Count Tolstoy would, of course, like to change mankind straightaway just by the power of words, and turn it from a war-loving into a peace-loving humanity. His words have been heard as far away as Japan, and even China, but have not prevented them from fighting each other.[7] His eloquence failed to impress even the Americans — those mainstays of the promoters of peace — and they even started a war. So it is more than permissible to doubt the effectiveness of his 'here and now' method of peace-making by words alone, however powerful and eloquent.

Wishful thinking is of no avail, because far deeper and more powerful causes impel people to adopt hostile attitudes towards one another. So long as these causes that make people quarrel and fight are not eliminated, not even

---

nutrition to industry, the nervous regulatory system to government, arteries and veins to roads and telegraph lines, and so on.

7. The Sino-Japanese war of 1894-5, for domination over Korea.

understood, war cannot be abolished. Even pacifists carry on such fierce debates with the advocates of war that their exchanges could become real warfare, had the contenders more power (duels have indeed occurred). So even the preaching of peace engenders militancy, and pacifists display aggressiveness and preach peace with hostility in their hearts. Such bitterness is quite comprehensible, when means as ineffective as words are used.

Standing as we do between the defenders of peace and the lovers of war, we suggest a method of reconciliation which would retain armies as a great force yet make war impossible. We, too, are filled with bitterness and resentment against both sides. The peace-lovers who demand the disbanding of armies and cry, 'Down with arms' forget that an army is a force and that this force, which spends itself in war, needs an outlet in some adequate activity. Industry cannot offer such an outlet. It can clothe, feed and provide for people — that is to say, it can prepare them for action — but it cannot satisfy them completely. Science and art in their present state are equally incapable of absorbing all the abilities of man.

The blindness of both lovers of peace and defenders of war is astounding, for they do not see the enemy against which they should both unite and turn their arms. Possibly, they do not notice this enemy, which is the blind force of nature, because it is present everywhere and always, within ourselves and without, and also because the defenders of both peace and war wish to have for their enemy not an unfeeling force but a being who can be made to feel their hate and anger, who can feel pain, and whose sufferings can be enjoyed by the lovers of peace. How can one otherwise explain such a passionate desire to see enemies only in one another, and in this enmity, despite constant bereavements, to forget the death-bearing force ; or, although they suffer from famines and are fully aware of their causes, such as droughts and rainstorms, how can one explain such a passionate desire to accuse other people just as helpless as they themselves are, of being responsible ? Neither can one blame nature for causing evil, because it is blind and because the rational force remains inactive. It is an inaction for which we all, not anyone in particular, are guilty, because we do not carry out the divine commandment laid down at the time of man's creation. And it is for this that we suffer punishment.

Foreword to a letter from F.M. Dostoevsky [1]

Letter to the Editor

Dear Vsevolod Grigor'evich,

Having come by chance across a letter of F.M. Dostoevsky's, which is important as an indicator of his religious convictions, we are anxious to have it published in your paper, with a few minor omissions that have no bearing on the particular idea of Dostoevsky's that impressed us.

The letter refers to an unknown thinker — but they are so numerous in Russia today, and of little concern to us. It is the thought of Fedor Mikhailovich that is of importance to us, an idea of amazing greatness and one that gives a meaning and an aim to human life at a time when such things are so desperately needed because, with the loss of purpose and sense, life too has lost all value. Dostoevsky says in his letter, 'Most essential is the duty to resurrect the ancestors who lived before us', that is to say, our duty, our task, consists in bringing back to life all who have died, all those whom, as sons

---

1. First published with Dostoevsky's letter (see Appendix I) in the Voronezh journal *Don*, n° 80, 1897. In 1876 N.P. Peterson had written to Dostoevsky asking him to publish in the *Diary of a Writer* an article apparently inspired by Fedorov. Dostoevsky did publish a long extract from it in the March issue of 1876 (chap. 2). The passage deals with associations, including trade unions, which the author regards as unbrotherly, since they cater for their own members to the exclusion of others. From Dostoevsky's answer it would appear that Peterson's letter contained an exposition of Fedorov's ideas which the latter expanded in his foreword.

and descendants, we lost — our fathers and ancestors. Of course, this duty is also a Divine commandment, which enjoins all humans as rational beings not merely to reproduce and populate the world but also to govern it. In other words, God's commandment demands from the human race that it transform the overpowering, blind, soulless force of the universe into one informed by the spirit, reason and will of all the resurrected generations. It is in this sense that we understand Dostoevsky's idea of the duty of all humans. However much we pondered on his thought, we could come to no other conclusion. Nor can it be understood otherwise since, according to Dostoevsky, the fulfilment of this duty would halt the procreation of children and would mean that nothing would happen unconsciously. Everything would be the result of reason, will and conscious work ; nothing would be gratis ; everything would be earned. Dostoevsky's idea deserves particular attention and a speedy implementation, because the ever-increasing human race is reaching the point of overpopulating the Earth. Within a century or two we shall have to pray to Jupiter or Allah (no such prayer can be addressed to the Christian God) that he permit destructive wars, plagues and other catastrophes capable of reducing the population. The alternative is to follow the Christian path and restore life to the decomposed dust of the deceased, and become capable of living beyond the confines of the Earth, in the Universe at large.

How puny by comparison are the aims proposed to man hitherto, such as comfort (even for all) and luxury (inessentials) ; or greater freedom of men from one another — that is, not union in labour to achieve a definite purpose, but freedom as something negative and devoid of positive content ; or, finally, progress, which adds to freedom and disunity the exaltation of the younger over the older, of sons over fathers, of the living over the dead — those 'loathsome ancestors', in the words of Ritschl.[2] To put it briefly, progress, being a sense

2. Probably Albrecht Ritschl (1822-89), German theologian, follower of Kant, who regarded metaphysics as distinct from theology and knowledge as

of major superiority over the fathers and ancestors and of a relatively minor superiority over animals, is at the same time an admission of one's insignificance before a blind, insensate force together with a servile submission to this force, thus excluding any sense or aim from human existence, as well as any notion of duty.

To advocate the resuscitation of ancestors as a most important duty follows obviously from an idea entirely different from that of freedom and progress, because what is necessary to implement this duty, as indicated by Dostoevsky, is not the worship of a blind, irrational force, nor the freedom of one man from another, but the union of rational beings in order to study this blind force which brings hunger, disease and death and to transform it from one bringing death to one bringing life. This entails that all become research workers and everything an object of knowledge — not sterile knowledge, but knowledge translated into action.

At a time when so much is written about universal compulsory education, the idea of making everyone a learner will not seem too bold, and one should note that the demand for such education is possible only in the name of a common duty, the duty mentioned by Dostoevsky, which demands that one should not live for oneself nor for others, but with all and for all. It requires the union of all the living for the resurrection of all the dead, the union of the sons to restore life to all the fathers. What could be more sublime than this ? It is neither egoism nor altruism, but something loftier than both. To demand universal education merely in the hope of driving out superstition, in the hope that it will put an end, for instance, to the sect of *skoptsy* (eunuchs), as is assumed by Mr. Vakhterov,* is to forget that Origen was no illiterate and that table-rapping (spiritualism) and other superstitions

---

distinct from faith. His name recurs in Fedorov's writings directed against Kant.

* *Russkaya mysl'* (*Russian Thought*), 1897, n° 1.

proliferate not among the illiterate but among the literate, even the very literate.[3]

The idea of involving everybody in the study of nature and making everything an object of knowledge is not new. We met it in the epigraph to the article 'Concerning a memorial to V.N. Karazin',* which says, 'Modern science is based on conclusions drawn from observations made by some, somewhere and sometimes, whereas it should be based on conclusions of observations carried out always, everywhere and by everybody.' Observations are only knowledge, and not action, whereas science will become action when experimentation is carried out by all, all over the world, according to a single plan.

In the foreword to 'A legend about the building of a church in Vologda in a single day',** a whole plan is outlined for building similar churches-schools, dedicated to the Holy Trinity as a model of unanimity and concord.[4] The author of the article assumes that it would be possible to introduce into these sacred churches-schools types of education that include research. It would therefore be possible to implement the idea of Karazin, who suggested combining instruction with meteorological observations and other observations of nature.

Together with Dostoevsky's letter we came across a small notebook — unfortunately incomplete — entitled 'What should a people's school be like ?'. This is probably a copy or a rough draft of an article referred to approvingly by Dostoevsky. It starts with the question, 'What must our

---

3. Vasilii Porfirovich Vakhterov (1853-1924), a progressive Russian educationist, very active in the promotion of universal primary education in Russia in the last quarter of the nineteenth century, author of widely used elementary textbooks. The Greek theologian and biblical scholar Origen (AD 185-254) is said to have castrated himself, taking literally v. 12, chap. 19 of the Gospel according to St Matthew.

* *Nauka i zhizn'* (*Science and Life*), 1894, N[os] 15 and 16.
** *Chteniya v obshchestve istorii i drevnostei rossiiskikh* (*Proceedings of the Society of Russian History and Antiquities*), 1893, vol. 166, n° 3.

4. Both the article on Karazin and the foreword to the legend are by Fedorov ; reprinted respectively in *FOD* I, pp. 644-50 and 650-5.

primary school be like ?' Must it teach permanent submission to the laws of blind nature, according to which the new absorbs the old, only to be in turn absorbed, in perennial submission to a blind force that cannot create without destroying, or give birth without killing ? Or should primary schools teach obedience to the Divine law, the Divine commandment, according to which whatever comes later should restore life to what came before, thus achieving its own immortality and fulfilling the duty of resuscitation mentioned by Dostoevsky ? Of course, the problem is solved in accordance with God's will, and not with the law of nature, which prescribes constant struggle — and on the basis of this General Dragomirov[5] recently defended the absolute necessity of perennial wars.

It was actually the 'Military note' in the *Novoe vremya* which quoted the opinion of General Dragomirov on the inevitability and absolute necessity of wars, that prompted us to hasten the publication of Dostoevsky's letter, since, according to this letter, the duty set before mankind, while making wars unnecessary, yet makes armed forces extremely necessary, if these are understood as involving obligatory lifelong service for all. What is most important is that General Dragomirov himself can contribute to the establishment of peace, so longed-for by mankind, as well as raise the status of the armed forces and prepare them for a great future.

General Dragomirov will probably be astonished that in defending the absolute and perennial necessity of wars he deprives the army of a truly great future. By denying, with Dostoevsky, the need for the eternal persistence of warfare, one can — or, better, one must — inevitably admit the continued existence of and need for armed forces, until such time as they vanquish that force that can be called a temporary

5. Mikhail Ivanovich Dragomirov (1830-1905), a senior general in the Russian army, took part in the Russo-Turkish war of 1877-8. A former Head of the Academy of the General Staff, and writer on military strategy, tactics and training, he stressed that soldiers should be educated to understand their duties, not merely drilled.

foe yet an eternal friend (nature). When this force has been conquered, the armed forces will embrace all humanity, which will become both consciousness and will — the Reason of nature — and will thus abolish the law which is in fact the blindness of nature to which all, even rational beings, bow down.

General Dragomirov's admission of the necessity of war leads to the denial of a great future for the armed forces, and results probably from the fact that, however strange it may sound, Dragomirov does not accept our definition of an army, a definition that would embrace every purpose for which an army can be used. Its purpose, it is usually said, is to defend the fatherland against external and internal foes. But what can we make of the following incident ? A fire started in a large provincial city. The flames spread towards a big ammunition dump, and people fled the town in terror. Only those who have to remain where they are, even when others flee, covered the roof of the dump with their bodies, on their own initiative. The soldiers knew that their sacrifice would neither earn them the St George Cross nor be regarded as an act of heroism, nor even a noteworthy one. This case is not unique. Another heroic act of self-immolation by Russian soldiers happened during the floods on the Sui-Fun, showing that acts of heroism are performed by the army even in peacetime. Here Koreans as well as Russians were rescued at the cost of kin. Indeed, for the Russian army, confronted by a common natural disaster, there can be no aliens, no foreigners. There have been instances of the army taking part in the fight against locusts and other dangers.

Evidently, in accordance with military law, armed forces are in fact obliged to fight not only individuals of their own species but also the blind forces of nature, to which the advocates of armies kowtow and wish to serve, in defiance of the second divine commandment. They may not accept the latter, yet they cannot, have no right to, reject what is an expression of human consciousness, of rational nature.

In an article signed S.U.T.-va in *Russkii Invalid*,* the expenditure on the army is justified on the grounds not only that it defends king and country against external and internal enemies, but also that it performs deeds of valour in the event of natural disasters ; and a plea is made for this type of army activity to be taken into consideration. However, it is not in these actions, however numerous yet fortuitous, that lies the army's great future. It lies in victory over those very laws in whose immutability those who accept eternal warfare believe, recognising solely *blind* nature and disregarding *rational* nature. 'Isn't man a creation of that same nature ?' asks General Dragomirov. Yet even if man is recognised to be a creation of nature, one must admit that this creation has begun to understand its imperfection, which consists in the elimination, the absorption, of the old by the new, the latter to be eliminated and absorbed in its turn. This imperfection arises from the disunion of worlds owing to which life on Earth manifests itself only as a succession of generations ; this imperfection is perceived as a law according to which nature destroys while creating, and war is regarded as subsumed under this law.

Yet man has always felt and recognised the imperfection of nature, and has never accepted it as law. He broke this law when he took his first step, because his vertical posture challenged gravity, the most universal law of nature. This upright position is not natural to man — it is supranatural — and he has achieved it artificially, through effort (by swaddling and other methods of adaptation). One cannot say of man that he is the creation of nature. On the contrary, he is the result of under-creation, of deprivation, of a natural pauperism which is shared by rich and poor alike ; he is a proletarian, a pariah among living creatures. Yet in this lay the origin of his future greatness ; deprived of natural cover and means of defence, he had to create all this himself by his own labour. Therefore man values only that which has been created by working, or

* 1896, n° 90.

which expands the area of application of work ; it is not difficult to guess that the culmination of this forward movement must be that everything on which human life depends will ultimately be achieved through work, so that humans will depend solely on their labour. Consequently the entire world, the meteorological, telluric and cosmic processes, will be the responsibility of man, and nature will be his work. Man is driven towards this goal by hunger, disease and every other calamity, so that whenever he delays in expanding the area of work, the scope for disasters expands. Thus nature punishes man by death for his ignorance and sloth, and drives him to ever-expanding labour.

The disastrous year 1891 and the present year 1897, which evidently is going to be no better, have failed to lead to an expansion of the realm of work, although there were reasons for doing so. The *Russkie vedomosti* wrote about the experiment in rain-making by means of explosives, that is, by using substances predominantly designed for mutual annihilation. This experiment had been carried out in America, though one would expect such experiments to take place in Russia, a country often afflicted by crop failures caused by drought and, occasionally, by excessive rainfall ; a country which urgently needs to control the meteorological processes and which possesses a considerable army, whose destiny might become the defence against cataclysmic weather. And the *Russkii arkhiv* very appropriately reminded its readers that nearly eighty years ago the famous Karazin had suggested experiments in rain-making by means of lightning-conductors raised on aerostats. The latter are now included in the army's arsenal. Furthermore, in its concern for Russia as well as for the whole planet, the journal mentioned not merely rain-making but also the general regulation of the entire meteorological process.[6]

6. A reference to Fedorov's own unsigned article, 'V.N. Karazin i gospodstvo nad prirodoi' ('V.N. Karazin and domination over nature'), *Russkii arkhiv*, 1892, n° 5, pp. 75-90.

However, the present generation is too frightened by the magnitude of time and space revealed by geology and astronomy, and has been so conditioned by four centuries of nature worship that it feels only its insignificance, and fears even to contemplate such an endeavour as weather control. Nevertheless, with a view to weather control and to the conversion of the army into a force for the study of nature (which would in no way impede its military might), it was suggested in *Russkii arkhiv* that the study of meteorological processes during peacetime training (particularly during firing practice) might be introduced, thereby being able to estimate the effectiveness of the American, the Karazin or any other method of affecting nature ; for such methods are bound to be discovered as soon as attention is focused on them.*

Incidentally, Karazin submitted his idea of rain-making experiments to Arakcheev,[7] who was then in Paris with Emperor Alexander I. Arakcheev ridiculed Karazin as a sorcerer. Yet even Metternich would not have dismissed the Holy Alliance as mere *verbiage*, had the monarchs who signed it included among the obligations of their armies the duty to carry out experiments of the kind suggested by Karazin, and thus initiated the transformation of instruments of destruction into means of salvation from famine, disease, pestilence and their fundamental causes. Not only in the years following the Napoleonic wars, but even in our time, when weapons of destruction have reached amazing perfection, our present pseudo-Christians forget that humanity constantly suffers from hunger ; they do not want to hear that the point of a sword, lance or pike raised on an aerostat (according to Karazin), as well as many other arms used in war, may become means of affecting atmospheric conditions and,

* 'Karazin and domination over nature', *Russkii arkhiv*, 1892, n° 5, p. 75, and the article, 'On managing the forces of nature' ('Penzenskie gubernskie vedomosti'), 1892, n°s 130, 132.

7. Count Aleksei Andreevich Arakcheev (1769-1834), War Minister and favourite of Alexander I. His name has become a byword for despotism and cruelty.

consequently, save everybody from famine and disease.* In any case, the transformation of instruments of destruction into instruments of salvation from calamities that harm everyone is worthy of investigation, worthy of becoming an object of thought and action. Yet our prophets preach non-thinking and non-doing.[8]

To transform instruments of destruction into instruments of salvation from hunger and pestilence is the universal and obligatory task of all the sons of man. The human race can unite not merely to make its existence independent of the blind force of nature, but also to make that soulless and death-bearing force into an instrument of its will, a will obedient to that of the God of the fathers. Herein lies the great future of the armed forces, or rather, the nations of the world transformed into an army, that is to say, the masses acting according to a single plan, because only such masses (as explained in the *Russkii arkhiv* article mentioned above), acting according to a unified plan, completely satisfy the basic conditions for the great Common Task — universality and communion.

The transition from a civilian to a military state, combining obligatory service with obligatory education and knowledge, will introduce superior moral principles into the world, principles based on the recognition of the imperfection (mortality) of the sons of man ; the sons of deceased fathers will demand resuscitation and immortality, ousting the present concern of protecting one's individual pseudo-dignity against others, in conformity with the present-day pharisaic morality.

With respect, I have the honour, dear Sir, to remain always at your service.

11 June, 1897, Voronezh.

* 'Concerning a memorial to Karazin', *Russkii arkhiv*, 1892, n° 5 and *Nauka i zhizn'*, 1894, n°s 15 and 16 ; also, the appendix by Mendeleev to his article on Explosives in the Brockhaus & Efron encyclopedia, vol. 11, p. 177 [207].

8. An allusion to L.N. Tolstoy, who preached non-participation in the armed forces and the civil government and, in general, non-resistance to evil by force.

Faith, deed and prayer [1]

Faithfulness to the God of the fathers, the God of Adam and of all the ancestors, is true religion ; all others are a betrayal of God and of one's forebears.

Living faith, according to St James the apostle, finds its expression in deeds ; according to St Paul it is the implementation (by action, of course !) of the hoped-for ; and, finally, faith is a promise, a pledge to fulfil the will of the God of the fathers, and is completely identical with that of the common people, the orthodox.

Only among the learned does faith become divorced from action and come to be mere representation.

Faithfulness to the God of the fathers and to each other is the expression of a faith inseparable from love, that is, from action, from service to God the Father, the God of the fathers.

Faith without deeds is a dead faith, it is unproductive, it does not create the Kingdom of God. Faith without prayer is cold, soulless ; it is not athirst for the Kingdom of God.

Faith is necessary ; action is necessary ; prayer, too, is necessary.

The faith of the unlearned, the faith of the people, is expressed (1) in prayer, (2) in commandments and (3) in the Common Task or the service of God. The prayer implied here is one that does not wish to make God into an implement of our will, but is ready to make us an instrument of God's will.

The collective prayer of *all* the living (sons and daughters),

---

1. From *FOD*, vol. II, section I, pp. 3-5.

the prayer of the whole community to the God of the fathers for the return of life, comprises the fullness of prayer. This *fullness of prayer* would coincide with *the fullness of faith* if it were accompanied by the action of all the living.

Faith includes the *prayer* for the Kingdom of God, the *full* or Lord's prayer, and the *short* prayer, that of the Thief, together with the Beatitudes. Similarly, in the service of God, in Divine deeds and Divine services, prayer is combined with the commandments, whereas in the catechism they are distinct.

The prayer of the Thief to be remembered in the coming Kingdom of God, and the prayer for the coming of that Kingdom and for participating in it ('Thy kingdom come, Thy will be done, on earth as it is in heaven'), is a prayer for union in prayer and deed, for daily bread — that is, for the realisation of the Kingdom of God and deliverance from the kingdom of the Evil One.

Prayer and faith are inseparable from the commandments. The commandments of the Old Testament are rules of what one should not do, and contain a creed, or *dogmas of faith* : namely, (1) the recognition of the God of the fathers and the rejection of other gods and (2) the honouring of the fathers by the sons, which is also faithfulness to the brothers and to unity.

On the other hand, the New Testament creed also comprises commandments. By transforming the Old Testament commandments of not doing into positive rules of doing, we get the Christian commandments.

What is called the Beatitudes is the praise of different states of our thoughts, feelings and desires. These commandments are addressed to listeners in the plural, not in the singular as in the Old Testament — a profoundly significant feature, indicating the need for collective salvation, not merely for personal, individual salvation. Furthermore, they are not orders, nor even advice, but praise of the states that lead to the Kingdom of God — which indicates the superiority of the voluntarily chosen way over the enforced. The first Beatitude, regarding the poor in spirit who are promised the Kingdom of God, encompasses all the others, for those who mourn cannot be proud and convinced of their superiority, nor can the meek, nor those thirsting for truth and righteousness, nor the merciful, be proud. To put it briefly, the way to bliss, to the Kingdom of God, leads away from the vain, commercial, industrial urban life, from upper-class pride to rural simplicity and humility, and hence to unification. The blessedness of unity is essential for the blessedness of resurrection. These two forms of blessedness bring together the first seven Beatitudes, while the two last are temporary and will be discarded when there are no longer any tormentors or tormented.

On the other hand, the ways to the kingdom of this world, the ways of sorrow, go in the opposite direction, from the countryside to the towns, from the outlying regions to the centres, forgetful of the cautionary threats : woe to towns, woe to ancient cities (Capernaum, Khorasin and, earlier, Tyre and Sidon, Sodom and Gomorrha, Nineveh and Babylon), woe even to Jerusalem, and a hundredfold more bitter woe to our modern cities for their growing sinfulness, catastrophes and impenitence.

Impenitence is contrary to the prayer of contrition which leads to unification and salvation. The prayer of the Thief, which united him with Christ and opened up to him the gates of His kingdom, was a prayer of repentance, agony and crucifixion. The cross has thus become the symbol of repentance, of suffering, of the supreme act of salvation and, at the same time, the banner of unification and victory. The translation of prayer into action transfigures the worshipper himself into a sign of the cross ; lifting his head towards heaven and spreading his arms, the praying figure seems to be calling upon his neighbours for help against an alien force which, because of its hostility, has forced him to stand up and take on a watchful (defensive) yet praying posture. Then the praying person makes the sign of the cross over *himself*. The external representation of the cross is a church, a place of reunion for all those risen from the dust of the earth, the dust of the fathers gathered together in an alien, hostile world. Taking on himself the shape of a cross, the worshipper represents it externally, and when it is enlarged in the form of a church he endows it with his image. The ultimate point in the development of prayer, embodied in the sign of the cross, will be the transfiguration of the entire world into a cross, that is, the translation of the image of the Son of Man into irrational nature. Both the daily and the annual divine services within the church, which educates and teaches the Common Task, will find their culmination in a service beyond the confines of the church, conducted by all the forces of the world in a liturgy beyond the confines of church buildings, in a universal Easter throughout the world.

Weather regulation as the implementation of the prayer, 'Give us [all of us] this day our daily bread' (that is, obtained by toil) [1]

To ensure against famine by developing industry that enables us to buy bread, or by developing a highly improved agriculture — which is nonetheless insufficient to feed the entire population, so that it is still necessary to import grain, or at least saltpetre or fertilisers such as guano from Chile* — does this not make one nation a privileged entity while reducing other people to doing the dirty work ? In total contrast, weather regulation requires that all unite to act according to a common plan. Regulation ensures that the needs of all nations will be met ; therefore, regulation is the implementation of the prayer, 'Give us this day our daily bread', because through regulation it is not the greatest profit from the land — 120 *puds* per *desyatina*[2] — that is obtained, but our daily bread. And it is obtained for today only, since regulation secures the necessary, and no reserves will be needed. To strive for union for the sake of weather control means to strive for natural, not artificial, ways of insuring against famine.

Therefore the Lord's Prayer, the prayer for the Kingdom of God, includes praying for regulation, that is to say, the

1. From *FOD*, vol. II, section XII, pp. 17-18.

* In fact, towns produce so much sewage that soon there will be enough of it to manure all the fields ; perhaps, even, the amount of sewage produced by towns will exceed what can be transformed into vegetation. Then how is this refuse to be transported to places where it may be needed without causing contamination at the points of loading and unloading ?

2. Approximately 5 tonnes per hectare.

fulfilment of the commandment given at Creation and the second commandment understood in the spirit of Christianity ; it also includes an entreaty for mutual forgiveness, for universal reconciliation as a precondition of Divine forgiveness ('Forgive us our trespasses, as we forgive them that trespass against us'). These two pleas contain the prayer for the eradication of the kingdom of iniquity, the kingdom of the Evil One ('Lead us not into temptation, but deliver us from the Evil One') ; while the first three are a prayer to Him Who reigns in Heaven for the spread of faith on earth, for the actual, real coming of His kingdom ; for His name to be truly hallowed and His will to be done on earth as it is in Heaven.

So often, when repeating the prayer for the Kingdom of God, the kingdom of Heaven on earth, we believe in its coming on earth, its realisation on earth — or is that praying for the impossible ?!!

The Orthodox burial rite and its meaning [1]

Dedicated to the Englishmen, the Archbishop of York and others, who visited Russia and saw the Orthodox burial ritual.

'Men bury their dead.'

The acceptance by Anglicans if only of a part of the Orthodox burial ritual, and even if they are only Englishmen from the upper classes, is nevertheless the beginning of a real reconciliation between the churches, whereas dogmatic reconciliation with the Old Catholics merely represents imaginary reconciliation and could never lead to real reconciliation, which would involve all classes. The Englishman in question had seen a part of the Orthodox burial ritual in his native land, and since he wanted to see it in its entirety he came to Russia for this express purpose ; while he was here, he came to the conclusion that it was vital to adopt it in its entirety.

It is easy to understand what this assimilation of an essential part of our burial ritual on the part of Anglicans should lead to. Logic and consistency should inevitably lead them to accept the whole of the Orthodox rite, because it could be said to be constructed on the model of the one basic rite, that of Holy Week, of Easter Week, the Easter of the Cross and the Easter of Resurrection, during which the very essence of Christianity is expressed. Our night service is not only by name a requiem to the saints (instead of a coffin and the body,

1. From *FOD*, vol. II, pp. 34-5.

there is an icon with a portrayal of the dead one on it) ; the offertory[2] is nothing other than the offering, by all the living, of a sacrifice on behalf of all the dead and all the living in a state of complete unification. The Eucharist is the culmination of the requiem and the offertory, albeit an incomplete one. The everyday church services consist of prayers for the dead and the sick, the reinterment of those who have died that day or have already been buried, with lamentations addressed to the righteous. And then the greatest of the services, of which the burial rite is but a dim reflection, is the service of Holy Week, which begins with the pre-death words of the Monday and Tuesday — in other words, with the threat of the end of the world and the reply which is used to show the Pharisees, the Sadducees and others the way to salvation, away from the threatened end. Its continuation is Great Wednesday — the preparation for burial (extreme unction) ; and Great Saturday — the day of the burial itself, culminating in resurrection.

Only the burial of Christ, however, has a real ending, a real conclusion ; it alone achieves its aim. None of the other burials, not even the discovery of the relics, concludes in the right way, since they do not yet achieve resurrection — indeed, here resurrection has apparently been forgotten. The actual word for the burial service, *otpevan'ye* (to read away, to sing away, to be nursed back to health from sickness and from death), has now acquired the completely opposite meaning. The word *otpetyi*, literally 'sung away' (in other words, having had the burial service read), has begun to express ultimate despair at the possibility of a return to life.

Why is it that the burial carried out in the actual place of worship fails to achieve its aim, the return of the dead to the living ? Obviously, it is because life outside the place of worship is mutual destruction. This means that we have a right to say that when the Anglicans accepted the most essential part of the Orthodox ritual, that part which actually points to

2. The offertory, *proskomidia*, is the part of the liturgy when the gifts of the Eucharist for the credence table are prepared for consecration.

the aim of unification implicit in the meaning of the burial, which is to say in coming to life or resurrection, they understood the real way to reconcile the churches, and even all religions.

The daughter of humanity as reconciler [1]

The parable of the prodigal son can also be applied to the daughters of humanity. Society ladies in general, and hetairai in particular, should be included among those who have abandoned the fathers, those who have forgotten the traditions of the fathers. 'Memento vivere !' — not in the sense of revitalising, but of giving pleasure — has become for such women the main precept of their lives. Socrates' Diotima numbers amongst them. Mary Magdalene corresponds to the youngest son in the parable : having returned to the father, she was elevated higher than those who had never abandoned him.

With those who have never abandoned the traditions of the fathers belong the women of the farming class, among whom devotion to the parents is expressed primarily in the burial ritual, which has now lost its real meaning. When she is preparing the funeral feast at the family home, the village woman is a priestess, in no way inferior to the vestal virgins, druidesses, Velledas,[2] to those inspired prophetesses. Indeed, she is even superior to them in her task, which she is meant to fulfil and which she must complete, while all the daughters of humanity are at one with her, and together they become as one daughter devoted to the fathers.

If, when a woman becomes a wife and mother, she remains a daughter, then even if she marries into a different family,

1. From *FOD*, vol. II, p. 40.
2. Velleda was a Germanic prophetess who twice led uprisings against the Romans in the days of Vespasian, who reigned from AD 69 to 79.

nation or race, this will not mean separation from the father, but unification of this other family or race with her own family and tribe. A daughter represents a great tool in the process of reuniting the race, in reconciling estates and nationalities. Certain commentators see the merging of hostile tribes exemplified in the marriages of Epimetheus and Pandora, of Peleus and Thetis.[3] But the significance that the daughter of humanity has unconsciously possessed for ages, she must now acquire consciously and after careful consideration ; and it is a significance with a more comprehensive, a more profound and ennobled meaning ; to her belongs not only an important, but also an honoured, place in the plan for universal reconciliation.

---

3. A reference to the marriage of a Titan and the first woman, of a mortal and a goddess.

The agapodicy
(the justification of Good)
of Solov'ev and the theodicy
(the justification of God)
of Leibniz [1]

The advocate of God would have achieved his aim, had he said that God created both nature, that is, a blind force engendering evil, and a rational force, and that it is only the inaction of the latter that allows the former to do evil. The advocate of Good could have shown its magnificence and power had he defined Good as 'the creation of brotherhood' *(bratotvorenie)* through the adoption and transformation of people into sons of man. Then Good would bring the prodigals to the God of the fathers in order to implement the duty of testamentary executor — that is to say, general resurrection. This is the very meaning of the liturgy. The liturgy is Good justifying itself and constituting the Common Task.

The spread of Christianity, the gathering together and the enlightenment, is the first phase of the Common Task; it is the liturgy of the catechumens. It teaches us to *pray* together for the sick, for those voyaging on the high seas or on land — to put it briefly, for all. This is the 'creation of brotherhood',

---

1. From *FOD*, vol. II, p. 177. The Orthodox liturgy consists of three parts : 1) the *proskomidia*, or preparation of the elements of the Eucharist, 2) the liturgy of the catechumens, during which passages from the Epistles and the Gospels are read (it also includes the litany with the prayer referred to by Fedorov on p. 176, 'For those who travel by sea and by land, for the sick and the suffering, for those in captivity and for their salvation, let us pray to the Lord'), and 3) the liturgy of the faithful comprising the consecration of the elements and the communion of the faithful. For Fedorov the liturgy should not be a *symbolic* commemoration of the resurrection of Christ and a *promise* of general resurrection, but an action contributing to it.

the transformation of people into sons of man, the return of the prodigals to the God of the fathers. The repentance of the prodigals — those outside the paternal homestead, guilty of the sin of alienation — and their baptism in the name of the God of unanimity and concord, the Triune God, make them into the faithful. Faithfulness is expressed in giving thanks to God (the eucharist) and to the fathers, and in the return of life to those from whom the sons received it.

Physical and moral sinlessness: a prerequisite of immortality [1]

Before talking about resurrection one must state firmly that, just as death is impossible where there exist sinlessness and knowledge that can control the forces of nature, so resurrection is impossible where there exist sin, ignorance and other misfortunes resulting from man's dependence on the blind forces of nature.

Neither the universal return to life, universal resurrection, nor even death itself, have hitherto been the subject of knowledge or well founded judgement. For there would have been full, detailed investigations into the reasons and conditions that have given rise to the phenomenon. For most people, death appears to be an absolute, inevitable phenomenon; but just how unfounded is this conclusion is obvious from the fact that it is considered acceptable to talk about the opposite of death, about immortality, and even about resurrection; and it is talked about as a possibility, in circumstances where all sorts of sins prevail among people, and all sorts of calamities and evils, arising from the folly of nature. But if the coexistence of the one with the other is unthinkable, since the one excludes the other, then can one talk about the possibility of death where there is moral and physical sinlessness, where nature shows such a benign attitude both within and outside man, of the sort that is deemed possible when man's knowledge and control of nature are complete?

1. From *FOD*, vol. II, pp. 202-3.

Even more senseless is the idea that immortality is possible for a few separate individuals, when faced with the mortality that is common to all mankind ; for this is as absurd as the belief in the possibility of happiness for a few, of personal happiness in the face of general unhappiness, in the face of a common dependence on so many catastrophes and evils.

How did art begin, what has it become and what should it be ? [1]

To solve the question, 'What should art be ?', will be to solve the contradiction between rational being and the blind force of nature, to fathom the most abnormal relationship between man and nature, to solve the question of the subordination of rational being to blind force. Will nature always remain blind and, in its blindness, a destructive force, while art remains the creation of nothing but dead imitations ? Will this division be temporary, or will it last for ever ? Perfection lies in the unity of nature and art.

Nature, within man, was conscious of the evil of death, of its own imperfection. So the rebellion of the living (the vertical posture) and the resurrection of the dead, in the form of tombstones, are natural acts for a feeling, rational being. It was when the living (who had suffered a loss) rebelled and turned to heaven, and when the dead were resurrected in the form of tombstones, that art began. Prayer was the beginning of art. Prayer and the (vertical) prayer posture constituted the first acts of art ; this was theo-anthropurgic art, which consisted of God creating man through man himself. For man is not only a product of nature but also a creation and concern of art. The last act of divine creation was the first act of human art, for man's purpose is to be a free being and consequently self-created, since only a self-created being can be free. In this act of self-creation —that is, in rebelling and turning towards heaven — man discovers God and God reveals himself to

---

1. From *FOD*, vol. II, pp. 239-40.

man ; or, more precisely, on discovering the God of the fathers, the being who has made the discovery becomes not just a man, but a son of man. And only in the abstract sense, forgetting the loss, is it possible to say that the being which has discovered God has become man.

When the vertical posture changed into one of cautious vigilance, then anthropurgic art was born, that is, secular, military art which, while making man on the one hand menacing and on the other sensually attractive, still tried to attach sacred importance to itself. Secular art has both a menacing and an attractive side to it. This could also be said of contemporary 'universal exhibitions', for from the outside they resemble an arsenal, while inside they offer a cornucopia of whimsical objects to satisfy sexual needs. To be menacing has become a mark of the ruling class, whereas to attract has become the sign of the 'weaker' sex.

In the act of rebelling (in the vertical posture) on the part of the living, and in the act of creating a likeness in the form of tombstones to the dead (in theo-anthropurgic art), man has raised himself above nature ; when man made of himself something menacing or sensually attractive (anthropurgic art), his fall was under way.*

* Among [aboriginal] Australians, the colour red used to denote not only entry into life but also parting from life, which they did not wish to regard as parting. Certain tribes would cover the deceased with thick, red, shiny ochre, which signified not a parting from life but an imaginary return ; that is, they gave the deceased the appearance of life. Conceivably the first colour primitive man painted himself with was simply the blood of a slain animal or wounded enemy. But just as the victors began to use red ochre instead of blood, so, quite possibly, the deceased were painted with blood : when the sons discovered they had blood and started rubbing it onto the pallid bodies of the deceased, they must have thought they were returning life to them.

Originally, mourning signified that the living were depriving themselves of life (co-dying), although this was only imaginary. The desire to deprive oneself of life was expressed by beating the breast and wounding oneself : later on, this came to express fear of being oneself deprived of life, fear of the soul wandering round the departed. In other words, it turned into a form of mythical hygiene. Later, the deceased were also painted to ensure that direct contact with the corpse did not lead to illness. In this way sacred art found its expression both in the painting of the deceased and in mourning. (N.F.F.)

If art in its beginnings was divine, whereas today it has become industrial-military — which means bestial and savage — then the question arises : How can art once again be given a course to follow which would correspond to its divine beginnings ? What should be set up to counter the industrial-military exhibition, which presents products which tempt, and weapons which destroy ? If the question, 'What has art become ?', is synonymous with 'What are the reasons for the unbrotherliness between people and for the rift in the relations beween nature and people ?', then the question, 'What should art be ?', is the same as the problem of establishing brotherly unity in order to transform the blind force of nature into a force guided by the reasoning powers of all the resurrected generations. In other words, what we are talking about is universal resurrection, since it is this that represents the complete restoration of kinship and that will provide art with the appropriate course to follow, and show it its goal. Transforming all the worlds into worlds guided by the reasoning powers of resurrected generations will constitute a complete resolution of the Copernican question and is at the same time identical to the primeval view — that is, the patrification of the heavens (the turning of the heavens into the fathers' abode), or catasterisation (the transferral of the fathers' souls to the stars) — which also finds its expression in church sculpture and painting. For children this primeval view is the most straightforward, an explanation and resolution of the Copernican question. To turn all the worlds into worlds guided by the reasoning powers of resurrected generations is also the most important goal of art.

The art of imitation
(false artistic re-creation)
and the art of reality
(real resurrection) [1]

Ptolemaic and Copernican art

Art as imitation — an imitation of everything in Heaven and on Earth — reproduces the world in the form in which it appears to the external senses ; it reproduces Heaven and Earth not as expressions of God's will, but as the effects of the blind forces of nature uncontrolled by rational beings, yet called gods (Uranus, Kronos) by them. The art of imitation depicts a sky which deprives us of life and an Earth which consumes the living. So the divine commandment denounces this art as paganism, as idol-worship or idolatry (bowing before idols which embody the blind forces of nature instead of controlling them) and as ideolatry (bowing before an idea which is not transformed into a deed, before the pointless, soulless and inactive knowledge of the learned). The reproduction of the world in the form in which it appears to the external senses and in which it is interpreted, either by the internal senses of the sons of humanity, who have retained their love for the fathers, or by the internal senses of the prodigal sons, who have forgotten their fathers, is in both cases the art of imitation ; but in the first case it is sacred art, and in the second, worldly art. Sacred art reproduces the world in the form of a church, in which all the arts are brought together : moreover, when the church is a work of architecture, painting and sculpture, it becomes a representation of

1. From *FOD*, vol. II, pp. 241-3.

the earth giving up its dead, and of the sky (the church's dome and iconostasis) being inhabited by resuscitated generations ; and since the church contains the singing during the funeral service, it is a voice to the accompaniment of which the earthly ashes, like a cemetery, come to life, while the sky becomes the dwelling place for the resuscitated.

> When referring to the singing and especially the lamentation for the dead, we mean the whole divine service ; this is the liturgy in the form of God's work, which is being fulfilled through the sons of humanity ; this is the all-night vigil and service for the deceased or their image, which corresponds to lamentations summoning them to rise up ; then during the day the coming together for instruction like catechumens, in preparation for the liturgy of the faithful, those faithful to the God of their fathers, when bread and wine are transformed from earthly dust into a living body and blood.

The art of the sons who have forgotten their fathers will reproduce the world in the form of a 'universal exhibition', in which industry is associated with all the arts. The exhibition itself represents woman, and the sons who have forgotten the fathers wish to devote all the forces of nature to serving her, in order to intensify the fascination of the sexual attraction ; they expect it to draw them towards life, but find instead death, and they find the only hope of a return to life in children.

Sacred art breaks the commandment only when it takes what it portrays to be reality, to be genuine resurrection, and the singing, the church liturgy, to be the extra-ecclesiastical task of resurrection. Secular art in the form of a universal exhibition breaks all ten commandments, and when it sets up sin in opposition to faith it sins even more against reason, since it subjects it to the blind force of nature, and compels it not to control nature but to serve her.

Truly defined, art is not cut off from science or morality or religion, and manifests itself as it actually is in the life of the human race and in history. Beginning with man's first uprising and his vertical position, the pain at losing those closest to him forced the bereaved one to lift up his face, to turn his whole being in the direction of the sky ; and this position expresses what was already a religious feeling, a newly awakened thought, both of which are recorded by art. (Orthodoxy demands that one stands, and allows one to sit only as a special dispensation ; this external expression, the standing position, makes Orthodoxy significantly different from both Catholicism and, especially, Protestantism.)

What will provide the transition from the art of imitation to the art of reality, from Ptolemaic to Copernican art, is a museum of all the sciences, in which the sciences will be combined together in astronomy ; connecting it with the idea of the church-school, this will be a museum with a tower from which to observe falling stars — in other words, to observe the continuing creation of the world as well as its fall, and to observe how, by changing martial art into natural-scientific, experimental art, the study of the stars will be transformed into experiment, into action.

Aesthetics is the science of reconstituting all those rational beings who have existed on this diminutive Earth — this little speck of an Earth, which is reflected in the whole Universe and reflects the whole Universe in itself — so that they might spiritualise (and control) all the vast heavenly worlds, which have no rational beings. It is in this reconstitution that the beginning of eternal bliss is to be found.

The manifestation of power in powerlessness is the law of terrestrial and extraterrestrial history, which together constitute the essence of Christianity as the opposite of, and as a means of salvation from, Buddhism. The Earth is a cemetery which, possessing history as it does, contains within itself more substance than all those worlds which have no history. Till now consciousness, reason and morality were localised on planet Earth ; by resurrecting all the generations who have lived on this Earth, consciousness will be disseminated to all the worlds of the Universe. Resurrection is the transformation of the Universe from that chaos towards which it is moving into cosmos — into the greatness of incorruptibility and indestructibility.

Just how profound and abundant wisdom is, is nowhere better expressed than in the salvation of the infinite Universe, a salvation which originated in that insignificant speck of dust, the Earth. The highest moral law requires that only the Earth, and no other worlds, should be populated. If the world is not a product of blind chance, then an expedient relationship beween the many dead generations and the multitude of worlds is possible, and this would mean that all the inhabitants of all the worlds could be created just from one blood and earthly dust. But were the world to be a product of chance, even then a rational, sentient being could not avoid making use of the multitude of forces to revivify so many generations deprived of life.

On the Earth itself we can find examples of localisation in an insignificant area ; whatever is localised is then disseminated all over the Earth. Palestine and the Hellenic world are examples of this sort of localisation — art and science in Greece, religion in Palestine, whence they then spread all over the Earth. But only when religion and science are united will it be possible to disseminate the influence of rational beings even beyond our Earth. Palestine and the Hellenic world represent East and West, and their struggle constitutes history.

Parents and resurrectors [1]

The day of destiny, expected since the original Fall, will only arrive when the present-day prodigal sons, endowed with reason, come to understand that power through blindness is not inevitable, but is only a divine disaster which has killed their fathers, and that it needs only rational guidance in order to be a vitalising force. It is the extreme moral torpor of the bookworm scientists and of that whole intellectual crowd that is the main obstacle to the advent of the day of destiny ; the consequence is that only terrible plagues and bad harvests, caused by the land being exhausted, will force them to turn to celestial power from the sun and other worlds, instead of to the hard labour of miners working underground. Only by uniting to control that meteorological process in which the sun's power is revealed, will the sons of humanity become capable of transforming the ashes of their forefathers (which are being extracted from the deepest layers of the Earth), and not by turning those ashes into food for their descendants, but by gathering them together into the bodies in which they originally belonged. The reverberation and quivering (vibration) of which molecules and the ashes of the dead are capable, and which cannot as yet be picked up by microphones since these are still a crude means of picking up sound, find a corresponding echo in the way in which particles shudder within live beings who are linked by kinship to the dead to whom these particles belonged. Such individual vibrations

1. From *FOD*, vol. II, pp. 273-4. Published in *Irish Slavonic Studies*, n° 4, 1983, pp. 109-11.

hidden in the secret depths of matter are only one possible key to the process of resurrection — a key which does not exclude other hypotheses. Hitherto hypotheses have been drawn up to explain the creation, building and development of the world, and these are hypotheses which could only be substantiated in isolated experiments in laboratories, whereas the hypothesis concerning the creation of the world demands a common experiment, embracing the whole of the Earth and all its layers.

In accordance with this hypothesis, the power extracted from air currents, which will then be conveyed to the various layers of the Earth, will produce the right reverberations in these layers, which will then replace the present destructive earthquakes — which do, nonetheless, set in motion the waters which collect the particles contained in the ashes of the dead. The science of endlessly small molecular movements, which can be picked up only by the sensitive hearing of the sons, who are endowed with the most delicate organs of sight and hearing, will not pursue precious stones or precious metals. For the pursuers will not be humanists to whom everything parental or paternal is alien, but the sons who are of age ; they will search for the molecules that form part of the beings who gave them life. The waters, taking the ashes of the dead out of the bowels of the Earth, will obey the common will of the sons and daughters of humanity, and will act under the influence of light rays, which will no longer be blind, like heat rays, nor coldly insensitive. Chemical rays will become capable of making a choice ; that is, under their influence the related will be united, and the alien separated. This means that the rays will become an instrument of the common beneficent will of the sons of humanity.

One can envisage that the various sorts of rays will be transformed into an instrument of the will in something like the following way and adopting the following course. The vibrations to which the particles found in the organism have been subjected will continue, even when the particles have left the organism and the body has been destroyed. The thick layers covering the particles will not remain insensitive to every sort of vibration. As the rays from these vibrations rise to the surface, they will travel along with both reflected and other rays, thereby forming not only an external image of the Earth and of those living on it, but also an internal image with the dead decaying in it. Once the movements of heavenly bodies other than the Earth have been guided or regulated, then the rays' reflections can be bounced back to the Earth, where, as we see, the particles which have been hidden deep down are brought to the surface. At this point the constructive activity of the rays begins. The rays, returned to the Earth, coming out of the Earth and moving away from the Earth — and in this order — bear within themselves images of live beings, then of dead ones, images of their bodies which have decomposed into particles ; when they encounter the particles, these same rays unite the gaseous molecules of the atmosphere with the solid-state molecules on Earth. The process by which mould or other vegetable forms have been unconsciously produced, will, in the presence of consciousness, unite the particles and turn them into the live bodies to which the particles used to belong.

But the question of resurrection is not only one of external forces, directed towards the combined reason of all, but also a personal matter for each person, whether son or other relative. If we are to compare our present petty family affairs with participation in the meteorological and cosmic processes of each and every one of us, in what is both a family and a personal affair, the resurrection of parents and relatives, then it becomes clear that all the spiritual powers, all the mental capabilities, which at present lie dormant because of the absence of any activity directed towards resurrection, will find a way to proceed and be utilised in this great task. The internal, mental, moral-artistic, psycho-physiological control of the process of nutrition, of internal growth, will transform the latter into the process of resurrection, instead of into the birth of a feeble creature with scarcely any feeling or consciousness.

On the day of destiny the Triune God will become an example to be copied by all generations all over the Earth, and will not be regarded as an unobtainable ideal. All the material worlds in the Universe, of which the sons of humanity will have become aware, will provide their souls with a means of expressing their likeness to the Immortal Trinity. The whole Universe, vitalised by all the resurrected generations, will serve as a shrine to the Immortal Trinity ; and the day of destiny is the day of the Trinity, the culmination of the festival of universal resurrection. The whole Universe will consist of innumerable worlds of immense heavenly space, with their multitudes united with those of the resurrected generations, who for innumerable centuries have been swallowed up by the Earth.

On the unity of the meteorological and cosmic processes [1]

Atmospheric particles should be numbered among shooting stars, asteroids — stars which have not yet fallen ; and aerolites — stars which have fallen. These particles are more closely concentrated than asteroids or particles forming the tails of comets, or even of comet clusters, which shower down to Earth as falling stars, such as the Leonids. These particles, or drops of water vapour, molecules (or even atoms) of elementary gases, including the recently discovered ones such as argon, coronium and helium, revolve just like the Moon around the planet Earth, even approaching quite near to its surface, then receding, circling it and undergoing even greater deviations and complex perturbations than the larger celestial bodies (planets and solar systems). Air currents can best be compared to streams of comets and, therefore, the meteorological process is also an astronomical phenomenon like the motion, course and progression of celestial bodies. Thus the regulation of the meteorological process already verges on the astronomical process. Regulation is a celestial Copernican task or art.

---

1. From *FOD*, vol. II, p. 301.

What the most ancient Christian monument in China can teach us *

No better way could have been found to honour the entry of Christianity into the twentieth century of its existence than by publishing a Russian translation of the Si-ngan-fu[1] inscription, which records the beginnings of Christianity in China (a Christianity not in need of armed support). This ancient monument, this simple stone, is more precious to us Russians than all the diamonds of South Africa, especially since the descendants of the Syrians (who, according to the inscription, brought Christianity to China) have been received into communion by our Orthodox Church.

The Si-ngan-fu inscription tells us of that first profoundly peaceful introduction of Christianity to China, in sharp contrast to the Christianity which appeals for armed support and arouses implacable hatred.[2] The monument to the introduction of the 'luminous faith' to the Middle Kingdom

---

* In connection with an article by S.S. Slutsky, 'The most ancient Christian monument in China', *Russkii vestnik*, 1901, n° 1 ; first published, unsigned, in *Russkii arkhiv*, 1901, n° 4, pp. 631-7 ; reprinted by N.A. Setnitsky in his *Russkie mysliteli o Kitae : V.S. Solov'ev i N.F. Fedorov* (*Russian Thinkers on China : V.S. Solov'ev and N.F. Fedorov*), Harbin, 1926.

1. Si-ngan-fu, now Hsian-fu, Shensi province, was the capital of China under the T'ang dynasty. This Nestorian monument, erected in 781, was rediscovered in the grounds of the Buddhist monastery of Chin-sheng-ssü in 1623, and became known in Europe through Jesuit missionaries who translated the Chinese and Syriac inscription into Latin in 1635.

2. A reference to the Boxer Rebellion (1899-1901), during which Chinese rebels attacked and destroyed railways and various European commercial enterprises as well as Christian missions.

stands in the old capital of the T'ang dynasty, a capital which reminds China of the best days of its long history, when the Celestial Empire was the largest and the mightiest on Earth,* and when the most important monarchies of the time, Persia and Byzantium, sought her support against the first 'Holy Wars' of Islam. In those days the Romano-Germanic West, which now rules the oceans and rampages throughout China, was weak and played no significant role ; its civic life was only just beginning to take shape on the ruins of that 'decrepit Rome' which it had destroyed. As to the Russian Slavs (a continental power, now a neighbour of China, her natural ally and perhaps her saviour from Western depredations), their civic life had not even begun. Neither Kiev nor Novgorod had been heard of, let alone Moscow.

In those days, in the heart of China and not in its outlying regions (Nanking and Peking),** because then China still belonged to the Chinese, there occurred something rather similar to what happened in Kiev in the tenth century.*** Owing to its central position, Si-ngan-fu was a meeting place for various religions : there were disciples of Zoroaster and Mani, Buddhists — already well established in China — and, probably, the ubiquitous Jews.

The seventh century saw the arrival in Si-ngan-fu of

---

* In the seventh and eighth centuries, under the T'ang dynasty, China held pride of place in world history. Even in the days of Christ, the Roman Empire, said to embrace the entire known world, was not the only empire. There were two. Yet in our so-called world histories the question is never posed as to which one was the most powerful and of greatest importance at different times. In fact history itself has answered the question, with the Huns, to the detriment of the Roman Empire. While leaving the mightiest — the Chinese — unmolested, the Huns overran the weaker Roman Empire and put an end to its existence. Christianity had not identified with it, and even rejoiced at the fall of 'the great Babylon'. The conversion of India and China, to complete the victory of peaceful Christianity, had been initiated already by the apostles Bartholomew and Thomas.

** Peking has been nicknamed 'the Chinese St Petersburg' by Siberian Old Believers who still seek for a pre-Nikon Russia in India and China.

*** The capital city of Lo-yang was for Buddhism in China what Kiev became for Christianity in Russia.

A-lo-pên, the great apostle of China who can be rightly compared to Saints Cyril and Methodius.* 'When a transcription of the Scriptures had been made in the Imperial Palace library', says the inscription, 'questions [discussions] were raised in the inner apartments of the Palace'. These words point to the internal state of China and her spiritual malaise, which affected especially the men at the helm, in the Palace. China had a Council — far more powerful than Vladimir's Duma — for China had already lived a long history, had felt and thought much in the persons of its philosophers — Lao-tse, Confucius and Mencius — before it heard the amazingly 'simple and luminous teaching' which called upon all to become pure, meek, like children, like the Son of Man, in order to know what is hidden and inaccessible to philosophers of all countries. Apparently, the Chinese scholars were particularly struck by the 'simplicity' of the doctrine as well as its 'profundity', the thirst to become perfect like the Heavenly Father, 'the beneficence of the doctrine for the people' and, at the same time, its 'rejection of everything impure and earthly'. That is how the Chinese scholars of the time perceived the teaching of Khe-le-tuze, our Christ.

Since, according to the inscription, the Emperor T'ai-tsung

* One can assume with some justification that 'good and sensible men' may have been sent to Syria for 'the probing of faiths'. At any rate the inscription mentions Ta-dzing (Syria), its boundaries and products, and the good mores of its inhabitants. Later, new converts went to Syria, possibly even to Jerusalem, just as Buddhists went on pilgrimages to Kapilavastu, recently rediscovered (by Fürer). Although the eventual victory of Buddhism was probably accompanied by the destruction of written and material records of Christianity, evidently not everything was destroyed, though our calendar of saints was probably enriched by many new martyrs who suffered at the hands of Buddhists. The excavations in Si-ngan-fu, designed to supplement the history of Christianity in China, could become an expression of friendship between Chinese and Russians because they would prove that once upon a time we were coreligionists. On the other hand, the discovery of Kapilavastu (Lun-bani), the cradle and the grave of Buddha, would probably engender a resurgence of Buddhism, the like of which could not be fomented within Christendom, even by the transfer to Moscow of the stone chronicle of Christianity in China, the Si-ngan-fu inscription.

sent his prime minister with a large retinue to meet the Syrian missionary, it is evident that A-lo-pên, the future apostle of China, was already well known and had been invited as the best exponent of the teaching of Christ, just as Saints Cyril and Methodius had been sent to the Slavs from Byzantium. Three years later (AD 638), after a deep and thorough study of the doctrine, it was recognised as 'true and right' in an imperial decree dated year 12 [of the Chen-Kuan period]. And the doctrine was not merely allowed : the decree prescribed that it be preached and taught, mentioning, alongside the Scriptures, 'images', that is, icons, meant for the illiterate, and it enjoined that the doctrine be disseminated throughout the Empire, which extended then to the Pacific in the east and nearly as far as the Caspian in the west.

The opening sentence of the decree contains, apparently, a justification for adopting the doctrine and for going beyond mere tolerance. It prescribed the building of a Syrian* church in the district of Peace and Justice. A considerable staff (twenty-one priests) were to be attached to the church, which points to the success and prospects of the new faith. The placing of an image of the Emperor in the church mentioned in the inscription may perhaps indicate the canonisation of T'ai-tsung, regarded as equal to an apostle.

In the reign of Kao-tsung, Christianity spread along 'the ten roads' of China. Churches were built in a hundred towns (at least, in many towns). A-lo-pên was awarded the title of Guardian of the Realm and Lord of the Great Law, with the right to transmit it, in accordance with Chinese custom, not to his descendants but to his ancestors ; this was an honour similar to that bestowed on Confucius. However, Christianity met also with opposition. At the turn of the seventh century an Empress of the Wu family, supported by Buddhists, carried out a palace revolution and transferred the capital to Lo-yang, a Buddhist centre. This shows that Christianity had become so strong in Si-ngan-fu that a government hostile to it could not

---

* Or Persian, according to a description of Si-ngan-fu in AD 1070.

remain there. Fifteen years later 'the luminous religion' was restored, the churches renovated, divine services were again celebrated in the palace and images of the emperors of the T'ang dynasty were placed again in the churches.

Christianity became particularly strong and widespread under the emperors Su-tsung and Hsuan-tsung (and consequently the Chinese Empire attained its greatest power and prosperity at that time). It was then that the Si-ngan-fu monument was erected and the history of Christianity in the Celestial Empire was preserved for us. The monument describes the advent of a golden age, and this is corroborated by Chinese chronicles. 'The T'ang dynasty was the most famous and glorious of those that ruled China... Under a long line of outstanding monarchs China attained its highest degree of enlightenment. At no time did the arts and sciences shine with greater splendour. This period was also marked by numerous contacts of Chinese with other nations' ; and, according to the Si-ngan-fu inscription, 'the Kingdom became rich, great and beautiful, and its families prosperous and happy'.

Most remarkable is the fact that, in the people's consciousness (implicit in the inscription), this external growth of the Empire and the successes of its internal prosperity are linked with high moral standards achieved by conversion to the 'luminous faith'. 'Families and kingdoms have been set on the path of righteousness by the sublime doctrine, and the pure dogma of the Trinity has furthered high morality through the truth of faith... The law has become part of life... Kindness has been upheld. So happiness and bliss have come about.' The emperors, the promoters of the faith, became the incarnation of virtue ; they 'surpassed the activity of the saints, overcame nefarious influences, attained supreme wisdom and humility, showing great mercy, doing unto others as to themselves and helping those in distress'. Those who copied the inscription, ending as it does with a reference to the beneficial moral revolution brought about by Christianity, exclaim : 'Not even of the greatest followers of Buddha had so much good ever been heard'.

Apparently, only natural disasters endangered the nation's welfare. And it is with a deep insight that the inscription expresses the desire to overcome also this ultimate cause of human catastrophes. 'If it were possible for rain and wind to come at the right time, the sublunar world would know peace... and nature itself would become pure, the living enjoy abundance, the dead know bliss and people govern themselves according to reason [come to reason].' One can conclude from this that they would seek to achieve a rational control of the blind forces of nature. By demanding that the 'movements of the soul' should not remain restricted within their inner world but 'manifest themselves outside', the chronicle of Christianity in China shows that it considers it a duty for the followers of the luminous creed to put the benevolent teaching wholeheartedly into practice.

What lesson can this brilliant forgotten page of history teach China in her present dark days, and the West, too ? Now that a great hatred of Christianity has been aroused in China, one must give up individual conversions. Indeed, it is wrong to speak of the modern introduction of Christianity into China as an innovation. One should speak of, and concern oneself with, the restoration of what has already existed, of the ancient past in China, whose antiquity is so glorious, and where respect for antiquity is so great.

Even if the present hatred of Christianity did not exist among the Chinese, a general conversion would be preferable to individual conversions, particularly as these are not influential in China. When a ship sinks and there is no hope of saving it, individual rescues are permissible, but we are not yet in this desperate situation. In China, where the relatives of a criminal are punishable for his crime and where rewards for acts of valour are extended to ancestors, how can one set aside individuals from the community and seek the salvation of a few, at the price of separating them from their neighbours ? We think (however bold it may sound) that universal conversion would not meet with insuperable obstacles if it were carried out in the right way. Such a general conversion would not be an unacceptable innovation for the Chinese, but a return to their ancient past. Naturally, China would wish for the restoration of that part of her past when she was the greatest state in the world, and that is inseparable from Christianity, Syrian Christianity, with which we Russians are now in communion... To make converts in China, a missionary must become a historian and an archaeologist...

Modern Christianity, as it is being introduced by China's Western 'enlighteners', can attract only rootless vagabonds bereft of fathers, and make them into a force hostile to China herself... Only through the study of the wild, tempestuous force of nature (in accordance with the philosophy of the Chinese themselves, as expressed in the Si-ngan-fu inscription) 'can the sublunar world be brought to peace', that is, to a correct alternation of rain and fair weather at the right times, ensuring the basic conditions for general welfare in a mainly agricultural country — indeed in any country.

...Maybe China, like Kievan Russia, was baptised without preliminary catechesis because, like our ancestors, she was convinced about faith not by reasoning, but by its overwhelming moral self-evidence. T'ai-tsung, 'who exceeded in justice all men', and Vladimir, who disbanded his harem and feared to execute even brigands, drew their peoples to a doctrine which gave rise to moral miracles of which they were themselves eye-witnesses. Both T'ai-tsung and Vladimir were like godfathers to their peoples, in undertaking to enlighten the new converts, by introducing obligatory education for all. Such an education, resulting from the building of churches alongside museum-schools, would today bring about conversion to *true* Christianity. At the same time this would promote spiritual union between two great continental realms.

These two powerful agricultural nations, which have defended themselves against nomads, the one (China) by erecting a stone wall (the Great Wall of China) and the other (Russia) by fortified earthworks, gradually came closer, enlarging the area of peace. The world, and Western Europe in particular, are indebted to them for halting the invasions of Mongols and other wild nomads...

From the dawn of history, Iran has struggled with Turan.[3] Darius understood, all that time ago, that victory over Turan was possible only if Turan met resistance from the north. However, this worthy heir of Cyrus could not pacify the steppes without being endangered by the Greeks. Therefore, instead of struggling against Turan, he was drawn into a war with the freedom-loving Greeks, so adept at discord. Similarly, the new Persian Empire found an enemy in Rome and was distracted from its pacifying task. Russia also, continuing Iran's struggle against Turan, was unsuccessful, owing to the perennial hostility of the West, a faithful ally of the nomads. The crusades were a temporary exception in this policy of the West's, which was later superseded by the alliances of Olgerd and Mamai, of Casimir and Ahmed,[4] and then of the West with the Turks... Such was the outcome of the distressing internecine war within the Aryan race...

Union in the struggle against the irrational force of nature could bring about that universal pacification suggested in our

---

3. A reference to the epic poem *Shah-Nameh* by the Persian poet Firdausi (940-1020), which contains ancient myths and legends in which Iranian heroes fight evil villains from Turan.

4. Olgerd, Prince of Lithuania (1341-77) ; it was actually his son Jagailo who allied himself to the Tartar Khan Mamai, but brought his army too late to save Mamai from defeat at the Battle of Kulikovo (1380), the first Russian victory over the hitherto invincible Tartars. Ahmed is probably the Sultan of Turkey Ahmed III (1673-1730), who gave refuge to Charles XII of Sweden in 1709 after the latter's defeat by Peter the Great at the Battle of Poltava. Ahmed supported Charles XII and the Polish King Stanislav Leszinski (not Casimir) in their war against Russia during which the Turks defeated the Russian army on the river Prut and nearly captured Peter himself. During the Crimean War (1853-6) French and British troops fought alongside the Turks and, after the Russo-Turkish war of 1877-8 for the liberation of the Balkan Slavs, the Western powers imposed on Russia the Treaty of Berlin, thereby thwarting Russia of the fruits of her hard-won victories and limiting the independence of the Balkan Slavs.

circular of 12 August,[5] which expressed the conviction that there is no fatal, ineluctable necessity for wars, and that they result from the sin of discord, which is a sin against the Holy Trinity. Firmly convinced of this, let us end our essay with a prayer preserved by the Syro-Chaldeans, and probably known to the Chinese who adopted the 'luminous faith' from them. This solemn yet touching prayer is read on 'the Wednesday of the general prayer of the Ninivians', but instead of speaking of the salvation of the Ninivians alone, it speaks of the salvation of the whole world.

> We pray for Thy mercy also towards all our enemies, all who hate us and conspire against us. We do not pray for judgement and vengeance, O Lord God Almighty, but for compassion, salvation and forgiveness of sins, because Thou wishest all men to be saved and to come to reason.*

---

5. The circular sent out by Tsar Nicholas II to all governments, which resulted in the convocation of the first Hague Peace Conference in May 1899 and the setting up of the International Court of Justice in the Hague. (See Appendix IV.)

* *Katolikos Vostoka i ego narod. Ocherki tserkovno-religioznoi i bytovoi zhizni Siro-Khaldeitsev*, St Petersburg, 1898, pp. 42-43.

On Turkestan
(from correspondence with V.A. Kozhevnikov) [1]

N.F. Fedorov's three letters on Turkestan [two of which are published here] belong to the material prepared for publication by the late V.A. Kozhevnikov and N.P. Peterson as the third volume of *The Philosophy of the Common Task*. This third volume, which was to comprise both Nikolai Fedorovich's correspondence and various pieces not included in the first two volumes, was almost ready for publication in 1916, but could not be published then because of the fall in currency and Kozhevnikov's financial difficulties connected with this enterprise. The subsequent deaths of both editors of *The Philosophy of the Common Task* (Kozhevnikov on 3 July 1917 and Peterson on 4 March 1919) held up publication of the material that N.F. Fedorov had left, and it is only now that brief fragments of what should have appeared in print ten years ago are beginning to creep into print.

The published letters relate to 1899, when Nikolai Fedorovich, on his friends' insistence, made several attempts to promote his ideas among his contemporaries via periodicals. He was also preparing several articles for publication simultaneously, and in collaboration with Peterson and Kozhevnikov, and working on the systematisation of material which subsequently went into the first volume of *The Philosophy of the Common Task*. This work was undertaken jointly with Peterson, with whom Fedorov usually spent the

---

1. First published in *Versty*, Paris, 1928, n° 3, pp. 276-88. The introductory note, signed 'S', is by N.A. Setnitsky, one of Fedorov's Harbin disciples.

summer months and with whom he worked during all his spare time. What is more, Peterson often acted as Fedorov's secretary. In that year, 1899, Peterson was transferred in connection with his work for the district court to the town of Askhabad. Nikolai Fedorovich visited him there at the end of the summer.

The letters published here are not only of interest as the impressions of a very thoughtful observer arriving for the first time in a new country. Their content makes them a composite part of N.F. Fedorov's whole conception of history, and it is precisely from this standpoint that they should be evaluated. Fedorov's theories in this field have not yet been researched, nor have they attracted sufficient serious attention. All the same, Nikolai Fedorovich Fedorov has posed the problem of East and West and Russia's relations with them, and has offered (in an unusually distinct way) his conception of the tasks and aims to which Russia has applied herself in the course of history. If his ideas have not attracted sufficient attention, one can only assume that the time has now come, and anyone trying to write on this topic should consider the views put forward by the author of *The Philosophy of the Common Task*.

'S'

8 September 1899

Dear Vladimir Alexandrovich,

I am very concerned that I shan't be able to tell you anything fascinating about Turkestan, this quite extraordinary country with its extraordinary desert expanses which demand from man so much activity. Krasnovodsk provides a suitable ingress into waterless Turkestan. It turns out that this city, so beautiful on account of its water,[2] in fact has no water of its

2. *Krasny* meaning 'beautiful' in old Russian, Krasnovodsk means 'Beautiful Water'.

own, but has it brought at the cost of anything from fifty kopeks to a ruble a bucket. There is a water distiller in Krasnovodsk, but apparently its water has a very unpleasant taste. After all I have seen, read and heard about Turkestan, I visualise it in the shape of a high pyramid, constructed of skulls and placed beneath a cloudless sky in the middle of a waterless, sandy desert. This symbolic representation of death, destruction and lifeless desert could even serve as Turkestan's coat-of-arms. A coat-of-arms like this would express the whole history and geography of Turan,* pointing not only to its past but also to its future, to what should be. Indeed, nowhere else is it so essential to deploy resources to remedy the lack of rain, and of water in general, as in this desert in the middle of the globe. More than four fifths of the Transcaspian region, which is about the size of France, consists of uncultivated land (desert), with only one fifth cultivated, and that includes mountain regions almost completely lacking in vegetation. A Report was compiled to draw the attention of scientists to this desert, which is apparently spreading and threatening to engulf the whole of Russia. It set out the need to make Turkestan, and Samarkand in particular, the venue for the next Conference of Naturalists and Physicians, as well as for an archaeological conference. After all, Samarkand lies at the foot of the Pamir mountains,** which are so very important not just for the natural sciences, but also for the relationship between history and archaeology. This Report was presented to the vice-president of the Tashkent Archaeological Society, Nikolai Petrovich Ostroumov, and was apparently well received by him, despite the fact that much of what many consider to be fantastic was left in.

I spent only a day in Tamerlane's city, so I won't talk about what I saw, only about what I did not have time to see and

* The flimsy (clay-built) towns we have built in Turkestan are obviously not intended to last, and vaguely resemble a mirage in the desert. N.F.F.
** A question was raised about the Pamirs at the 10th Archaeological Conference, a fact which was pointed out in the Report. N.F.F.

which you can examine in more detail if you come to Turkestan. Some ten kilometres to the south of Samarkand lie some ruins, Kyafir-Kol', the Christians' last fortress in Turkestan. This is where the Russian Samarkand ought to be built. Not far from these ruins there are some caves, called Kyafir-mola (the graves of the infidels, that is, the Christians). Here is that very cave in which the last remaining Nestorians, who so revered the prophet Jonah and the apostle Thomas, were asphyxiated by smoke on Tamerlane's instructions. The Nestorians are now rejoining Orthodoxy, so it would be a good idea to build a memorial Novopechersky[3] monastery near this cave and make it the principal monastery of all Turkestan. Also, a day should be chosen to commemorate these martyrs which would become a local, or even an all-Russian, feast day.

In Russian Samarkand they honour the mythical grave of Dan'yar, that is, the prophet Daniel, since they have no other sacred places.

In imitation of Eastern custom I press my hand to my heart — this replaces the bow — since this gesture best expresses that good will and gratitude with which I remain

N. Fedorov

I am enclosing the first page of the article 'On churches built by a community in a single day' (*O khramakh obydennykh*).[4]

---

3. Novopechersky — New Pechersky. Ascetic monks sometimes went to live in caves; the most famous Russian 'Monastery of the Caves' was that near Kiev, dating back to the eleventh century, where, in the early days of Christianity in Russia, many ecclesiastical books were translated from the Greek and the first Russian chronicles compiled. The monastery was closed down in 1961 as part of the Communist anti-religious campaign. Part of it was returned to the Orthodox Church in connection with the celebration of the millennium of Christianity in Russia in 1988.

4. The reference is probably to the article in *FOD*, vol. I, pp. 685-731. 'On the significance, in general, of churches built by a community in a single day and, in particular, in our time (with the calling of a world peace conference). In connection with the 10th Archaeological Conference in Riga'.

15 September 1899

Dear Vladimir Alexandrovich,

I am hastening to reply to your question about excerpts from the article on churches built in a single day. The more excerpts you include the better...

Something could also be said about temples in Turkestan. The erection of stone temples in Turkestan demanded the combination of a great number of human forces, just as the building of wooden churches in one day did in our country. A church built by a community in a single day represents a victory over time. A stone temple in Turkestan, erected in a place where there is no stone, represents a victory over space, the more so in those places furthest removed from any area where stone is available. What is voluntary in our country has been replaced here by the compulsory. Legend attributes the building of huge mosque-monuments to the emir-sultans, who used their vast hordes on these constructions, assembling them in lines stretching from the quarries to the place where the temple was being constructed.

...

In issue 33 of the newspaper *Nedelya* a letter from Rome was published under the heading 'The elimination of hail'. E.L. Markov* sent the page containing this article about hail from Voronezh to N.P. Peterson, adding 'Just what you are hoping for'. A short note about this letter from Rome was written and forwarded to Markov, requesting him to send it on, if possible, to the editorial office of *Nedelya* to which, apparently, he contributes. The note begins with words taken from a lecture which Nazzari, a retired officer, had delivered to a huge audience. 'If,' said the former officer, 'cannon were fired not at people's chests, but at those storm-clouds which carry destruction to the poor peasants, then this would be

---

* E.L. Markov, a landowner of Voronezh province, father of the well known Markov 2nd [later a member of the Duma]. S.

more worthy of humanity.'* Speaking frankly, or, in the words of the note, to tell the truth, he did not remain faithful to the truth, but betrayed it immediately. Instead of talking about transforming weapons of destruction, the firearms in the hands of the fighting forces, into weapons of salvation from hailstorms, he started talking about a different sort of artillery which rural landowners were introducing.

Nedelya thinks that, by referring to Nazzari's lecture, it is introducing Russia to a completely unknown issue. The note, citing newspapers and journals, proves not only that this question is a familiar one, but that, on the one hand, it has fierce opponents (Archbishop Amvrosy),** while on the other, it has been put forward as a theory, as a general problem concerning the relation of rational beings to blind, insensate nature. Instead of being seen as two forces existing from time immemorial (like Ormuzd and Ahriman, white god and black god), it is seen as one force which has temporarily split into two. The more influential the rational one becomes, the blinder becomes the other. By making herself into an instrument of the Unconditional Being, that is, by making herself into a Christian country and uniting all of humanity, Russia, Iran's successor, will be eliminating that evil — in other words, death — caused by the inactivity of the rational force, and restoring good, that is, life. By the way, the article says nothing about Iran and Turan, nor about Ormuzd and Ahriman, but talks about a higher morality, whereby good does not depend on the existence of evil, nor is it, like present-day morality, doomed to doing good without being capable of eradicating evil...

---

* The lecture was read at Frascati. It would be curious to know what the liberal Pope's attitude would be to cannon aimed at storm-clouds. Would he, like Amvrosy of Kharkov, regard such a cannon salute as an insult to God ? N.F.F.

** He spoke in a sermon about anti-hail firing into the clouds as a profane act. N.F.F.

From the foot of the Parapamisus mountains
on the borders of Iran and Turan

19 September 1899

Dear Vladimir Alexandrovich,

Up to now all travellers who have come here have been either specialists or people with little understanding of the universally historical significance of the country they have come to. Neither Pamir, nor Iran, nor Turan aroused any feeling in them, nor did they find here anything sacred. Indeed, these travellers are no different from the Russian traders, bureaucrats and officers living here. They are, of course, very liberal, but to them the history of this country is quite alien, despite its world significance. They are not at all shocked that, in this country of Zarathustra, Dzhemshid, Afrosiab, Gistashen,[5] Alexander the Great and Tamerlane, streets should be named after Pushkin, Belinsky, Dobrolyubov, Saltykov-Shchedrin — such dwarfs in comparison with those giants. New, secular Russia cannot understand the greatness of Iran and Turan, is unaware of the vibrant historical life of this country.

The only place one could say is of equal importance in this respect is the Pacific coast of China where Russia joined forces with China to confront the united forces of the West. She encountered its advance detachment (England) even earlier at

---

5. Heroes of the epic poem *Shah-Nameh*, see note 3 to 'What the most ancient Christian monument in China can teach us', p. 203.

There were still vestiges of the Iran-Turan conflict in Fedorov's time. The Turkic-speaking tribes in northern Turkestan were still nomads (and pillaged Russian caravans on the way to the prosperous oases in the south). Here the population, though racially mixed, was still largely of Iranian stock. Farsi (Persian) survived as the language of culture, and was even the official language in Bokhara. Centuries before the rise of Islam, Iran's religion was Zoroastrianism ; later, Christianity, in both Orthodox and Nestorian forms, spread to Iran, which became also the cradle of Manicheism. Islam itself diverged into Shi'ah and Sufism, and during the Middle Ages it lacked the aggressive fanaticism of its Arab, Turkish and Mongol converts.

the Pamir, which was also Russo-Chinese. It could be said that it is at these two points that the pulse of history beats most strongly, that basic issues concerning the life of the human species are being resolved, issues which lie concealed beneath political ones. It is quite another question which of these two points is the more important, or whether the Chinese problem is to serve to divert attention from the Indian, or vice versa. Whatever the case may be, one has to admit that eventually these two points bring together the two circuitous movements, one by land and the other by sea. The internal significance of these movements needs to be understood. Yours is an enviable role, to be the first to take a serious look at this country — this 'heart of the world', to use your expression — not from the liberal-commercial point of view but from the universally historical, from the moral-religious point of view.

It was in Turkestan that the struggle between North and South, between Iran and Turan, between the settled tiller and the nomad, between Near East and Far East, took place, and this at a time when not only was there no Far West, but even the Near West had hardly emerged ; so this is still a prehistoric epoch. And insofar as history begins with the struggle between East and West, then countries that border the seas and later oceans begin to figure. However, this is only oceanic history, which is being mistaken for world history. There is yet another history, which begins with the struggle of Iran and Turan : this is the history of a continent, and only if oceanic forces combine with those of the continent will history become truly universal.

What, then, is Turkestan and where are its borders ? And what is Iran ? Turkestan was not always the Turks' camp ; it had been the Mongols', and had belonged to the Chinese, becoming Buddhist, peasant, then Muslim, before becoming Russian or Zendo-Slavic. Nor has it always been a desert, even when it belonged to Iran, for Iran was the enemy of deserts and lifelessness. And this Turan — both the Western, now Russian, and the Eastern, that is, Chinese — only constitutes the central part of a belt of deserts and steppe lands which stretches from the Western to the Eastern oceans, across the whole of what was formerly the Pamir continent. If being desert is a characteristic feature of Turkestan in the physical sense, then it is difficult to define Turan's boundaries to the south and north because the desert is spreading further and further northwards and southwards, just as the Pamirs are rising higher and higher, thereby becoming colder and colder. So one is forced to acknowledge that Turkestan is a desert which was formed where two northern continents came together, making of it a country cut off, on the one hand, from the ocean and, on the other (by high mountains), from the warm seas ; a country open to the very cold sea, and one from which desert and barrenness are spreading to all countries. If being desert is a characteristic of Turan, and if the saying, 'Where the Osman's foot treads, no grass will grow' is true of the Turks, then the name Turkestan, meaning Turks' camp, is quite appropriate. What is more, one should not assert that the northern border of the Turkic race is the Urals, or even the Volga or Oka rivers. What one should concede as being close to the truth is the identification of the desert with fatalistic Islam, and that being so, even the eastern border of Turkestan keeps moving eastward, which means that Turkestan is squeezing, and may even squeeze out, the Chinese. So Islam, as a religion, and the Turkic race, nurtured by the desert and by fatalistic Islam, turn out to be allies of the desert, the more so as Islam does not forbid giving in to blind nature or to blind passions (polygamy, and Holy Wars against non-Moslems).

If real victory over paganism consists not in destroying idols but in controlling the powers embodied in pagan gods, then... the Turkic race can only be vanquished in the desert, where it came into being, just as the desert can only be vanquished by bringing water to it from the sky, thereby transforming it into pasture and cornfields. This should be the task of Iran's northern successors. However, to do this it is vital to make an ally of the West, of the two Britains. Yet the West was always Turan's ally in its struggle with Iran, both in the ancient and the new worlds. This alliance led to the downfall of ancient Iran and, if it also leads to the downfall of the new Iran (now misnamed Turan by the West), then just as the Black King (the German Emperor) predicted in the well known image (the yellow peril) before he travelled to the East, the West will have the chance of seeing real Turanians.[6]

To bring down water from the sky represents a victory over a formidable force, the victory of rational beings over a blind, insensate force, the victory of Ormuzd over Ahriman, of White God over Black God, of the White tsar (Ahpadishah) over the Black tsar (Kara-padishah), of Christianity over anti-Christianity, of good over evil, that is, of Iran over Turan. Iran and Turan are not symbols of good and evil, but synonyms ; and not in any abstract, arbitrary sense, but in a concrete sense, which is related to the whole of world history, where good is life and evil is death. The triumph of good over evil means the victory of life over death, a return to life, resurrection. So Turan coincides with anti-Christianity and Iran with Christianity, with real, active Christianity. The black prophet (Nietzsche) of the Black King, ally of three hundred million Moslems,[7] that is, of Turan, is an anti-Zarathustra, a false Zarathustra, who cannot possibly deny that those who build both pyramids and pillars of skulls are 'supermen',

6. Fedorov has in mind the anti-Russian view held in the West, that Russians are not Europeans but Tartars, Huns, nomadic barbarians from Asia who have only just 'taken the wheels off their carts and waggons' in the words of the French *philosophe* Louis de Bonald, writing in 1812. In Fedorov's terminology, such a culture would have meant 'Turan'. On the other hand, many Russians considered that Western Europe had been able to develop its brilliant civilisation through being shielded against the devastating invasions of Asiatic hordes by Russia, which had borne the full brunt of their destructiveness. Cf. Aleksandr Blok's well known poem *Skify* (*The Scythians*), 1918.

7. An allusion to a speech made in Damascus by Kaiser Wilhelm II during his trip to the Middle East in 1898, when he said that 300 million Moslems could count on him as a friend, and to his admiration for Caliph Saladin (1137-93), who defeated the Crusaders and put an end to the Christian kingdom of Jerusalem.

beyond the boundaries of good, and realise the ideal of evil.

Will the whole Earth (a heavenly body) submit to this blind force ? Will it turn into Turan, that is, into a desert, a cemetery, aimlessly floating through innumerable spheres, unguided by reason and moving towards downfall and destruction ? Or will the whole Earth become Iran, paradise, Eden ? This will only be possible when the rational, sentient force on this Earth which bears the ashes of the forefathers transforms itself into an instrument of God's light and goodness, and returns consciousness and life to dust (the ashes of the fathers), so that countless worlds deprived of reason can be populated with resurrected generations of sentient beings, who will save them from downfall and destruction.

The Parapamisus mountain range, rising as it does between Iran and Turan, prompts this very question : What is the Earth to become, Iran or Turan ? Turan, the world as it is, that is, a struggle, or a yoke (oppression) ? Iran cannot represent peace while Turan is armed, while Turan stands for the world as it is, while Turan is the world, and not peace.[8] Iran can stand for peace only in the sense of a projected transformation of ignorant Turan and of the dishonourable West, which so misuses knowledge, into a place fulfilling the duty of piety. No matter how vast and powerful wicked Turan is in its alliance with the West — which has admitted itself to be an instrument of the blind power of nature — Iran, as the instrument of the God of light, can and should become boundless and all-powerful, because Turan's power is based on discord and the inactivity of the power of reason (Iran).

To experience the appropriate feelings in fathoming a country lying at the foot of the Pamirs, it is not enough to dash about by rail, in carriages with buffets, cafés chantants and the

---

8. This is an untranslatable pun, the word *mir* in Russian meaning both 'peace' and 'world'. In old Russian they were distinguished by different spellings.

like.* One should undertake not just a journey, but a pilgrimage, since, other than Palestine, there is no holier place than the Pamirs. So if you come to Askhabad and want your journey to be productive, you should spend several days here — a minimum of three. From here you should arrange a short journey, not by train, but by camel and donkey, taking if possible a Russian-speaking donkey-driver. It would be best to start the journey in Anaou, where there are ruins of a large ancient mosque, which is in no way inferior to those of Samarkand. It is no more than ten kilometres to Anaou, which is the first railway station on the way to Samarkand. You cannot get a true picture of Turan unless you make such a journey. The distance is not great, but it is sufficient to give you an impression of what this region was like in ancient times, long before Islam. You shouldn't use the usual sort of camel encountered in Askhabad for the journey, but rather the sort we came across in Tashkent. Camels in Askhabad have a pathetic appearance, whereas those in Tashkent look majestic. The road runs along the foot of the Kopet-Dag, the ancient Parapamisus, to the border of Iran and Turan. Unfortunately, we do not know what it is called in the *Zend-Avesta*, if there is a name for this mountain range in it, but you can find out in Moscow from Ritter, *The Iranian World* (in Russian, *Iran*), c/o Darmstetter, the new edition of the *Zend-Avesta*. These mountains can also be seen from a railway carriage, though the caravan trail runs even closer to the foot of the mountains, so you can see these black ridges more clearly, as fantastic as dreams — at least, that's how they seem to us who haven't seen any other mountains. Here is just about the southernmost part of our territory. One can say that here in June there are never any shadows, not even from the tallest trees, because the sun is apparently at its highest point. At night when there is a clear sky — and we haven't yet seen

---

* There aren't any cafés chantants in the trains yet, but the liberal-commercial agents who are in charge won't be slow in arranging things so that a traveller in a train in the depths of Asia will feel as though he was in Paris.

one that wasn't — sitting on a camel you can see a phenomenon unknown in the north, the setting of the Great Bear, even though it is not quite complete.

You have to organise your journey so that it takes part of the day and part of the night, and travel in the eastern fashion, by camel, with a drum, and a driver dressed in a suit of the sort worn since Abraham's or even Adam's day, and in this way the journey not only suggests but even transports one into biblical and pre-biblical times. The proximity of the railway, the new means of moving from place to place, will only serve to give a more forceful impression of the old. Railway and caravan trail — how many millennia between them! The sound of the cylindrical bell round the camel's neck and the train's piercing whistle in the desert!

But to get an all-round impression from a journey like this, you must do some detailed preparatory reading. On your first day in Askhabad you should have a look at the new Russian Askhabad, this eighteen-year-old built of ephemeral material, literally of dust, for here dust is used as building material — one might call it the fifth element. Perhaps you won't have the time to see it, in which case I will tell you how easily this clay town was erected: on to the street itself, knee-deep in dust, water was poured making a kind of dough, to which finely chopped straw was added — this is the material for the simplest walls, between the doors and windows. Not all buildings are built like this: the less simple ones are made of adobe bricks, baked by the Turkestan sun, while others have stone foundations. Stones are found scattered between the hills and the town. Those bricks baked not by the sun but by fire are used only for surfaces, for decoration, as an expensive extra.

They say there are two gardens and a park in the town, whereas in fact the whole town is within a garden, which the ancient Greeks would have called *Pantikapeia*. The streets, which have tendentious names with which the ordinary people are not familiar, are so monotonous, and the buildings so alike, that it is difficult to tell which street you are on.

Askhabad doesn't remind one of old Russian towns, for it has too few churches — only four, including the Armenian one and the one at the cemetery. A fifth is being built. In the main square, rightly named Skobelevsky,[9] is a single-domed cathedral with a five-domed bell-tower such as we've never seen elsewhere. Askhabad has a museum, two monuments, and a third is being built... By the way, it is impossible to describe everything, for that would involve 'selling Kiev for the paper and Chernigov for the ink', so come and see for yourself.

The second day of your stay I suggest a morning trip to the hills and *auls*.[10] This too is a journey into the past, into Old Testament history. The evening of that day, go for a stroll along the three-kilometre-long avenue to Keshi, to the nursery garden, where you will get to know the flora of the steppes. You'll see there also the almost leafless Haloxylon (*saksaul* or *sazak*), the *sazen*, which is a bit like our silver birch only with a pale-pink bark and with roots many metres long, the *cherkes* and *kandysh* bushes, the little *burdzhak*, and the *erken-selim* and *urkachi-selim* grasses, which are the best for fodder. Nursery gardens like these exist in almost all the towns built by the Russians. It's as if they want to show that, by contrast with the Turks, where the Russians tread, trees and grass grow, to prove that we're not just *Polyane* but also *Drevlyane*.[11]

I'll put the rest of the details for your stay in Askhabad and the journey from Krasnovodsk to Samarkand at the foot of the Pamirs in the next letter. I'm waiting for your article on churches built by the community, about which I spoke in my

---

9. In honour of General Mikhail Dmitrievich Skobelev (1843-82), whose campaigns against the Khans of Kokand and Khiva contributed to the conquest of Turkestan by Russia and reduced the Khanates of Khiva and Bokhara to mere Russian protectorates.

10. *Aul* is a Tartar word for 'village'.

11. Polyane and Drevlyane : these were Slavic tribes deriving their names respectively from *pole*, a field, and *drevo*, a tree — hence 'steppe dwellers' and 'forest dwellers'.

last letter when replying to your request to take excerpts from that manuscript you are familiar with, which would be very desirable. In the same letter I also told you about what I sent to Markov, and after that I sent Ostroumov in Tashkent an article entitled 'So-called stone images',[12] the first monuments to be placed on graves, together with the articles with which you are familiar on stone images, published in the newspaper *Don*. In Turkestan, where one frequently comes across the expressions *'Babá-Gamber'*, *'Imam-Babá'*, used in connection with cemeteries — for this is what they are called — I have become convinced that one has to read or pronounce it not as *kamennaya bába* as in Russian, but as in the Turkestan language, as *babá*, which does not mean woman, but father. So you have to write 'stone fathers' instead of 'stone women'.

Askakal
Karaskakal[13]

12. *Kamennye baby* — literally, 'stone women'.
13. White Beard and Black Beard : the names by which Fedorov and Peterson, respectively, called themselves.

Paradise and hell ?
Or purgatory ? [1]

Paradise, if understood in the Christian Orthodox sense, transforms itself into purgatory, because if domination is rewarded then pride ceases to be vice, and, conversely, if pride is a vice, then domination is no virtue. If anger is a vice, then Crusaders and those possessed of noble wrath, who fought for faith, are in need of purification.

Hell without egress is alien to Orthodoxy.

However, if paradise descends into purgatory, then hell must rise towards it, so as to form a single purgatory, which is in fact our history confined to the realm of sense experience. It is out of this that paradise must be created, a paradise far superior to Dante's, because it will be created not by contemplation or words but by action, and within it there will be neither domination nor condemnation.

Although hell came to exist because we know not what we are doing, there is nothing astonishing in its depriving so many of hope, and in its seeming eternal.

All instruments of punishment such as tempests, floods, droughts, extremes of heat and cold, stinking infection-breeding swamps, are but perversions of beneficent air currents, rain, warmth and so on. If these forces, capable of being beneficent, often manifest uncontrollable destructiveness, pointless savagery and deadly blindness, this is because rational forces are diverted into activity engendered by the

1. From *FOD*, vol. II, p. 13.

seven deadly sins, and for these sins we are punished by the irrational forces of nature.

'They know not what they do' can only become forgiveness and deliverance from hell when we learn what we need to do, what we must do. Our vices are perversions of virtues. So long as man has no outlet for his craving for action, he will waste it on exalting himself above others, on envy, hatred, anger and the accumulation and squandering of wealth. Even the tremendous power of the sexual urge will then find an adequate outlet in re-creation. Only the discovery of a field of activity directed towards saving life can free humanity of vice. This is a hypothesis. There is, however, no doubt that vice will dominate until scope for a lofty and life-saving activity is discovered.

The conditionality of prophecies concerning the end of the world[1]

There can be no better way to begin this article than by quoting the following prayer of the Syro-Chaldeans:

> We also ask Thy mercy for all our enemies and those who hate us and devise evil against us. We do not pray, Almighty God, for judgement and retribution, but for compassion and salvation, and the forgiveness of all sins, because Thou desirest all men to be saved and to come into wisdom.

This prayer is not unique among the Syro-Chaldeans, who have entered into communion with us and from whom it would be most timely to borrow such prayers, because objections to the cause of conciliation are being derived even from the prophecies concerning the end of the world.

A discussion of the conditionality of these prophecies should be prefaced by an explanation of 'the Law and the Prophets', both from the scholarly and from the religious points of view. The religious interpretation of the books of Holy Writ differs sharply from that of the scholars. The former does not speak of dogma but of *law* ; in other words, it demands *action*. It does not separate history from prophecy, action from word. However, for scholars a prophet is a contemplative, that is, a scholar whose object is knowledge of the future — a predetermined, fatal event. Yet the Gospel in

---

1. From *FOD*, vol. II, pp. 13-16.

accordance with the ancient religious classification speaks of 'the Law and the Prophets', that is to say, the Law and those who denounced its transgression. Transgression brings punishment on town or people, or on the world, though *not with fatal consequences* ; this would accord with the scientific but not the religious view, or would be true only for a class of people limited to thought without action.

The Gospel speaks of the Law and not merely of those who denounce law-breaking, that is, sin, which is the cause of death and catastrophe. Scholars seek to discover law in history, which as fact is sheer lawlessness. They accept determinism, fatalism, the inevitable, and refuse to recognise history as a project for universal redemption which would imply the negation of determinism and fatalism. According to the Gospels, 'the Law and the Prophets' mean the Kingdom of God, the union of all — peace. The prophets are those who denounce the kingdom of this world, with its divisions and exclusions — the world as it is. At the same time the prophets are those who restore the Law, that is, peace. If one takes the two commandments that are the foundation of the Law and the Prophets, their observance would consist in the wholehearted love of everyone for the God of the fathers.

...The conditionality or unconditionality of the end of the world depends on one's interpretation of 'the Law and the Prophets'. An analysis of the prophecies regarding the end of the world should begin with those relating to the doom of Nineveh. If the Book of Jonah, the first prophet of the first world empire, is taken as a general introduction to the prophetic books of both the Old and the New Testaments, then what is said there against the unconditional destruction of Nineveh can apply with even greater force to the prophecies regarding the unconditional destruction of the whole world, because the God of the prophet Jonah is also the God of the author of the Apocalypse. It would be great boldness indeed to assume that Christ might express regret that the prophecy about the destruction of the world should not come true. It would also be strange for the apostle of love not to express gratitude that the revelations concerning the doom of the world were not realised.

Let us listen to what the prophets had to say on behalf of God the Judge, as well as God the Father.

'Sometimes,' says Jeremiah, 'to a nation here, a kingdom there, I pronounced my sentence, for the uprooting and undoing of it, for its utter destruction. Let but that nation repent of the crimes I brought against it, I too will repent of the punishment I thought to exact.'* 'The Lord is ever gracious and merciful,' exclaims Joel, 'threatens He calamity, even now He is ready to forgive. Who knows but that He will relent ?' These are the testimonies of the prophets themselves, yet those who refer to them dare assert, 'For sure He will not relent ! He cannot relent.'

Whether the end of the world will be a catastrophe or a peaceful transition without wars and natural calamities will depend on whether men continue to oppose God's will and persist in the state of perennial enmity or, on the contrary, unite to become the instrument of God's will in the task of transforming a destructive into a creative force.

For many, the very question of the conditionality of the end of the world, and even the desire to see it saved, sounds like a heresy. These pitiless thinkers turn *the Creator* of the world into its *Destroyer*, forgetting the words of *the Saviour* that he desires not a single man to perish but that *all* be saved and come into the wisdom of truth. Apart from such obvious parables as those of the prodigal son, the lost sheep, the lost piece of silver and the labourers in the vineyard, even those usually adduced to prove that the end of the world will be followed by eternal damnation contain in fact the same idea that the salvation of all is possible. If the parable of the ten virgins ends with the words, 'Therefore, be watchful !', it obviously aims at the salvation not of the five but of all ten virgins, so that all ten may become wise. Significantly, it is followed by the parable of the talents, which expresses the

* Jeremiah 18 : 7 ff.

different attitudes of people to their work, an approach alive to differences in ability and calling. It is clear that, for the salvation of all, not only is the union of all men necessary, but the utilisation of their *diverse* abilities also. The conclusion of the parable of the talents — 'He that hath ears to hear, let him hear' — clearly shows it to be a predication, a sermon, perhaps even a threat, but not an unalterable prophecy. To preach is to tell what *must* and consequently *can* be fulfilled, but not necessarily what must inevitably happen.

Only the failure to fulfil the demands of these parables, that is to say, the refusal to unite all the forces of all people in the task of universal salvation, brings about the punishment described in the last parable about the goats and the sheep : threatening the former with eternal torment and the latter with its contemplation.

Appendix I

Translation of letter from F.M. Dostoevsky to N.P. Peterson, first published, in abridged form, in the Voronezh newspaper *Don*, n° 80, 1897. Full text in A.S. Dolinin (ed.), *Pis'ma F.M. Dostoevskogo*, Moscow, 1959, vol. 4, n° 620, pp. 9-10.

Dear Nikolai Pavlovich,

With reference to the books for the Kerensk library, I have already given instructions for them to be sent, and you will by now have surely received them.

Now, concerning the original of the unsigned letter in the December issue. I did not include any answer in the *Diary* because I hoped to find your address in the directory of subscribers (Kerensk, according to the postmark) and to correspond with you personally, but, because of lack of time and ill health, I have been postponing doing so from one day to the next. Eventually, your letter of 3 March arrived and explained everything. Again I failed to respond because I fell ill. So may I ask your forgiveness for the delay.

Firstly, a question : who is the thinker whose ideas you have transmitted ? If you can, please let me know his real name. I have become so interested in him. At least let me have some details about him as a person — if possible.

Secondly, I must say that in essence I completely agree with his ideas. I read them as if they were my own. Today I read them (anonymously of course) to Vladimir Sergeevich Solov'ev, our young philosopher, who now lectures on religion — his lectures are attended by crowds nearly a thousand strong. I deliberately waited for him to read your account of your thinker's ideas because I found in his views much similarity. This gave us two excellent hours. He sympathises with your thinker and was intending to lecture next week very much on the same lines (he still has four more lectures to give out of the twelve). However, here is a positive and definite question which I was intending to ask you in December.

In the account of your thinker's ideas, undoubtedly the most essential is the duty of resurrecting former ancestors ; this duty, if it were carried out, would stop the procreation of children and would lead to what the Gospel and the Apocalypse call the first resurrection. However, your exposition does not say how you understand this resurrection of the ancestors, how you imagine it and whether you believe in it. Do you understand it as somehow mental, allegorical, perhaps like Renan, who envisages it as an enlightenment of the human consciousness at the end of humanity's existence, making it quite clear to people of the future, for instance, how much and in what way such and such an ancestor influenced humanity, so that the role of every person who has lived will be revealed ? And their work will be appraised (by science, the power of analogy) so minutely that we will realise also how much these ancestors, having influenced us, have come to be reincarnated in every one of us and, therefore, in those future harmonious humans who will know everything and who will witness the end of humanity.

Or does your thinker assume definitely and literally, as hinted at by religion, that resurrection will be real and personal, that the chasm which separates us from the souls of our ancestors will be closed, will be overcome by victory over death, and that they will come to life not merely in our consciousness, not allegorically, but really, personally, actually, in bodies. (NB Of course, not in present-day bodies, because with the advent of immortality, marriage and childbirth will come to an end, which shows that bodies in the first resurrection, destined to live on earth, will be different from present-day bodies, and possibly similar to the body of Christ after His resurrection but before His ascension and the descent of the Holy Spirit.)

An answer is needed to this question — otherwise, everything becomes incomprehensible. I must forewarn you that we here — that is, at least Solov'ev and I — believe in a real, literal, personal resurrection and that it will happen on earth.

Let me know, highly esteemed Nikolai Pavlovich, if you can and are willing to, how your thinker envisages it, and, if you can, in as much detail as possible.

As to the purpose of primary schools, I am of course quite in agreement with you.

My address is as previously : next to the Greek church, Greek Prospect, Strubninsky House, flat n° 6. NB This is my address till 15 May (however, you can write to me here after that date. Although I will be away, letters will reach me).

With profound respect,
F. Dostoevsky

Appendix II

Two letters from Vladimir S. Solov'ev to N.F. Fedorov, both undated but probably written in 1882. First published by V.A. Kozhevnikov in the appendix to his book *Nikolai Fedorovich Fedorov*, Moscow, 1908, pp. 317-19 ; reprinted in E.L. Radlov (ed.), *V.S. Solov'ev : Pis'ma*, vol. 2, St Petersburg, 1909, pp. 345-7.

Deeply respected Nikolai Fedorovich,

I read your manuscript with greed and spiritual delight, having devoted to it the whole night and part of the morning ; and during the two following days I gave much thought to it.

I accept your 'project' *unconditionally* and without argument ; it is not the project itself that needs discussing, but some of its theoretical premises and assumptions and, also, the first practical steps for implementing it. I will return the manuscript to you at the museum on Wednesday, and we must meet one evening at the end of the week. I have much to say to you. But for the time being I will say only that since the emergence of Christianity your 'project' is the first movement forward of the human spirit along the path of Christ. As to myself, I can only recognise in you my teacher and spiritual father. However, your aim is not to make proselytes or to found a sect, but to save humanity by uniting it in a common cause, and to this purpose what is necessary is for your project to become universally accepted. What means can bring this about in the near future ? This is what I would like to discuss with you during our meeting.

Keep well, dear teacher and comforter.

Your totally devoted
Vladimir Solov'ev

Dear and highly respected Nikolai Fedorovich,

My friend Tsertelev left Petersburg back in May and has not yet returned to his country house, and I do not know when he will, so for this reason (amongst others) I cannot fulfil my wish to meet you in Kerensk. Consequently, we shall meet in Moscow, where I am going presently. But I would like to talk to you before then.

The cause of resurrection as a process, and *its very purpose*, depend on conditions. The simple physical resurrection of the dead cannot be a goal in itself. The resurrection of people at a stage when they seek to devour each other, to resurrect humanity at the stage of cannibalism, would be both impossible and quite undesirable. Therefore the goal is not a simple resurrection of the human *personnel*, but its restoration *in the state it should be*, that is, when all its parts, all its individuals, do not exclude or replace, but include and complement, each other. Of course, you agree with this. If humanity as it should be (as it will be after the resurrection of the dead and the life hereafter) is merely desirable but not yet real, then one cannot speak about real humanity as if it were as it should be, because if humanity, as it should be (when God is all in all), does the will of the Father, then God Himself is directly and undividedly instrumental in all human activity ; and this being the case there is no need for any special acts of God.

However, this is not at all the situation with real humanity, which fails to do the will of the Father and is in no way a direct expression or form of the Deity. Insofar as our actions do not conform to the will of God, this will expresses itself in its own special actions, which are for us something external. If human activities were to coincide with those of the Deity (as in your future psychocracy), then indeed one would not perceive God behind the people. But it is not yet so ; we do not identify with God, and therefore divine action (grace) manifests itself beyond our activity, and in all the more strange (miraculous) forms the less we ourselves correspond to our God. Whereas an adult son may achieve such inner solidarity with his beloved father that in all his actions he does the will of his father without external direction, in the case of a child the will of the father is of necessity to a certain extent an external force and an uncomprehended wisdom which requires instruction and direction. We are all children still, and need the guidance of external religion. Therefore, in positive religion and in the church we have not only the beginning and prefiguration of resurrection and the future Kingdom of God, but also a genuine (practical) path and effective means towards this goal. Consequently, our task must have a religious, not a scientific, character, and we must seek the support of the masses of the faithful and not that of ratiocinating intellectuals. Briefly, this is my justification of the feelings that I expressed to you recently in Moscow.

Au revoir, my dear teacher. May God keep you. Take more

care of your physical health — of the rest you have an abundance. Do you keep your manuscripts ? It would be a good idea to prepare them for the autumn to be lithographed.

>Your truly loving and deeply respectful
>Vlad. Solov'ev

Appendix III

Letter from A.A. Shenshin (the poet Fet) to N.F. Fedorov, published by V.A. Kozhevnikov in the appendix to his book *Nikolai Fedorovich Fedorov*, Moscow, 1908, pp. 319-20.

Moscow, Plyushchikha, own house 6 December 1887
N° 481

Deeply esteemed Nikolai Fedorovich,

These last days, since it started snowing, I have been intending to drive to the Museum and thank you personally for your double kindness, both in enabling Ekaterina Vladimirovna to explore the Museum and for providing such precise information in answer to my inquiry. But as ill-luck will have it sudden fits of my chronic asthma have prevented me from carrying out this pleasant duty. So I am reduced to doing this in writing in order not to appear in your eyes in an unfavourable light. I will never forget the words of Lev Nikolaevich [Tolstoy] about you in those days when we met with you in such a friendly way and conversed together in his home. He said : I am proud to live at the same time, to be a contemporary of such a man. One must have much sprirtual capital to earn that kind of appreciation. Indeed, I know of no one who knows you and who does not express himself in a similar way. If I did not feel it embarrassing to say so I would boldly count myself among their number.

> Please believe in the respect and gratitude
> of your obedient servant
> A. Shenshin

Appendix IV

Russian circular note proposing the first peace conference*

The maintenance of universal peace and a possible reduction of the excessive armaments which weigh upon all nations represent, in the present condition of affairs all over the world, the ideal towards which the efforts of all Governments should be directed.

This view fully corresponds with the humane and magnanimous intentions of His Majesty the Emperor, my august Master.

Being convinced that this high aim agrees with the most essential interests and legitimate aspirations of all the Powers, the Imperial Government considers the present moment a very favourable one for seeking, through international discussion, the most effective means of assuring to all peoples the blessings of real and lasting peace, and above all of limiting the progressive development of existing armaments.

During the last twenty years aspirations towards general pacification have particularly asserted themselves in the consciences of civilized nations. The preservation of peace has been made the aim of international policy ; for the sake of

---

* Handed to the diplomatic representatives August 12/24 1898, by Count Mouravieff (Murav'ev), Russian Minister for Foreign Affairs, during the weekly reception in the Foreign Office, St Petersburg. English text in *British Parliamentary Papers*, vol. 110, Russia, n° 1, 1899.

peace the Great Powers have formed powerful alliances, and for the purpose of establishing a better guarantee of peace they have developed their military forces in an unprecedented degree, and continue to develop them without hesitating at any sacrifice.

All these efforts, however, have not yet led to the beneficent results of the desired pacification.

The ever increasing financial burdens strike at the core of public prosperity. The physical and intellectual forces of the people, labour and capital, are diverted for the greater part from their natural application and wasted unproductively. Hundreds of millions are spent in acquiring terrible engines of destruction which are regarded today as the latest inventions of science, but are destined tomorrow to be rendered obsolete by some new discovery. National culture, economical progress, and the production of wealth are either paralysed or developed in a wrong direction.

Therefore, the more the armaments of each Power increase, the less they answer to the objects aimed at by the Governments. Economic disturbances are caused in great measure by this system of excessive armaments, and the constant danger involved in this accumulation of war material renders the armed peace of today a crushing burden more and more difficult for the nations to bear. It consequently seems evident that if this situation be prolonged, it will inevitably lead to that very disaster which it is desired to avoid, and the horrors of which make every humane mind shudder by anticipation.

It is the supreme duty, therefore, at the present moment of all States to put some limit to these unceasing armaments, and to find means of averting the calamities which threaten the whole world.

Deeply impressed by this feeling, His Majesty the Emperor has been pleased to command me to propose to all Governments who have Representatives at the Imperial Court the meeting of a Conference to discuss this grave problem.

Such a Conference, with God's help, would be a happy

augury for the opening century. It would concentrate in one powerful effort the strivings of all States which sincerely wish to bring about the triumph of the grand idea of universal peace over the elements of trouble and discord. It would, at the same time, cement their agreement by a united affirmation of the principles of law and equity on which rest the security of States and the welfare of peoples.

Count Mouravieff

St Petersburg, 12 August 1898

On 30 December 1898 Mouravieff handed out a second circular letter, suggesting that the conference should not sit in the capital of any of the Great Powers where were centred so many political interests that might impede the progress of the conference, and detailing the aims of the conference under the following eight heads :

1. An understanding not to increase for a fixed period the present effective of the armed military and naval forces, and at the same time not to increase the Budgets pertaining thereto ; and a preliminary examination of the means by which a reduction might even be effected in future in the forces and Budgets above-mentioned.

2. To prohibit the use in the armies and fleets of any new kind of fire-arms whatever and of new explosives, or any powders more powerful than those now in use either for rifles or cannon.

3. To restrict the use in military warfare of the formidable explosives already existing, and to prohibit the throwing of projectiles or explosives of any kind from balloons or by any similar means.

4. To prohibit the use in naval warfare of submarine torpedo-boats or plungers, or other similar engines of destruction ; to give an undertaking not to construct vessels with rams in the future.

5. To apply to naval warfare the stipulations of the Geneva

Convention of 1864, on the basis of the Additional Articles of 1868.

6. To neutralise ships and boats employed in saving those overboard during or after an engagement .

7. To revise the Declaration concerning the laws and customs of war elaborated in 1874 by the Conference of Brussels, which has remained unratified to the present day.

8. To accept in principle the employment of good offices, of mediation and facultative arbitration in cases lending themselves thereto, with the object of preventing armed conflicts between nations ; to come to an understanding with respect to the mode of applying these good offices, and to establish a uniform practice in using them.

Select Bibliography

Aksenov, G. 'Mir dan ne na poglyadenie...' ('The world is given not for just gazing...'), *V mire knig* (*In the World of Books*), 1980, n° 8, pp. 71-2.

Altaisky, K. 'Moskovskaya yunost' Tsiolkovskogo' ('Tsiolkovsky's youth in Moscow'), *Moskva*, 1966, n° 9, pp. 176-92.

Arlazorov, M. *Tsiolkovsky*, Moscow, 1962.

Bely, Andrei (pseudonym of B.N. Bugaev) *Moskva*, Moscow, 1926.

Berdyaev, N.A. 'Religiya voskreseniya' ('The religion of resurrection'), *Russkaya mysl'*, 1915, n° 387, pp. 75-120. 'Tri yubileya : L. Tolstoy, Gen. Ibsen, N.F. Fedorov' ('Three jubilees : L. Tolstoy, H. Ibsen, N.F. Fedorov'), *Put'* (Paris), 1928, n° 11, pp. 71-94. English translation of section on Fedorov, 'N.F. Fedorov', *Russian Review* (New York), 1950, n° 9, pp. 124-30.
Russkaya ideya, Paris, 1946. English translation *The Russian Idea*, New York, 1948.

Borisov, V. 'Ideal'ny bibliotekar'' ('An ideal librarian'), *Al'manakh bibliofila*, 1979, n° VI, pp. 201-6.

Bradovi, M. & Louz, L.J. *Fedoroviana Pragensis*, Prague, 1962 (description of file n° 142 containing unpublished letters of N.A. Setnitsky and other material in Literarni Archiv Narodni Museum, Prague).

Bryusov, V.Ya. *Khvala cheloveku* (*In Praise of Man*) (poem), 1908.

'O smerti, voskresenii i voskreshenii' ('On death, resurrection and resuscitation'), in *Vselenskoe delo* (*The Ecumenical Task*), Odessa, 1914, p. 49.

Bulgakov, S.N. 'Zagadochny myslitel' ('An enigmatic thinker'), *Dva grada* (*Two Cities*), Moscow, 1911, part 2, pp. 260-77.
Svet nevecherny (*Unfading Light*), Moscow, 1917. Both reprinted by Gregg International, Farnborough, 1971.

Byers, H.E. 'History of weather modification' in W.N. Hess (ed.), *Weather and Climate Modification*, New York, 1974.

Chayanov, A.N. *See* Kremnev.

Correspondence regarding the Proposal of His Majesty the Emperor of Russia for a Conference on Armaments, *Parliamentary Papers*, 1899, vol. 110, Russia, n° 1.

Dollezhal, N. & Koryakin, Yu. 'Yadernaya energetika : dostigeniya i problemy' ('Nuclear energy : achievements and problems'), *Kommunist*, 1979, n° 14, pp. 19-28.

Dostoevsky, F.M. 'Letter to N.P. Peterson', *Don*, Voronezh, n° 80, 1897 ; full text in Dolinin, A.S. (ed.), *Pis'ma F.M. Dostoevskogo* (*Letters of F.M. Dostoevsky*), Moscow, 1959, vol. 4, n° 620, pp. 9-10.

Edie, J., Scalon, J., Zeldin, M. & Kline, G.(eds) *Russian Philosophy*, Chicago, 1965, vol. 3, pp. 16-54.

Fedorov, N.F. *Filosofiya obshchago dela, stat'i, mysli i pis'ma*. Kozhevnikov, V.A. & Peterson, N.P. (eds.), vol. I, Verny, 1906 ; vol. II, Moscow, 1913. Reprinted with a preface in English by N.M. Zernov, under the title *The Philosophy of the Common Cause*, by Gregg International, Farnborough, 1970, and (without preface) by L'Age d'Homme, Lausanne, Switzerland, 1985.
2nd edn, incomplete, with a biographical essay by A. Ostromirov, 3 issues, Harbin, 1928-30.
'Pis'mo v redaktsiyu' ('Letter to the Editor' or rather a foreword to Dostoevsky's letter to Peterson) *Don*, Voro-

nezh, 1897, n° 80 ; reprinted in *Vselenskoe delo*, n° 1, Odessa, 1914, pp. 24-30.
'Chemu nauchaet drevneishy khristiansky pamyatnik v Kitae', *Russky arkhiv*, 1903, n° 4, pp. 631-7. Reprinted in N.A. Setnitsky, *Russkie mysliteli o Kitae : V.S. Solov'ev i N.F. Fedorov*, Harbin, 1928.
'Iz tret'yago toma *Filosofii obshchago dela*' ('From the third volume of *The Philosophy of the Common Task*'), *Put'* (*The Way*), Paris, 1928, n° 10, pp. 3-43.
'Iz posmertnykh rukopisei N.S. Fedorova' ('From the posthumous manuscripts of N.F. Fedorov'), *Put'*, 1929, n° 18, pp. 1-24.
'Chto takoe dobro ?' ('What is good ?'), *Put'*, 1933, n° 40, pp. 3-15.
'Iz perepiski N.F. Fedorova s V.A. Kozhevnikovym o Turkestane', *Versty*, Paris, 1928, n° 3, pp. 278-88.
For a complete list of articles attributable to N.F. Fedorov not included in the two-volume edition of *Filosofiya obshchago dela* (*The Philosophy of the Common Task*), see George M. Young, *Nikolai F. Fedorov : An Introduction*, pp. 248-55.

Ginken, A. 'Ideal'ny bibliotekar' — Nikolai Fedorovich Fedorov', *Bibliotekar'*, 1911, n° 1, pp. 12-26.

Gor'ky, Maxim (pseudonym of A.M. Peshkov) 'Gor'ky i sovetskie pisateli : neizdannaya perepiska' ('Gor'ky and Soviet writers : unpublished correspondence'), *Literaturnoe nasledstvo*, vol. 70, Moscow, 1963, pp. 134-6, 335, 584, 587 and 589.

Gornostaev, A.K. (pseudonym of A.K. Gorsky) *Rai na zemle : k ideologii tvorchestva Dostoevskogo : F.M. Dostoevsky i N.F. Fedorov* (*Paradise on Earth : Some Ideological Aspects of the Works of Dostoevsky : F.M. Dostoevsky and N.F. Fedorov*), Harbin, 1928.
Pered litsom smerti : L.N. Tolstoy i N.F. Fedorov, 1828-1903-1910-1928 (*Facing Death : L.N. Tolstoy and*

N.F. Fedorov), Harbin, 1929, both pamphlets reprinted, Clamart, France, 1928.

Gorsky, A.K. *See* Gornostaev and Ostromirov.

Grechishnikov, S.S. & Lavrov, A.V. 'Andrei Bely i N.F. Fedorov', *Toimetiged : acta et commentationes Universitatis Tartuensis*, Tartu, 1979, n° 459, pp. 147-64.

Hagemeister, Michael 'Neue Materialen zur Wirkungsgeschichte N.F. Fedorovs, M. Gor'kii und die Anhänger Fedorovs in Moskau und Harbin', *Studia Slavica*, Beiträge zum VIII Internationalen Slawistenkongress in Zagreb 1978, Giessen, 1981, pp. 219-43.
'Die "Biokosmisten" — Anarchismus und Maximalismus in der frühen Sowjetzeit' in G. Friedhof, P. Kosta & M. Schütrumpf, *Studia Slavica in Honorem Viri Doctissimi Olexa Horbatsch*, Munich, 1983.

Kiselev, A. 'Varsonof'ev i N.F. Fedorov', *Novy zhurnal*, New York, 1977, n° 110, pp. 296-9.

Koehler, Liudmilla *N.F. Fedorov : The Philosophy of Action*, Pittsburg, 1979.

Kozhevnikov, V.A. *Beztsel'ny trud, 'Ne-delanie' ili Delo ? Razbor vzglyadov Em. Zola, A. Duma i gr. L.N. Tolstogo na trud (Aimless Labour, 'Non-doing' or a Task ? An Analysis of the Views of E. Zola, A. Dumas and Count L.N. Tolstoy on Work)*, Moscow, 2nd edn, 1894.
'Nikolai Fedorovich Fedorov', *Russkii arkhiv*, 1904, n° 2, pp. 315-25 ; n° 3, pp. 390-401 ; n° 4, pp. 545-54 ; n° 5, pp. 5-26 ; n° 9, pp. 106-24 ; n° 10, pp. 225-61 ; 1905, n° 1, pp. 180-200 ; n° 2, pp. 333-65 ; n° 7, pp. 417-70 ; 1906, n° 1, pp. 63-102 ; n° 2, pp. 260-301. Reprinted in book form, Moscow, 1908, with an appendix containing the letter from Dostoevsky to Peterson, the two letters from Solov'ev translated here (see pp. 229-32), one from the poet Fet to Fedorov (see pp. 232-3) and one from Tolstoy to Ivakin.

Kozodoev, I. 'Bibliografiya Filosofii obshchago dela', *Vselenskoe delo*, n° 2, Riga, 1934, p. 188.

Kremnev, I. (pseudonym of A.V. Chayanov) *Puteshestvie moego brata Alekseya v stranu krest'yanskoi utopii*, Moscow, 1920. English translation by R.E.F. Smith, 'The journey of my brother Alexei to the land of peasant utopia', *Journal of Peasant Studies*, 1978, n° 1, pp. 63-117.

Laptev, I.D. *Planeta razuma* (*The Planet of Reason*), Moscow, 1973.

Lodge, Sir Oliver *Lightning Conductors and Lightning Guards*, London, 1892.

Lord, R. 'Dostoevskii and N.F. Fyodorov', *Slavonic and East European Review*, June 1962, pp. 409-30.

Ludwig, Emil *Kaiser Wilhelm II*, London, 1927.

Lukashevich, Stephen *N.F. Fedorov (1828-1903), a Study in Russian Eupsychian and Utopian Thought*, Newark, 1977.

L'vov, Vladimir 'Zagadochny starik' ('An enigmatic old man'), *Neva*, 1974, n° 5, pp. 65-116.

Mamedov, N.M. 'Ekologicheskaya problema i tekhnicheskie nauki' ('The ecological problem and the technical sciences'), *Voprosy filosofii*, 1980, n° 5, pp. 111-20.

Mayakovsky, V.V. *Pro eto* (*About This*), 1923. English translation by H. Marshall, *Mayakovsky*, London, 1945, pp. 161-216.

Mikulinsky, S.R. 'Tak li nado otnositsya k nasledstvu ?' ('Is this how to treat a heritage ?'), *Voprosy filosofii*, 1982, n° 12, pp. 151-7 (a critical review of Semenova's edition of *FOD*).

Murav'ev, V.E. *Ovladenie vremenem* (*Control over Time*), Moscow, 1924. Reprinted with an introduction in German by M. Hagemeister, Munich, 1983.

Ostromirov, A. (pseudonym of A.K. Gorsky) 'Nikolai Fedorovich Fedorov, 1828-1903-1928, biografichesky ocherk' ('A Biographical Essay'), published as preface to the 2nd edn of *Filosofiya obshchago dela*, Harbin, 1928, pp. i-xx.
Nikolai Fedorovich Fedorov i sovremennost' (*N.F. Fedorov and Our Time*), four issues, Harbin, 1928-33 :
1st issue, 1928, 20 pp.
2nd issue, *Bogoslovie obshchago dela* (*The Theology of the Common Task*), 1928, 51 pp.
3rd issue, *Organisatsiya mirovozdeistviya* (*The Organisation of Action on the World*), 1932, 40 pp.
4th issue, *Ostrie mirovogo crizisa* (*The Sharp Edge of the World Crisis*), 1933, 51 pp.

Pasternak, L.O. *Zapisi raznykh let* (*Notes from Various Years*), Moscow, 1973.

Pazilova, V. 'Proekt obshchego dela N.F. Fedorova' ('N.F. Fedorov's Project of the Common Task'), *Nauka i religiya* (*Science and Religion*), 1983, n° 3, pp. 26-9 and n° 4, pp. 17-20 (a critical review of Semenova's edition of *FOD*).

Peterson, N.P. *N.F. Fedorov i ego kniga* Filosofiya obshchago dela *v protivopolozhnost' ucheniyu L.N. Tolstogo o neprotivlenii i drugim ideyam nashego vremeni* (*N.F. Fedorov and his Book* The Philosophy of the Common Task in Opposition to the Teaching of L.N. Tolstoy on Non-Resistance and to other Ideas of Our Time), Verny, 1912.

Powers, Edward *War and the Weather*, Chicago, 1871 ; 2nd rev. edn 1890.

Reade, Winwood *The Martyrdom of Man*, 1st edn Trübner, London, 1872.

Russky biografichesky slovar', Moscow, 1914, vol. 4, pp. 67-8 ; vol. 18, St Petersburg, 1904, pp. 299-304.

Sacki, P.J. *The Nestorian Documents and Relics in China*, Tokyo, 1937.

Schmemann, Alexandre *Ultimate Questions : An Anthology of Modern Russian Religious Thought*, Mowbray's, London & Oxford, 1965.

Semenova, S.G. (ed.) *Nikolai Fedorovich Fedorov — Sochineniya (Works)*, Moscow, 1982.
'N.F. Fedorov — zhizn' i uchenie' ('N.F. Fedorov — Life and Teaching'), *Prometei*, 1977, n° 2, pp. 88-104.
'K publikatsii stat'i N.F. Fedorov *O Fauste*', *Kontekst*, 1975, pp. 312-32.

Setnitsky, N.A. *Russkie mysliteli o Kitae : V.S. Solov'ev i N.F. Fedorov (Russian Thinkers on China : V.S. Solov'ev and N.F. Fedorov)*, Harbin, 1926.
Kapitalistichesky stroi v izobrazhenii N.F. Fedorova (N.F. Fedorov's Account of Capitalism), Harbin, 1926. Reprinted in *Versty*, Paris, 1928, n° 1, pp. 259-78.

Shklovsky, V.B. *O Mayakovskom*, Moscow, 1940.

Solov'ev, V.S. *Tri razgovora (Three Conversations)*, St Petersburg, 1900. Excerpt translated by Barnes, N.I. & Heynes, H.H. as *The Antichrist*, Edinburgh, 1982.
Pis'ma (Letters), ed. E.L. Radlov, St Petersburg, 1908-23 : vol. 2, 1909, vol. 4, 1923.

Stoffel, Charles *Résurrection*, Paris, 1840.

Sukhikh, L.I. 'M. Gor'ky i N.F. Fedorov', *Russkaya literatura*, 1980, n° 1, pp. 160-8.

Teilhard de Chardin, Pierre *Œuvres*, Paris, Editions du Seuil, 1955 onwards :vol. I, 'Le Phénomène humain', 1955 ; vol. VIII, 'La Place de l'Homme dans la Nature', 1956. *Cahiers I*, 'Construire la Terre' (multilingual), Paris, 1958.

Teskey, Ayleen *Platonov and Fyodorov : The Influence of Christian Philosophy on a Soviet Writer*, Avebury (England), 1982.

Tolstoy, L.N. *Polnoe sobranie sochineny* (*Complete Collected Works*), Moscow, 1928-58. References to N.F. Fedorov in vol. 49, p. 58 ; vol. 63, pp. 80-1 ; vol. 82, pp. 179-80 ; article 'Ne-delanie' ('Non-doing'), vol. 29, pp. 173-201.

Young, George M. Jr 'Fyodorov in Baker Library', *Dartmouth College Library Bulletin*, part I, April 1976, pp. 54-61 ; part II (Fyodorov bibliography), April 1977, pp. 74-88.
Nikolai F. Fedorov : An Introduction, Belmont, 1979.

Zabelin, I.M. 'Chelovechestvo — dlya chego ono ?' ('Humanity — what is it for ?'), *Moskva*, 1966, n° 8, pp. 172-86 and 1968, n° 5, pp. 147-62.

Zola, Emile 'La propriété littéraire', *Nouvelle Campagne*, Paris, 1896.

INDEX

absolutism and morality, 51
Abyssinia, source of energy for Africa, 147
Ackermann, 76
Adam, 124, 169, 217
aerostats, 69, 94, 167
aesthetics, 105, 125, 189
Afrosiab (in epic *Shah-Nameh*), 211
agapodicy (justification of Good), 180-1
agnosticism, 50
agriculture, 91-3
Ahmed III (Turkish sultan), his alliance with Casimir, 203
Ahpadishah (white tsar), 134, 214
Ahriman (black god), 210
akakia (dust), 139
Alexander the Great, 211
alienation, 37-8, 118
All Saints' Day, 126
Allah, 160
Alliance, Holy, 167
Alma-Ata (Verny), 19
A-lo-pên (Chinese apostle), 198-9
Alps, as source of energy, 147
Altaisky, K., 17, 237
altruism, 60, 119, 161
Ambrosius (Amvrosy), Bishop of Kharkov, 34-5, 210.
America, 13, 94 ; and rain-making experiments, 144-55
Americans, as supporters of peace, 156
amorisation, 27
ancestors, 12, 18, 26, 54, 96, 121-2 ; and school-museum, 138 ; cult of, 65-6, 125, 140 ; return to life of, 98 ; *and see* resurrection, supramoralism
'Andrei Bely i N.F. Fedorov', (S.S. Grechishnikov, A.V. Lavrov), 21, 240.
Anglicans, and Orthodox burial rite, 175-6
Anglo-Russian scientific expedition, 18

245

annihilation, 34, 55, 81 ; instruments of, 138
anti-Christianity, 214
Apocalypse, 130, 223
Apostolic rules, 175
Arakcheev, Count A., 167
Archaeological Society, Tashkent, 207
Archbishop of York, 175
argon, 195
Aristotle, 56
Arlazorov, M., *Tsiolkovsky*, 17, 237
armaments, 63, 82
art, 105, 123-5 ; anthropurgic, 185 ; as imitation, 187-90 ; as pornographic pleasure, 61 ; German, 124 ; Copernican, 128, 187-91, 195 ; Kant's philosophy of, 51 ; participation in, 40 ; phases in, 184-6 ; Ptolemaic, 128, 187-90 ; theo-anthropurgic, 184-5 ; and vertical posture, 124, 184-5 ; mythological, 56 ; martial, 189 ; *see also* science, industry, knowledge, painting, religion
Aryan(s), race, 203 ; tribes, 71 ; of Iran, 86
asceticism, 110, 113, 118-19, 141
ashes, 126, 188, 191-2, 215 ; *see also* kremlins

Asia, 17, 18 ; as source of energy, 147 ; and struggle with Europe, 77 ; South-East, 77 ; Western, 86
Asiatic hordes, 215
Askhabad, 216, 218 ; Peterson transferred to, 206
assembly, 46
Assumption, Cathedral of the, Moscow, 124
astrology, 167
astronomy, 42-3, 123, 195
atheism, 66
atoms, 102, 132, 141, 195 ; man recreated from, 134
atonement, 108, 116
Aul (Tartar village), 218
Austria, and meaning of 'constitution', 130 ; floods in, 145
autocracy, 122, 130-1 ; Russian, 108
Autocrat, 17, 140-1 ; as godfather to all, 138 ; Russian, 139

Babá-Gamber, 219
Babylon, 171, 197
balloons, *see* lightning conductors
baptism, 106, 142
Bartholomew, apostle, 197
Baudouin, F., 152
Beatitudes, 105, 170
Being, Divine, 71 ; Immortal, 70 ; Triune, 71, 76,

83 ; Unconditional, 210
believers, 33, 115, 117-18, 137, 139-40
Belinsky, V., 211
Bely, A., 21, 237, 240
Berdyaev, Nicholas, 'The religion of resurrection', 19 ; *The Russian Idea*, 237 ; 'Three jubilees : L. Tolstoy, H. Ibsen, N.F. Fedorov', 20, 237
bereavement, 114
Berlin, Congress of, 18 ; Treaty of, 67, 203
Bible, 26
black god, *see* Ahriman
Black King, 214
black prophet, *see* Nietzsche
Black tsar, Kara-padishah, 214 ; German, 134
Blok, A., and *Scythians*, 215
bodies, 100 ; resurrected, 228-9
Bogorodsk, Peterson in, 14
Bokhara, 211
Bonald, Louis de, 215
Boxer Rebellion, 196
brain, 107
Britain, 213
British Parliamentary Papers, 233
brotherhood, 11, 18, 29, 33, 40, 42, 74-5, 84-5 ; creation of, in liturgy *(bratotvorenie)*, 180 ; nadir of, 55, 131 ; of sons, 116
Bryusov, V., 21, 237

Buddhism, 65, 74, 189, 196, 200 ; and nirvana, 132, 212
Buddhism in Comparison with Christianity (V.A. Kozhevnikov), 17, 240
Bulgakov, S., Father, 20, 238
burial rite, Orthodox, 175-8 ; aboriginal Australian, 185
Byers, H. E., 27, 238
Byzantium, 77, 86, 197-9

cables, globe-encircling, 69 ; telegraph, 70, 95 ; telephone, 70
Caesar, *see* Tsar
cafés-chantants, 216
camp, *see* school-camp
cannibalism, 230
cannon, 235 ; to fire at clouds, 210
Capernaum, 171
capitalism, 24
capital punishment, 78
Casimir, his alliance with Ahmed, 203
Caspian, 199
catasterisation (transfer of father's souls to stars), 186
catechism, 83
Catholicism, different from Orthodoxy, 189 ; authoritarianism of, 77
Catholics, Old, 175
Caucasus, Indian, 87 ; water-

247

falls of, 147
Celestial space, explorers of, 96
cemeteries, 26, 67, 121, 122. *See also* Earth
Central Committee of CPSU, 13
chaosography, 50
chastity, 17
Chateaubriand, F.R. de, 73
Chayanov, A. V., *see* Kremnev
Chen-Kuan period, 199
Chile, importation of guano, 173
Chileans, mining of mountain passes, 154
China, 28, 77, 86 ; ancient Christian monument in, 196-204 ; Council of, 198 ; icons of, 199 ; Sino-Japanese war, 156 ; Great Wall of, 202 ; the Celestial Empire, 197 ; problem of, 212 ; *see also* positivism
Christ, 64, 83, 122 ; adulthood of, 44 ; and apostle Thomas, 89 ; last prayer of, 106 ; as Khe-le-tuze, 198 ; risen, 125 ; *see also* son(s)
Christianity, 64, 73, 117, 175, 189, 208-11 ; and Byzantium, 77 ; and idea of God,' 72 ; and Iran, 214 ; and natural science, 35 ; and physical resurrection, 23 ; *see also* Orthodoxy
Chrysostom, John, homily of, 126
church, 67, 121, 187 ; and cross, 171-2 ; sculptures, 186-7 ; symbolism of, 124, 187 ; of God of fathers, 125 ; of Immortals, 71 ; built in one day, 162, 208-9 ; *see also* school-church
citizenship, as cause of 'unbrotherliness', 42
civilisation, as cause of 'unbrotherliness', 42 ; synonymous with struggle, 43
class, agricultural, 91 ; rural, 38, 91 ; urban, 38, 91
cleansing, *see* baptism
co-dying, 119, 184-5
collective mind, 102
collectivisation, 21
colonialism, 40
comets, 195
commandments, 105, 137, 142, 188 ; and faith, 170 ; and the Autocrat, 139 ; *see also* God
Commission for plan of common action, 59
Common Task, *see* Task
communal land tenure, 93
Commune, agricultural, 93-4, 96

Communism, 77
Comte, A., 17, 155
Conductors, *see* lightning
Conference, 10th Archaeological (Riga), 208 ; of Brussels, 236 ; of naturalists and physicians, 207 ; Peace, 135.
Confucius, 198-9
Congress, US, 27
consciousness, 40, 108, 118, 131, 164 ; disseminated round universe, 189 ; of nature, 106-7, 115 ; in resuscitation process, 193, 215
Constantine, 86
Constantinople, 17, 29, 69, 77, 86, 87
constitutions (self-will), 130-1
consumer goods, 24, 29, 39
Copernicus, 124, 127, 186
coronation, meaning of, 126
coronium, 195
cosmology and Kant, 50, 116
cosmos, 25, 128, 190
Cossacks, 96
cottage industries, 62-3, 96, 139
Court of Arbitration, Permanent, 144
Creator, 97, 101, 106-7
Crimean War, 203
criminologists, 63
critical philosophy, 49-51
crop rotation, 93
cross, and Constantinople, 81 ; as symbol, 171-2
Crusaders, 214, 220
Crusades, 203
cult, 49 ; of ancestors, 65-6, 125 ; of fathers, 121 ; of graveyards, 121 ; of woman, 120-1, 140 ; urban, 120

Dante, 135
daughter(s), 74, 75 ; as reconciler, 178-9 ; and union with fathers, 65 ; and union with souls, 65, 119, 140-1, 169
death, 11, 12, 18, 23, 24, 33, 34, 35, 42, 56, 66, 72-3, 83, 98-9, 110, 121 ; and desert, 207 ; and Kant, 50 ; and sex, 43, 188 ; as organic evil, 91 ; penalty, 115 ; venerated, 76
decomposition, 25, 89-90, 99
deforestation, 114-17
defraternisation, 129
deism, 66, 111-12
Delphi, 115
Descartes, R., 115
desert, and Iran, 212 ; and Turan, Turkestan, 207
desertification, 29
despotism, 30 ; enlightened, 51
determinism, 42
Diary of a Writer (F.M. Dostoevsky), 14
disarmament, 23, 29, 34,

144 ; manifesto (12 Aug. 1898), 126
discord, 11, 14, 25, 59, 71, 79, 97, 111, 122, 129 ; and Roman eagle, 134 ; internal, 45 ; and Turan, 214-15
disintegration, 23
dissension, 25
disunion, 165 ; morality of, 119
disunity, 37, 45, 59, 71, 74 ; Kant and vice of, 51 ; as lack of brotherhood, 60
Divine Being, 71
divinisation, 27 ; of woman, 120
divinity, 27
division, 106
Dobrolyubov, N., 211
dogmatics, 105
Dollezhal, N., 70, 238
Don (Voronezh journal) 14, 159, 219, 227
'Dostoevskii and N.F. Fedorov' (R. Lord), 15, 241
Dostoevsky, F.M., 14, 15, 238 ; and foreword to letter of, 159-69 ; and Ilyusha and bodily resurrection, 15 ; and letter to Peterson, 14, 227-9
Dragomirov, General M.I., 163-5
Drevlyane (Slavic tribe), 218
drought, 34, 88, 102 ; of 1891, 144-54
drug abuse, 47, 98
drunkenness, 98
Dukhobors, and Tolstoy, 22
Duma, Vladimir's, 198
dust (of fathers), 109, 120, 125-7, 129-31, 138-42, 160, 188, 215 ; *see also* father(s), resurrection
duty, 12, 36-8, 76, 99, 112, 138 ; Dostoevsky and, 159-61 ; to deceased fathers, 43, 120-1 ; to return life to ancestors (supramoralism), 105, 228 ; *see also* surpamoralism
dynamite, 34
Dzhemshid (in epic *Shah-Nameh*), 211

eagle, Roman, 134
Earth, 23, 35, 70, 80, 90, 97, 107, 122, 141, 190 ; New, 25 ; and Dante, 135 ; as graveyard, 42, 69, 97, 123, 142, 189, 214 ; as heavenly body, 42-3, 68-9 ; as bearer of salvation, 88 ; control of its motion, 98, 135 ; in relation to sun, 87 ; destiny of, 96-7 ; magnetism of, 25, 69, 95 ; *see also* dust, Universe
East, Far, 212 ; Near, 212 ; and oppression, 72 ; and

West, 82, 206 ; represented by Palestine, 190
Easter, 105, 125-7, 131, 138, 140, 172 ; disappearance of, in West, 126 ; of the Cross, 175 ; of Resurrection, 175
Eastern Question, 40, 44, 147
'The ecological problem and the technical sciences' (N.M. Mamedov), 70, 241
education, compulsory, 142, 161, 168 ; system, 24
egotism, 119, 161
electricity, atmospheric, 27 ; Lodge's studies of, 28
electromagnetic cycle, 100
Elementary Lessons in Astronomy (Sir J.N. Lockyer), 95
emigration, 25, 97-8
Empire, Roman, 197 ; *see also* China
energy, electrical, 147 ; solar, 28
England, 87, 211
English, visitors to Russia, 175 ; workers, 62
Enlightenment, Age of, 63
Epimetheus, and marriage to Pandora, 179
equality, limitations of, 84
ethics, 105, 128
Eucharist, 176, 180
Europe, Asia and, 77 ; Eastern, 147 ; sees Russia as enemy, 86 ; Western, 76, 94
Evil One, 170, 174
evolution, its cosmic force, 27 ; of species, 79
Exhibition, French (Moscow, 1891), 36, 67 ; Universal, 120-1, 124 ; universal exhibitions, 88, 185
exorcism, 48
explosives, 33, 67, 235 ; *see also* rain-making
extermination, mutual, 34, 79, 108, 131, 133
Ezekiel, 86

faith, 63, 89, 169-73 ; and knowledge, 125
Fall, the, 128, 191
famine, 11, 23, 27, 34 ; of 1891, 33, 36
Farsi, 211
fatalism, oriental, 156
fatherhood, and sonship and autocracy, 131
father(s), 26, 36, 42, 54, 70, 79, 106, 116-17 ; against son, 122 ; deceased, 111-12, 168 ; destroyed by lust, 113 ; displaced by sons, 53, 112 ; dust of, 109, 120, 131 ; forgotten by sons, 43, 45, 106, 128, 188 ; love of, 42 ; of all nations, 17 ; mourned by sons, 72 ; resurrection of, 60 ;

stone, 219 ; *see also* son(s)

Fathers and Sons (I.S. Turgenev), 53

fauna, 24, 92

Fedorov, Nikolai Fedorovich, background, 11-30, 205-6 ; article on Goethe's *Faust*, 19 ; complete writings, *see* Young, G.M., and 238-9 ; *Filosofiya obshchago dela (The Philosophy of the Common Task)*, 12, 17, 19, 205-6 ; foreword to letter of Dostoevsky, 14

fertilisers, 173

Fet (A.A. Shenshin), 232

Fichte, J., 115

filiation, 26

Finland, 147

Firdausi (Persian poet), 203

flora, 24 ; of steppes, 218

fly, Hessian, 93

force, irrational, 108 ; life-giving, 33 ; rational, 111 ; of feeling, 107 ; of motion, 107 ; sensient, 119 ; sensuous, 119 ; telluric, 80 ; telluric-solar, 99-100

forefathers, 18, 26 ; and iconostasis, 124

forerunner, and iconostasis, 124

France, and meaning of 'constitution', 130 ; Russia's material struggle against, 155

Franco-Russian alliance, 67

French, need for union with, 67 ; Revolution, 14, 73, 77, 83, 85 ; *see also* Exhibition

Gagarin, Prince Ivan, 15

Gagarin, Prince Paul, 15

galaxy, electromagnetic cycle of, 100

Galilee, 128

Gandhi, M., 23

genealogies, 26

genetic engineering, 13

Geneva Convention (1864), 236

geology, 167

Germans, in A. Chayanov's *Journey of my Brother Alexei to the Land of Peasant Utopia*, 21

Germany, and Russia's peace initiatives, 144 ; and militarism, 67 ; Russia's material struggle against, 155 ; workers in, 62

Ghost, Holy, *see* Spirit

Ginken, A., 70-1, 239

Gistashen *(Shah-Nameh)*, 211

God, 26-7, 36, 89, 99, 114, 122 ; and nature, 111 ; as ruler and judge, 83, 224 ; his commandment,

159-60 ; existence of, 34-5 ; and fulfilment of his will, 110, 115, 169, 231 ; and his transcendence, 70-1 ; in Kant's *Critiques*, 50-1 ; Kingdom of, 40, 61, 75, 97, 119, 132, 135, 169-71, 173, 223 ; likeness to, 112 ; of the fathers, 41, 60, 66, 112, 117, 169 ; of the living, 111 ; scourge of, 86 ; Triune, 54, 65, 66, 71, 76, 83, 121, 127, 142, 153, 181, 194 ; *see also* Creator

Goethe *(Faust)*, 19
Gomorrha, 171
Gorky, M., 21, 22, 239
Gornostaev, A.K. (pseudonym of A.K. Gorsky), 15-16, 239
Gorsky, A.K., *see* Gornostaev, Ostromirov
Gospels, 75, 222-3, 228
Graeco-Persian wars, 77
Graeco-Turkish war, 144-7
graves, 26, 106 ; orgies on, 131
graveyards, 122 ; *see also* cemeteries
gravity, 165
Great Powers, 234-5
Grechishnikov, S.S., on Bely and Fedorov, 21, 240
Greeks, against Iran, 203 ; against Turks, 144

guilt, 121
gunfire, to control atmosphere, *see* rain-making
gunpowder, 81-2

Haeckel, E., and monism, 40
Hagemeister, Michael, 22, 240
Hague Peace Conference (1899), 126, 204
Harbin, 19, 205
Heaven, Kingdom of, 63
helium, 195
hell, 220-1 ; and lechery, 133
Hellenic world, art and science in, 190
Hess, W.N., 27
history, 77-88, 123 ; extraterrestrial and terrestrial, 189 ; via art, 124
Holy, Wars of Islam, 197, 213 ; Week, 175 ; Writ, 222 ; *see also* Spirit
Homer, 82
humanism, 111-12 ; nineteenth-century negation of, 63
humanity, as crew of celestial craft, 97
Humanity — what is it for ? (I.M. Zabelin), 29, 244
Huns, 197, 215
hypnosis, 47-8

iconostasis, 124, 188
ideolatry, 111, 187
idolatry, 111, 187

253

immortality, 23, 25, 50, 76, 93, 121 ; and baptism, 106 ; and sinlessness, 182-3 ; of soul, 99
Immortals, Church of the, 71
Imperial Court (St Petersburg), 234
India, 28, 77, 86, 87 ; conversion of, 197 ; problem of, 212
individualism, Western, 156
industrialism, 122 ; and church, 125 ; and sex, 119
industry, and art, 186 ; luxury, 120; manufacturing, 37, 62, 139 ; scientific, 120
insects, 92-3
Institute of Philosophy of USSR Academy of Sciences, 13
intelligentsia, 13, 137, 140 ; weakness of, 148
International Court of Justice (the Hague), setting up of, 204
international library loans, 17
Iran, 210-19 ; Aryans of, 86 ; against Turan, 18, 203 ; and Christianity, 214 ; as paradise, 214-15
Irish Slavonic Studies, 191
iron, revolution in production of, 62
Islam, 213 : Arab converts to, 211 ; Christian circle surrounding, 87 ; Turkish converts to, 211 ; 1877-8 war against, 65
Italy, and meaning of 'constitution', 130

Japan, Russia's material struggle against, 155 ; Sino-Japanese war, 156
Jerusalem, 171, 214 ; Old, 126 ; New (Monastery of the Resurrection), 127
Jews, and Galilee, 128 ; in China, 197
Joel (prophet), 224
Jonah (prophet), 130, 208, 223
Journal of Peasant Studies, 22
Judgement, Last, 20, 29, 129-30

Kaiser Wilhelm II, 241 ; his letter to Nicholas II, 144
kamennaya bába, 219
Kant, I., 17, 50, 95, 116 ; *Critiques* of, 49-51, 155
Kapilavastu, 198
Kara-padishah (Black tsar), 214
Karazin, V.N., 28, 35, 94-5, 100, 152, 156, 162, 166-7
Kazakhstan, 19
Kerensk, 14, 227, 230
Kharkov, *see* universities
Khazars, 18

254

Khorasan, 112
Khorasin, 171
Khorovod, 112
Khvala cheloveku (V. Bryusov), 21
Kiev, 218 ; and China, 200 ; and Russian Christianity, 197
Kingdom, Middle, monument to, 196
kinship, 18, 26, 33, 37, 43, 45, 48 ; lack of, 38-9, 44-5, 77, 80, 83, 118 ; restoration of, 60, 75, 186 ; misinterpreted by socialism, 61
Kiselev, A., 'Varsonof'ev i N.F. Fedorov', 21, 240
knowledge, 22-4, 39, 41, 74, 94, 116, 123 ; and action, 11, 17, 24, 45, 56, 105, 109, 161-2 ; and art, 124-6, 141 ; and faith, 125 ; and unbelievers, 118 ; and class, 56, 60 ; and Germans, 67 ; Haeckel on, 40 ; Kant and the positivists on, 50 ; obligatory, 168 ; of all by all, 60 ; three subjects of, 105 ; universal, 56
Koehler, L., *N.F. Fedorov : The Philosophy of Action*, 13, 21, 240,
Kontekst, 19
Kopet-Dag (mountain), 216

Koreans, 164
Koryakin, Yu., 70, 238
Kozhevnikov, V. A., 16, 17, 19, 205, 232, 240 ; *Buddhism in Comparison with Christianity*, 17 ; *The Philosophy of Feeling and Faith*, 17
Krasnovodsk, 206-7, 218
Kremlin (Moscow), 129 ; and Easter, 126 ; as cemetery fortress, 142
kremlins (citadels protecting fathers' ashes), 138
Kremnev, I. (pseudonym of A. V. Chayanov), 21-2, 241
Kronos, 187
Kronstadt, French navy visit to, 67
Kulikovo, Battle of (1380), 203
Kyafir-Kol' (Christians' last fortress in Turkestan), 208
Kyafir-mola (Christians' graves), 208

Lake Saimen, 147
Lao-tse, 198
Laplace, P., 95
Laptev, I. D., 29, 241
Lavrov, A. V., on Bely and Fedorov, 21
law, divine, 163 ; and the Prophets, 222-3 ; courts, 83

lawyers, 113
learned, the, 24, 26, 36-9, 82, 109, 115-16, 131, 187 ; and artificiality, 106 ; and the unlearned, 23, 33, 40-5, 65, 77, 89 ; and history, 77-8
Lenin Library, 19 ; *see also* Rumyantsev Museum Library
Leonids (falling stars), 195
Leopardi, G., 76
lightning, as source of energy, 28 ; conductors, 28, 36, 69, 94, 152, 156, 166
Literaturnaya gazeta, 13
Literaturnoe nasledstvo, 22
liturgy, 26, 131, 172, 180, 188 ; extra-ecclesiastical, 129
Lockyer, Sir J., 95
Lodge, Sir Oliver, 28, 152 ; *Lightning Conductors and Lightning Guards*, 241
Lord, R., 15, 241
Lo-yang, 199
Ludwig, E., 144, 241
Lukashevich, S., 13, 241
lust, 113 ; as will, 119, 132 ; sterile, 116 ; world as, 113

'M. Gorky and N. F. Fedorov' (L. I. Sukhikh), 22, 243
magnetic, field, 95 ; pole, 70 ; storms, 100
magnetism, *see* Earth
Magog, 86
Mamai (Tartar Khan), his alliance with Lithuanian Olgerd, 203
Mamedov, N., 70, 241
Man, his *raison d'être*, 97
Mani, 197
Manicheism, Iran as cradle of, 211
Markov, E. L., 209, 219
The Martyrdom of Man (W. Reade), 27, 242
Marx, K., 24
Mary Magdalene, 178
materialism, 13 ; scientific, Haeckel on, 40 ; moral, Haeckel on, 40
Mayakovsky, V. V., *Pro eto (About this)*, 21, 24
medicine, 99
meditation, 80
Mediterranean, 86
melanite (in gunpowder), 81
memorials, erection of, 124
memory, 25
Mencius, 198
Mendeleev, D. I., 148, 154, 168
metaphysics, 50
meteorology, 100 ; and volcanic, plutonic or cosmic phenomena, 122, 195 ; control of, 37, 62, 68, 94, 134, 147-50, 166 ; distortion of, 88 ; *see*

also weather
Metternich, 167
microphones, 191
Middle Ages, 63, 211
migration, 40, 44
militarism, 11, 24, 67, 119-21, 125 ; and Germans, 67
Military, and scientific research, 154-5 ; service, 82-3, 138, 155 ; *see also* rain-making
Milton, J., 133
miners, 62, 191
Ministry of Education, 55, 152 ; *see also* Karazin
Ministry of Transport, 145
minority, 75, 128
minors, 131, 140 ; Dante's paradise for, 132-6
molecules, 91, 132, 191-3, 195 ; man re-created from, 134, 141-2
Monastery of the Caves (Kiev), 208 ; of Novopechersky, 208 ; of the Resurrection (Voskresensky), 127 ; of Chin-sheng-ssü, 196
Mongols, 18, 202, 208, 211 ; and Turkestan, 212 ; *see also* Mamai, Tamerlane
monism, 44, 57-8, 122 ; *and see* Noiré
Montenegro, 18
moon, 195
morality, 105, 119, 138 ; theo-anthropic, 26 ; zoo-anthropic, 26
Morris, William, 21
mortality, 99 ; as imperfection, 168
Moscow Archives of Ministry of Foreign Affairs, 16
Moskovskie vedomosti (Moscow Gazette), 20
Moskva (A. Bely), 21, 237
mosque-monuments, 209
multi-unity, 71, 102
Murav'ev, Count M.N., 144, 233-4
Murav'ev, V. E., 241
muscular system, 100
museums, 17, 46, 121, 124-5 ; and need for new cemeteries and schools, 26, 67 ; *see also* school-museum, Rumyantsev Museum Library
Muslim, 71, 212, 214
mythology, 56

N. F. Fedorov and his Book The Philosophy of the Common Task *in Opposition to the Teaching of L. N. Tolstoy on Non-Resistance and to other Ideas of our Time* (N. P. Peterson), 14, 242
N. F. Fedorov (1828-1903), a Study in Russian Eupsychian and Utopian Thought (S. Lukashevich), 13, 241

Nanking, 197
Napoleonic wars, 167
Narva, 147
nationality, 122
nature, 18, 23, 33-5, 38-40, 113, 139 ; as a death-bearing force, 36, 42, 51, 76, 90, 109 ; as uncontrolled force, 46, 53, 137 ; becoming conscious, 106-7 ; God and, 111 ; plunder of, 79, 113 ; regulation of, 20, 29, 48, 55, 114, 123
Nauchnoe obozrenie, 17
Nauka i zhizn', 162
Nazareth, 128
Nedelya (The Week), 209
neo-Kantianism, 49
nerves, motor, 107 ; sensory, 107
nervous system, 100
Nestorian, 196, 208, 211
'Neue Materialen zur Wirkungsgeschichte N. F. Fedorovs, M. Gor'kii und die Anhänger Fedorovs in Moskau und Harbin' (M. Hagemeister), 22
Nicholas II, Tsar, 204, 233-5
Nietzsche, F., 17, 116 ; as (black) prophet of German emperor, 214
Nikolaevsk, 69
Nikolai Fedorovich Fedorov — Works (S. G. Semenova), 13, 15, 19, 243
Nikolai F. Fedorov — An Introduction (G. Young), 13, 29, 244
Nikon, Patriarch, 127 ; and Old Believers, 197
Nineveh, 171, 223
nirvana, 132
Noiré, L., 44
nomadism, 120, 121
noosphere, 13
Northern Lights, 100
Novoe vremya, 144
Novopechersky, 208
Novy zhurnal, 21
Nuclear power stations, USSR, 70

Obermann (Senancour), 73
Odessa, 16, 69 ; Technological Society of, and artificial rain-making, 145-6
Oka (river), 213
Okna (Kherson province), 15
Old Believers, Siberian, 197
Olgerd (Lithuanian prince), and alliance with Mamai, 203
O Mayakovskom (V. B. Shklovsky), 21, 243
organs, 101, 108 ; artificial, 96
Origen, 161
Ormuzd (white god), 210
orphanhood, 120
Orthodoxy, 18, 29, 108, 122, 127, 130 ; and standing,

189 ; replaces action by symbolism, 77 ; *see also* burial rite
Osman, 213
'*O smerti, voskresenii i voskreshenii*' (V. Bryusov), 21, 238
Ostromirov, A. (pseudonym of A. K. Gorsky), 15, 19, 242
Ostroumov, N. P. (Tashkent Archaeological Society), 207, 219
otpevan'ye (burial service), 176

Pacific, the, 199 ; coast of China, 211
pacifists, 157 ; *see also* Tolstoy
paganism, 71, 76, 112, 117, 125 ; and Dante, 134 ; and fall of Byzantium, 77 ; how to overcome, 213 ; its religions, 55
painting, church, 186-7
Palestine, 190, 216
Pamir, 18, 69, 87, 147, 207, 211-18
Pandora, and marriage to Epimetheus, 179
pantheism, 66, 71
Pantikapeia, 217
paradise, 132 : and Dante, 133-6 ; and hell, 220-1 ; and Iran, 214
Paradise on Earth : Some Ideological Aspects of the Works of Dostoevsky (A. K. Gornostaev), 15, 16, 239
Parapamisus mountains, 211, 215-16
parents, 129, 132, 140 ; and resurrectors, 191-5 ; universal love for, 118-19
Paris, 216 ; Count A. A. Arakcheev and Alexander I in, 167
particles, 10, 91, 99, 191-3 ; atmospheric, 195 ; molecular structure of, 101
paschal questions, 108, 110, 131, 139-40
Passion, mythical, 43 ; sexual, 118-19
Pasternak, L., 16 ; *Notes from Various Years*, 242
patrification, 124, 127, 139 ; *see also* resuscitation
patriotism, 42
pauperism, artificial, 109
peace, 33 ; proposed conference (1898), 233
peasantry, 24, 26, 39, 117 ; Fedorov's and Tolstoy's views on, 22
Pechenegs, 18
Peleus, and marriage to Thetis, 179
perfection, 27 ; and Kant, 50 ; in unity of art and nature, 184

Persia, 197 ; her empire, 203
pest control, 92-3
Peterson, N. P., 14, 19, 159, 205-6, 227, 242
Pharisees, 176
philanthropy, 14, 19, 63, 159
philosophes, 86
philosophy as idle contemplation, 88, 115
The Philosophy of Feeling and Faith (V. A. Kozhevnikov), 17, 240
planet Earth, 13, 25, 90 ; conscious of its fate, 97 ; finite resources of, 94 ; inevitable extinction of, 96
Planeta razuma (I. D. Laptev), 29, 241
Platonov, A., 21
Platonov and Fyodorov : The Influence of Christian Philosophy on a Soviet Writer (A. Teskey), 13, 21, 243
Plevna, 82
plutonic phenomena, 122
politics, 42
Polovtsy, 18
Polyane (Slavic tribe), 218
Polybius, 86
polygamy, 213.
Pope, the, 134, 210
positivism, 17, 48-9, 51, 58 ; as modification of theological scholasticism, 48 ; and resurrection, 56-7 ; Chinese, 49
Powers, Edward, 27-8, 33, 145, 242
prayer, 169-72 ; the Lord's, 173
press, the, 142
prodigal, *see* son(s)
Pro eto (About This, V. V. Mayakovsky), 21, 241
progress, 52-6, 92
proletarianism, 92
proletariat, and weather control, 148
prophecies, their conditionality, 222-4
prophets, 86, 127 ; on iconostasis, 124 ; *see aslo* Jonah
proskomidia (part of Orthodox liturgy), 26, 176, 180
Protestantism, different from Orthodoxy, 189 ; individualism of, 77
Providence, 34
pseudopatrification, 124
Pskov-Chud basin, 147
psychocracy, 44, 50
psychology, 25, 50
Ptolemaic world view, 124, 127 ; *see also* art, superstition
purgatory, 220
Pushkin, A., 101, 211
Put' (The Way), 19-20
Puteshestvie moego brata Alekseya v stranu kres-

t'yanskoi utopii (I. Kremnev), 21-2, 241

radiation, to reconstitue bodies, 142
radicalism, 13
railways, 216-17
rainfall, 13
rain-making, artificial, 27, 33, 145-55 ; using explosions, 35, 166 ; *see also* War and the Weather
rationalisation, 120
Reade, W., 27, 242
reanimation, 100
reason, 23, 108, 150 ; transforming power of, 27 ; peasant, 118 ; practical and theoretical, 105, 110, 115-18, 130-1, 137 ; *see also* Kant, *Critiques*
Re-creation, 112, 139, 220
redemption and history, 223
regulation, *see* nature
religion, 112, 125 ; science and art united in, 138
religionisation, 112
Renaissance, 63, 73, 76-7
Renan, E., 228
repentance, 73
representation, 61, 113-16, 122
research, 24, 25, 29, 39, 41
resurrection, 12, 20, 25-6, 61, 64, 76, 108, 112, 135, 216 ; and baptism, 106, 228 ; conscious, 90-1 ; and Easter services, 176 ; of Christ, 80, 105-6, 142 ; of fathers, 44 ; requires perfection, 155 ; positivists' opinion of, 51 ; process, 193 ; religion of, 111 ; task of, 117 ; transcendental, 129 ; universal, 182, 186 ; *see also* paschal questions, resuscitation
Resurrection (Tolstoy), 14
Résurrection (C. Stoffel), 27, 243
resuscitation, 25, 43, 55, 56, 60, 71-2, 82, 87, 93, 97, 100, 109, 113, 116, 119, 124-6, 131, 142 ; and freedom from hunger, 90 ; and nature, 106 ; centre for, 129 ; history as, 77-9 ; of fathers, 108, 168 ; as supreme task, 80, 89, 132, 135
Richelieu Lyceum, Odessa, 16
Riga (10th Archaeological Conference), 208
ring-dances, 112, 117, 126
Ritschl, A., 160
roburite (in gunpowder), 81
rocketry, 16
Roman Catholics, 135
Romania, 18 ; and Russo-Turkish war, 82
Rossiya, 16
Rumyantsev Museum Libra-

ry (Lenin Library, Moscow), 16, 68, 232
rural, communes, 96 ; communities, 38, 43-4 ; problem, 39 ; schools, 26 ; way of life, 106, 121
Russia, 41, 816 ; ancient, 128 ; her armies, 82 ; and electricity, 147 ; and the West, 148 ; and lack of rain (1897), 145 ; secular, 211 ; *see also* science
Russian Review, 20
Russian Technological Society, 28
Russian Thinkers on China : V.S. Solov'ev and N.F. Fedorov (N. A. Setnitsky), 243
Russkaya literatura, 22
Russkaya mysl', 19, 161
Russkie vedomosti, 166
Russkii arkhiv, 19, 167-8
Russkii vestnik, 196
Russky invalid, 153, 164
Russo-Turkish war, 18, 163 ; and Plevna, 82
Rybachi peninsula, 69

sacrifice, 49, 60
Sadducees, 176
Saladin, Caliph, 214
saltpetre, 173
Saltykov-Shchedrin, M., 211
salvation, 12, 97, 110, 141, 190 ; collective, 170 ; from hunger, 34
Samarkand, 207-8, 216
sanitary problems, 90-102, 109, 110
San Stefano, treaty of, 18
Satan, 153
Schéquet, L., 76
scholasticism, 48
school, 46, 138 ; -camp, 138, 142 ; -church, 138, 142, 162 ; -museum, 138, 143 ; museum-schools in Kiev and China, 202
Schopenhauer, A., 17, 113
science, 45, 94, 122-3, 132 ; and art, 105, 128, 138, 140, 157 ; fragmentation of, 36 ; Russian, 41
scientists, responsibilities of, 29
selection, natural, 66
self, -consciousness, 107 ; -creation, 107, 184 ; -government, 107 ; -indulgence, 114 ; -improvement, 107 ; -organisation, 107 ; *see also* constitutions
Semenova, Catherine, 15
Semenova, S. G., 13, 15, 19, 243
Semites, 71
Senancour, E., 73
sensuality, 43
Serbia, 18
Setnitsky, N. A., 19, 205, 243
Sevast'yanov, V. I. (astro-

naut), 13
sewage, 173
sexuality, 18, 26, 66, 118-20, 124, 139, 185, 188, 220
Shah-Nameh (epic poem), 203, 211
Shenshin, A.A. (Fet), 232
Shi'ah, 211
Shklovsky, V. B., *O Mayakovskom (About Mayakovsky)*, 21, 243
siderolite, 95
Sidon, 171
sin, 90, 220 ; as cause of death, 108, 142-3 ; international, 144 ; original, 85, 106,
Si-ngan-fu, Chinese inscription, 196-200
sinlessness, physical and moral, 182-3
Skobelev, General M.D., 218
skoptsy (eunuchs), 161
Slavs, 67, 86 ; Balkan, 18, 203 ; and Berlin Treaty, 67 ; and Cyril and Methodius, 199 ; Russian, 197
Slutsky, S. S., 196
Smith, R. E. F., 'Note on the sources of George Orwell's *1984*', 22
social contract, 38
socialism, 24, 62, 119 ; its abuse of 'brotherhood', 61 ; semitic, 85
socialists, 37, 38

Socrates, 115
Sodom, 171
solar, energy, 68 ; system, 100-1, 122, 141 ; heat to power cottage industries, 62 ; radiation, 37, 95 ; world, 87
Solov'ev, Vl.S., 15, 227-8, 243 ; in L. Pasternak's *Three Wise Men*, 16 ; and the justification of Good, 180
Solzhenitsyn, A. K., 21
son(s), 18, 43, 74-5, 79, 108, 119-20, 126, 160 ; and consciousness of nature, 106 ; and daughters, 140-1, 192 ; brotherhood of, 42 ; immortality of, 108 ; of God, 75 ; of man, 41, 44, 74, 83, 106, 116, 121, 125, 137, 185 ; prodigal, 38, 52, 66, 74, 78, 106, 121, 178, 180, 187, 224 ; *see also* father(s)
sonship, 131
South Africa, diamonds, 196
Soviet Union, 13
space, 16-17, 25, 27, 29 ; explorers in, 96 ; outer, 96
Spanish-American war (1898), 154
Spencer, H., 17, 60
Spirit, and its feminine form, 75 ; Evil, 48 ; Holy, 75,

263

101, 116, 127, 142
spiritualism, 47, 98, 161
St Cyril, 198-9
St Francis of Assisi, 16
St George Cross, 164
St James, apostle, on faith, 169
St Methodius, 198-9
St Paul, on faith, 169
St Petersburg, 69, 147, 233 ; Chinese (Peking), 197
St Sergius of Radonezh, 65
Starkov, A., 148
stars, 87-8, 195 ; fathers' souls transferred to, 186 ; extinction of, 87-8
starvation, 34, 35
statehood, in preference to 'citizenship', 42
steam power, 147
Stirner, M., 116
Stoffel, C., 27, 243
Sufism, 211
Sukhikh, L. I., 22, 243
superman, 121, 214
superstition, 75, 116-17, 161 ; nineteenth-century, 63 ; philosophical, 99 ; Ptolemaic, in Dante, 136
supramoralism, 105-37 passim
Suslov, M. A., 13
Svet nevecherny (S. N. Bulgakov), 20, 238
swaddling, 165
Syria, 198
Syriac, 196 ; ancient, 75

Syrian, Christianity, 200 ; church built in China, 199
Syrians, 196
Syro-Chaldeans, 204, 222

T'ai-tsung, 198, 199, 202
Tamerlane, 208, 211 ; city of (Tashkent), 207
T'ang dynasty, 197, 200
Tantalus, sufferings of, 86
Tartars, 18 ; Western view of Russians as, 215
Tashkent, 216 ; *see also* Tamerlane
Task, Common, 12, 18, 25, 36, 43-4, 83, 85, 110, 117, 138-9, 168, 172, 180, 230 ; lack of, 37 ; and Kant, 50
technology, 120 ; modern, 29
Teilhard de Chardin, P., 13, 243
telegrams, 70
temples, 124 ; in Turkestan, 209
Teskey, A., *Platonov and Fyodorov : The Influence of Christian Philosophy on a Soviet Writer*, 13, 21, 243
Testament, New, 170, 223 ; Old, 170, 218, 223
theodicy (justification of God), 180
Thetis, and marriage to Peleus, 179

theurgy, ethico-aesthetic, 128 ; mystical, 135
Thief, prayer of, 170-1
Third World, 29
Thomas, apostle, 89, 197
'Three jubilees : L. Tolstoy, H. Ibsen, N.F. Fedorov' (N. A. Berdyaev), 20
Tibet, 147
Tolstoy, L. N., 20-3, 156, 232, 244 ; in L. Pasternak's *Three Wise Men*, 16 ; and *Resurrection*, 14 ; and his doctrine of peace, 42 ; and his school at Yasnaya Polyana, 14 ; an nonresistance to evil, 168 ; and his preaching, 22
tombs, as places for research, 99
tombstones, 184-5
town-dwellers, 25, 118, 146
toys, 'industrial', 24, 29, 109-10, 113, 122-3, 129, 132
Trade Unions, 159
transformism, 79
Trans-Pacific Telegraph, 69
Trinity, 26, 34, 66, 71, 87, 129, 142, 156 ; 162-200 passim, 204 ; and Dante, 135
Triune, *see* God
Troy, 82
Tsar, and God, 130-1 ; *see also* Black tsar, White tsar

Tsargrad, *see* Constantinople
'Tsiolkovsky's youth in Moscow' (K. Altaisky), 17, 237
Tsiolkovsky, K., 16-17
Turanians, 86
Turgenev, I., 53
Turkestan, 205-36 passim ; Russia's victories over, 67
Turkey, floods in, 145
Turkic race, 213
Tyre, 171

unbelievers, 33, 34, 115, 118 ; *see also* believers
unbrotherliness, 41-2, 186 ; of relations, 118 ; state of, 40-2 ; *see also* brotherhood
unification, 67, 108, 142
union, morality of, 120 ; of sons, 44
United Nations Environment Programme, 29
unity, 36, 43 ; negation of, 38
universality, need for, 66
Universe, 88, 122-3, 128, 139, 141-2, 160, 189, 194 ; government of, 107 ; insects' role in destiny of, 92 ; and Laplace and Kant, 95 ; unification of, 107, 127 ; spiritualisation of, 115
universities, 121-2, 125 ; Birmingham, 28 ; Kharkov,

265

28, 34-5 ; Fedorov on, 24
unlearned, the, 33 ; memorandum from, 65 ; and history, 80, 82 ; faith of, 169 ; *see also* learned
Urals, 213
Uranus, 187
utopianism, 12

Vakhterov, V., 161-2
'Varsonof'ev i N.F. Fedorov' (A. Kiselev), 21, 240
Velleda (Germanic prophetess), 178
Venus, power of, 135
Verny, 14, 19
Versty, 19, 205, 124
Vestal virgins, 224 ; and village women, 178
vlad (phoneme), 69
Vladikavkaz (Ordzhonikidze), 69
Vladimir, Prince of Kiev, 202
Vladivostok, 69
Volga, 145, 213
Vselenskoe delo (The Ecumenical Task), 21

war, 34, 36
War and the Weather (E. Powers), 27-8, 33, 145, 242
weapons, 39, 49 ; of destruction, 38
weather, 23 ; regulation, 146-8, 173

West, 89, 94 ; against East, 82, 211, 213 ; and disunity, 72 ; expected war against, 65 ; hostility to Russia of, 77 ; moral short-sightedness of, 87 ; represented by Hellenic world, 190 ; Romano-Germanic, 197
Western powers, 18 ; maritime, 77
white, god (Ormuzd), 214 ; tsar (Ahpadishah), 134, 214
Wilhelm II, Kaiser, 214
will, 138 ; divine, 115 ; rational, 137 ; to procreate, 119 ; to resuscitate, 119
World Health Organisation, 29

'Yadernaya energetika ; dostigeniya i problemy' (N. Dollezhal, Yu. Koryakin), 70, 238
Young, George M. Jr, *Nikolai F. Fedorov : An Introduction*, 13, 29, 244

Zabelin, I., 29, 244
'Zagadochny myslitel'' (S.N. Bulgakov), 20, 238
Zarathustra (in *Shah-Nameh*), 211
Zend-Avesta, 216
Zernov, N., 19

Zola, E., 244 ; and International Copyright Agreement, 22
zoology, 123
zoomorphism (secular philosophy of history), 79
Zoroaster, 197
Zoroastrianism and Iran, 211